ESCAPE:

How animation went mainstream in the 1990s

ESCAPE:

How animation went mainstream in the 1990s

by G. Michael Dobbs

to Stasia:
Thanks for your interest!
And good luck!
Mike Dobbs

Published in the USA by:
BearManor Media
P O Box 71426
Albany, Georgia 31708
www.bearmanormedia.com

ISBN 1-59393-110-7

Printed in the United States of America.

Book design by Darlene Swanson of Van-garde Imagery, Inc.
Cover design by Mark Martin. © 2007 by Mark Martin

Contents:

Acknowledgments:

Many, many people have contributed to my interest in animation over the years and, ultimately, to the creation of this book. However, there are a few people whose assistance and encouragement have loomed large.

Therefore, this book is dedicated to:

Rosalie and the late Myron Waldman. Their support has always been deeply appreciated.

My mother and late father. My dad used to question my interest in comics and cartoons but he bought me my first movie camera. My mom was willing to typeset my fanzine and help underwrite other projects. I've been blessed.

Most of all, to my wife Mary. Her love and encouragement have allowed me to accomplish so much in life. Thank you.

Introduction:

What's grown man doing watching cartoons?
By himself? Aren't they just for kids?

It doesn't seem so odd nowadays that people in their 20s through 60s quote Bugs Bunny or collect animation art or look forward to a new animated DVD chock full of extras. When this Baby Boomer was growing up in the 1950s and '60s, cartoons were definitely kid's stuff.

Oh sure, adults watched *The Flintstones*, which was shown during prime time. And *Rocky and Bullwinkle* had jokes I didn't get but my parents did. Generally, though, cartoons were thought of as the programs children watched on Saturday morning or feature films that were deemed suitable entertainment.

By the late 1980s the status of animation had begun to change.

The fact is if you were 25 years old in 1965 and loved cartoons, many people would have thought you had some sort of arrested development. Today, there's nothing wrong with adults decorating their cubicle at work with Loony Tune action figures or a Betty Boop toy.

This book is more than just a collection of updated articles, interviews and reviews I wrote for my two animation magazines, *Animato* and *Animation Planet*. It is also a look at how animation went from being perceived as a throwaway medium aimed at kids to a commercial art form for both adults and children.

How did this change take place? How did an adult fan base for animation emerge? Several key factors made this shift take place.

From nearly the beginning of the medium in the late 1890s, animation was something designed for both adults and children. In the earliest days of the motion pictures when the nickelodeons and the vaudeville stages were the venues for movies, the work of J. Stuart Blackton, Emile Cohl and Winsor McCay undoubtedly played before predominately adult audiences.

McCay has remained the best known of this first generation of animators and showmen, largely because many people have incorrectly been told that his *Gertie the Dinosaur* was the first animation cartoon. It was not, of course. It was not even McCay's first production.

One of McCay's subsequent productions, *The Sinking of the Lusitania*, was definitely adult as it recreated in grim detail the event that helped propel the United States into the First World War.

As motion pictures grew into a more mature business, producers began giving exhibitors the sort of programming building blocks that mirrored vaudeville. In vaudeville, exhibitors would build a program with a combination of different kinds of acts that would support the headliners or main acts.

By the time of the First World War, a similar philosophy was seen guiding movie programs. A program of short subjects – a newsreel, a serial chapter, a 20-minute comedy and a cartoon, supported the main feature film, for example.

The serial, for instance, in 1914, was considered adult fare. *The Perils of Pauline* was so much a hit that the Hearst newspapers printed a weekly synopsis of the motion picture action. In fact, this seminal serial was more popular than the features it accompanied, proving the power of a well-received supporting short.

It may be difficult for today's movie audiences to conceive of a time when the material shown before the feature was not simply a barrage of commercials or previews of coming attractions. There was once a highly de-

Winsor McCay's depiction of the act that drew America in World War I remained for years an example of what animation can do outside of humor or sentiment.

fined sense of showmanship in the motion picture industry and exhibitors knew that to build audience loyalty one had to present films audiences wanted to see.

This showmanship existed at a time when bills at motion picture theaters changed at least once a week. This practice started in the pre-1920s era and continued at many venues through the end of the 1940s. The growing popularity of commercial television starting in 1948 altered forever the motion picture industry and the concept of a program.

Before television, exhibitors had to compete not only for their share of the audience, but to keep the audience coming back to their theater. Many people had a once-a-week movie habit; some, if they could afford it, went multiple times.

I have a "herald" in my collection for the Lyric Theater in Elkin, N.C., for one week in September of 1937. A herald was a small paper handout that showed what films were playing during a particular week.

One gets a sense of just how busy a theater could be, even a small-town theater such as this one. On Monday and Tuesday, *The Rage of Paris* with Douglas Fairbanks, Jr., was featured. On Wednesday, *Stolen Hearts* with Gene Raymond was the main attraction. "Brought back to delight you" was a reissue of the MGM's *David Copperfield* for just Wednesday. For Friday, not only was *Penitentiary* with Walter Connolly and John Howard shown, but there was also a midnight show as well, *Mr. Moto Takes a Chance* with Peter Lorre. Saturday was the time for a Western and this one was *Cheyenne Rides Again* with Tom Tyler.

All of these films were accompanied by "news events," cartoons, comedy short subjects and, for the Saturday cowboy film, a serial chapter.

The cartoon was not something just aimed at children, although it was clear that children liked cartoons. All cartoon afternoons were common programming for a Saturday "kiddie matinee."

During the silent era, many cartoons were originally part of a "screen magazine," or a self-contained collection of supporting shorts. Being packaged with a newsreel, definitely an "adult" feature, undoubtedly helped people think that the cartoon was entertainment for all.

In the 1920s, the power of a popular cartoon to help draw audiences to a theater was shown with the popularity of Felix the Cat and of Ko-Ko the Clown. Otto Mesmer's Felix shorts inspired merchandise and references outside of movie circles. The *Out of the Inkwell* shorts with Ko-Ko the Clown were popular enough that its producer, Max Fleischer, became a bit of a celebrity himself.

Fleischer's earliest work, for instance, was from the J.R. Bray Studio, which supplied cartoons to Paramount. One's first reflection after seeing this bit of work is 'why doesn't Mr. Fleischer do more.' After a deluge of pen and ink 'comedies' in which the figure moves with mechanical jerks with little or no wit to guide them it is a treat to watch the smooth motion of Mr. Fleischer's figure and enjoy the cleverness that animates it."

Also in the 1920s there was a growing trend for an animation studio to align itself with a motion picture studio for better distribution to theaters, rather than trying to set up a distribution system for itself. This move reinforced the idea that a particular cartoon supported the work of a particular studio.

Fleischer's earliest work, for instance, was from the J.R. Bray Studio, which supplied cartoons for Paramount. Pathé distributed Paul Terry's *Aesop's Fables*.

This move allowed the studios to offer a more complete line of features to exhibitors to build their programs.

The trend of treating animation as entertainment for both adult and child was reinforced by the critical acceptance of Walt Disney's Mickey Mouse cartoons in the late 1920s. Whereas most cartoons normally only received scrutiny from industry critics in trade publications, the Disney cartoons were the subjects of adoration from writers for the popular press.

Beginning with *Steamboat Willie* in 1928, the Disney shorts were the dominant animated cartoons in the minds of mainstream critics who seldom mentioned such productions.

Although there had been successful merchandising efforts for animated cartoon characters prior to Mickey Mouse, the Disney line of licensed products starting in the 1930s simply set the standard for the movie industry.

Merchandising created another value for a successful animated cartoon. There was not only money in the rental of the cartoon itself, but there was income from toys, games and dolls of popular characters.

Unlike today, with some animation merchandise marketed squarely at adults, the merchandise then was definitely for children.

In 1948, commercial television, which had been put on hold by World War II, began its fight to conquer the hearts and minds of Americans. It really wasn't much of a battle.

Television changed everything in the motion picture business. The lure of "free" entertainment at home provided a slow but sure death to a number of types of movies. The classic B picture series, such as Westerns, the *Blondie* films, Charlie Chan and the like, were made unprofitable by their video equivalents of the sitcom and the half-hour and hour adventure shows.

Also in 1948, the Supreme Court ruled that studios could not own theater chains and the practice of block booking was ruled illegal. Block booking was a common practice among studios. In order for an exhibitor to book a film he or she really wanted, other less desirable films were also forced upon them.

The major studios saw their clout slipping away and there was an end of an era in how they did business.

There was less and less call for the kind of supporting shorts as the tactics studios used to regain an audience changed. The 1950s saw many shifts in the movie industry. More and more films in color were produced to combat the black-and-white images of television. Widescreen formats such as Cinema-Scope and Cinerama were introduced to give audiences a more dramatic picture. Three-dimensional systems were also tried, but proved to be just a fad.

The growing phenomena of the independently-owned drive-in theater, plus the changes in the demographic of the American family, also had a deep impact. The 1950s and '60s saw the rise of producers outside of the Hollywood mainstream – such as Roger Corman, Herman Cohen, Richard and Alex Gordon and others – creating exploitation films that were embraced by the growing youth market.

The content of films was also changing. In 1953, *The Moon is Blue* was released without the approval of the Breen Office, the self-censorship arm of the movie industry. Just a few years ago this would have been a kiss of death with exhibitors refusing to show it; now it became a hit.

The result of all this change was the closing in the mid- to latter 1950s of the animation arms controlled by the major studios. Warner Brothers, Paramount and Metro-Goldwyn-Mayer all closed their doors. Only Walter Lantz, who owned his studio independent of his distributor Universal, remained in production, although it would take longer and longer for him to recoup the costs of his Woody Woodpecker cartoons as there were fewer theaters wanting them.

Interestingly enough, the decade of the 1950s had opened with the rise of UPA, a studio releasing its cartoons through Columbia Pictures. The different look and animation techniques behind the UPA *Mr. Magoo* and *Gerald McBoing-Boing* cartoons revolutionized the industry and captured the attention of the critics.

While the Disney artists strove for realistic movement and lush background, the UPA shorts were almost abstract. Backgrounds could be minimal and the animation itself dared to be limited.

Despite the mainstream attention the UPA shorts captured, by the end of the 1950s, theatrical short subjects of any kind were primarily a thing of the past.

Television, ironically, saved the day – sort of.

William Hanna and Joseph Barbera, who had headed the most commercially successful unit at MGM with their *Tom and Jerry* cartoons, were the first studio refugees to tackle the project of bringing original animation to television audiences.

Although the *Crusader Rabbit* cartoon series holds the distinction of being the first animated show designed for television, it was barely animated.

The sale of packages of cartoons to television stations – some dating back to the silent era – had shown that TV viewers still wanted to see cartoons. The cartoons were also proving to be dependable fodder for the many stations that produced local programs for children.

Hanna and Barbera downsized the level of animation, hired highly talented voice actors who could provide characterization when the images couldn't and developed formats that, in the worse cases, reduced their productions to predictable formulas.

The UPA model showed that detailed and lush backgrounds were not necessary and since so much emphasis was placed on dialogue rather than action, having money-saving close-ups could stretch the budget.

While their first series, *Ruff 'n' Reddy* in 1957, scored a hit and their subsequent characters of Huckleberry Hound and Yogi Bear proved even more popular, it wasn't until the prime-time success of *The Flintstones* that the team reached the kind of audience it once had in theaters.

The success of the sale of the Fleischer and Famous Studio Popeye cartoons to television stations was not lost on King Features Syndicate, which controlled the Popeye character. King Features produced over 200 new color shorts for the television market in 1960 and 1961 using a number of different studios. Some of the people were veterans of the theatrical Popeye shorts, while other studios turned out cartoons that were only marginally related to the classic character.

By the mid-1960s, cartoons were the chief form of children's television programming. CBS had bought the Paul Terry studio and its library and was producing new cartoons itself. Hanna-Barbera had gone from being down-and-out studio rejects to a major force in television. The team produced prime-time shows as well as shows for Saturday morning.

Their shows, though, were very formulaic. The Hanna-Barbera prime-time shows were too often either parodies of other television shows (*The Flintstones/The Honeymooners*; *Top Cat/ The Phil Silvers Show*) and their programs for kids seemed to feature a two-character funny animal format that seldom seemed too funny.

But, frankly, whether or not the cartoons were funny is beside the point. The point is that they were a principal amusement for almost the entire Baby Boom generation.

As it is defined today, "prime time" was when the networks began their national programming. The difference was that over 40 years ago, prime time began at 7:00 p.m. network execs obviously felt a show such as *The Flintstones* was a good one for a time slot in which children were watching.

The early 1960s also saw the prime-time premiere of a Bugs Bunny program, which used clever new animated framing sequences to introduce classic theatrical cartoons, and Jay Ward's *Rocky and Bullwinkle*. Rocky may have been crudely animated, but the stories and voice work provided both children and adults with a sophisticated humor that the Hanna-Barbera shows never did.

Hanna-Barbera's greatest gamble was *Jonny Quest*, a prime-time adventure show developed by cartoonist Doug Wildey. It didn't have a long run, although the shows made an impression with the children who watched them and have spawned revivals and updated versions over the years.

This peak of activity for animation aimed at a general audience was relatively short-lived. Although *The Flintstones* had a respectable run, the other shows were on the air for several seasons and then gone.

During that time, Jay Ward's series, after the prime time Rocky and Bullwinkle, were either syndicated or seen on Saturday mornings. Although Hanna-Barbera tried other prime-time shows, none clicked like *The Flintstones* and that company also concentrated on Saturday morning fodder.

American audiences were also having greater exposure to non-Hollywood animation. Although the major studios experimented in the 1960s with reviving theatrical shorts (the Chuck Jones/*Tom and Jerry* cartoons and the *Pink Panther* shorts, for instance), with the decline of the Hollywood product other kinds of cartoons gained prominence.

Just take a look at the Academy Awards nominations. In the late 1950s, there were still animated shorts from Disney and Warner Brothers to be considered for nomination. As the 1960s dawned there were more and more independent shorts.

The category could no longer survive on just Hollywood product.

In 1959, John Hubley's *Moonbird* received the Oscar for Best Animated Short Subject. The competition was *Mexicali Shmoes* from Warner Brothers, *Noah's Ark* from Disney and *The Violinist* from producer Ernest Pintoff.

The next year, *Munro*, based on a Jules Feiffer cartoon and produced independently by Rembrandt Films, went home with the statue. There were two Warner Brothers shorts and one Disney short also nominated.

In 1963, for the first time, there were no mainstream Hollywood-produced animated shorts being considered for the Oscar. *The Critic*, released by Columbia, but produced by Ernest Pintoff, won the award.

Make no mistake, though, that even if a slight, but growing number of people saw animation as an artistic medium with great potential, most people continued to see it as a step-child to other kinds of filmmaking.

In the entertainment industry when something makes money, people pay attention.

In the early 1970s, the rating system developed by the Motion Pictures Producers Association allowed filmmakers to use subject matter that up until then had frequently lurked at the fringes of the mainstream: sex, nudity and violence.

In the annual "Sex in the Cinema" article written by Arthur Knight and Hollis Alpert for the November 1971 edition of *Playboy*, the authors noted the explosion of sexually-charged content in mainstream movies.

One photo layout included three stills from *Fritz the Cat*, which the authors predicted would be X-rated. They described it as "a raunchy romp through Harlem and Greenwich Village created by underground commix artist Robert Crumb."

Although there had been animated stag shorts circulating for years through the underground circuit of bachelor parties and smokers, *Fritz the Cat* was different. It was mainstream, not hidden. It was chic, not sleazy.

With the success of Ralph Bakshi's *Fritz the Cat* in 1972, the idea that animation was only a medium for children was shattered. For the first time in years, many film critics were looking at animation in a completely different way, as were many audiences.

Bakshi also hit another home run with *Heavy Traffic*, also rated X like *Fritz the Cat*. Undoubtedly some of the box office success of both came from the notoriety of an "adult" cartoon, the fact remained that Bakshi was able to do something that no one had accomplished until then. He used animation to attract a strictly adult audience to a widely released and profitable film.

Of course, lightning doesn't strike in the same place over and over. The non-Bakshi sequel, *The Nine Lives of Fritz the Cat*, was a disaster and Bakshi's *Coonskin* was, for all intents, banned.

Animation had also become a preferred medium for many college students in film courses at that time. Unlike live-action films, animation was something a small crew – or a single person – could do on a limited budget. Kodak sponsored a long-running contest open to young filmmakers and many of the winning entries were animated.

Animation programs were popular at colleges in the 1970s and animation giants such as voice actor Mel Blanc and director Bob Clampett toured campuses giving talks on their careers to packed halls.

Undoubtedly many students just felt nostalgic, but some clearly welcomed the chance to discover the adult appeal of their childhood entertainment. In the mid- to late 1970s, the initial fan core was being built.

Horror, science-fiction and fantasy films had already a well-established fandom that communicated through fanzines (amateur publications that were often very professional) and comic book fans had not only fanzines, but fan gatherings dubbed "conventions," as well.

Mike Barrier's *Funnyworld* emerged in the late 1960s and was one of the first fanzines that treated cartoons seriously. Barrier presented articles on animation as well as comic book creators.

ASIFA, an international organization devoted to the study and celebration of animation, also was formed at this time.

In 1976, the prestigious magazine *Film Comment* devoted an entire issue to classic Hollywood animation with a wide range of articles. It's safe to say that a film magazine had never taken mainstream Hollywood animation quite as seriously.

David Mruz's *Mindrot* (later known as *Animania*) was another well-read fanzine that treated animation seriously. People were selling 16mm prints of shorts in its pages and there was a group of collectors who were presenting films at conventions and other shows.

Soon, though, nearly everyone could be a collector.

It is one of those happy coincidences that by the time Boomers started having families, the VCR burst onto the scene. With home video, people could program their own entertainment and the Boomers who watched so many cartoons as kids were able to share that experience with their children.

The VCR changed everything for film fans. Generally serious movie fans that didn't live in metro areas with multiple television stations, a revival theater or two and museums with film programs led a life of reading about many movies instead of seeing them.

With the popularity of home video and the flood of movies into rental stores, suddenly people who were vicarious film fans now could see the movies they had only heard of.

This resulted in an explosion of books, professional, semi-pro and amateur magazines about all aspects of film as well as recognition by the business world of a new and growing film fandom.

There were now adults who were willing to buy a movie poster of their favorite film, wear T-shirts with the images of stars of yesteryear and seek out reproductions of famous movie props.

Articles on animation were popping up on a regular basis in magazines such as *Comic Scene* and *Fantastic Films*, as well as mainstream publications.

Independent animators such as Bill Plympton and Sally Cruishank were being noticed for their idiosyncratic work that blended both commercial and art house sensibilities.

The VCR allowed parents to do their own television programming for their children and they sought out animation from their youth as well as new productions.

The push animation received from home video was accelerated by several developments in the 1990s.

The success of *The Simpsons*, which began its run in December of 1989, showed that prime-time animation could capture both kids and adults and effectively compete against more traditional sitcoms and dramas. The impact of that show can't be underestimated. When FOX put it up against the highly popular Bill Cosby program on Thursday nights, there was a national debate if that horrid Bart Simpson could win viewers away from the wholesome Cosby television family.

The Simpsons proved a prime-time animated show could be very edgy and still be a hit in the mainstream.

The success of that program has led to a parade of prime-time animated programs, some of which have become hits – *Family Guy* – some of which deserved to be hits – *Dilbert* – and too many of which were flops.

Unlike what happened during the 1960s, the networks, which now include the cable channels, kept trying animation in order to strike that *Simpsons* gold again.

The founding of the Cartoon Network as a basic cable channel and the beginning of Nickelodeon producing its own animated series had a major effect on animation and its intended markets. One of those Nickelodeon series, *Ren & Stimpy*, was replayed on sister network MTV and a phenomenon was born in 1992.

What was happening was that animation could no longer be put neatly into a category and, in broadcasting terms, *Ren & Stimpy* crossed demographics in a way no one had anticipated. A ten-year-old could see *Ren &*

Stimpy on Nickelodeon while his older brother and sister were watching it on MTV. Merchandise could appeal to both groups – children and teens.

Ren & Stimpy's creator, John Kricfalusi, became the first animation director in years that actually became a celebrity among young people.

With the success of *Beavis and Butt-Head*, which debuted on MTV in 1993, there was a new kind of thinking for television animation – consciously create a series that would be seen as cutting edge and would capture that all-important 18-to-34 age group coveted by advertisers.

Between the animation block on the WB Network (*Animaniacs, Pinky and the Brain*), the shows created for the Cartoon Network (*Powerpuff Girls, Cow and Chicken, Courage the Cowardly Dog*) and Nickelodeon (*Invader Zim, The Fairly OddParents* and *SpongeBob SquarePants*) there has been plenty of evidence of cross-demographic success.

The incredible rise of *South Park* in 1997 showed that there are new limits in taste to be reached and broken. Its enduring success has proven that it hasn't been a fad.

The development of computer-generated animation has also fueled the mainstreaming of animation. Pixar's success with *Toy Story* and its subsequent films initially caused people to think that traditional cel and stop-motion animation were dinosaurs on the road to extinction. Instead, the financial success of such films as *The Nightmare Before Christmas*, the *Wallace & Gromit* shorts and feature and others have shown that computer animation is simply another tool an artist can use.

Adding more fuel to the fire was anime. Several companies began importing anime – Japanese animation – to this country and a dedicated subfandom was created. There are anime fans that are not interested in American animation, but are die-hards for the varied productions from Japan.

The Japanese produced animation in a dizzying number of genres, including hardcore pornography, and has had a huge impact on American audiences – just consider the effect of *Pokémon* on younger children and *Akira* for adults, just two instances.

The success of such series as *Beavis and Butt-Head* led to an animation rush
on MTV that had such misfires as *The Brothers* Grunt. © MTV

And with the rise of interest in animation, came a new industry: animation art merchandising. Aimed squarely at replicating the kind of collectible
fever comic books and sports trading cards had created, cels, drawings,
storyboards from both classic theatrical cartoons and television series drew
big bucks from collectors. Limited edition cels featuring artwork by some of
the legends of the medium were created to cash in on the collecting mania.
Some collectors loved the art, while others were speculators.

Because of the speculation, the bubble burst on animation art in the
late 1990s. Just as the "value" of comic books and sports trading cards
had been manipulated and overstated, the limited edition cels were too
often sold as "investments."

The field became crowded with cels that had images derived from
publicity art and signed too often by people with marginal association
with the subject matter.

Animation merchandizing continues to boom, however, in other fields.

Within just a few years, animation had gone from primarily residing in
a kiddie ghetto to a medium that could appeal to all age groups. Whether

it was a Boomer seeking out a piece of artwork from a Tex Avery cartoon or a 22-year-old buying a Stimpy doll that passed wind, animation had entered a new era of popularity.

With that popularity came publications that catered to the new audience.

Animation Magazine was a trade publication that in its earliest years also wanted to appeal to the fan audience.

In Toon covered animation art and *Storyboard: The Art of Laughter* was dedicated to all things Disney.

Animato had been a rough-looking fanzine that was published in Boston for a group of cartoon fans. Under the editorial guidance of Harry McCracken, the magazine blossomed into having a very professional look and tone. McCracken relinquished the editor's job back to publisher Michael Ventrella, who wrote that he needed help with the publication of the magazine.

I had written a column on the Fleischer Studios for several issues and I offered to edit the magazine and Ventrella hired me. Suffice to say the arrangement was moot when I discovered that an unpaid printing bill and no available financial resources would prevent any further issues.

When I was ready to quit, my friend and fellow animation fan Patrick Duquette suggested we buy the magazine by retiring the printing bill. Ventrella accepted the offer and we were in the magazine business.

The first issue under our ownership, number 23, was released in the fall of 1992 and, thanks to the assistance of Donna and Tim Lucas of *Video Watchdog*, we were able to make distribution arrangements with about six distributors that serviced both large chain and independent bookstores. Several distributors had told us that *Animato* was considered "dead."

It was an uphill effort. Initially, many thought – including Patrick and me – that our biggest market would be comic book shops. We learned, though, that our greatest sales came from bookstores. Comic book fans were not necessarily animation fans.

At a comic book shop promotion in our hometown, one customer

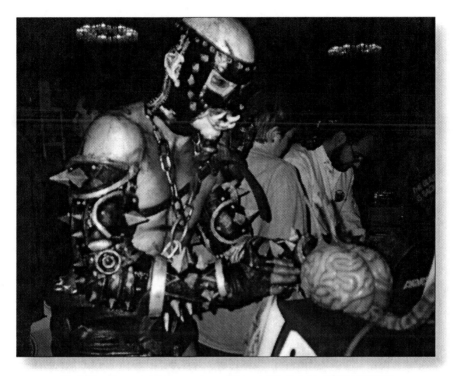

Marketing the magazine meant meaning a table at many Chiller Theatre Conventions in New Jersey. Here a member of Gwar shows his approval.

quizzed us for minutes before making a purchase and wanted to know what we thought the value of the issue would be in a few years.

Patrick and I produced issues 23 through 37, the last being the Spring 1997 issue. He was the publisher and I was the editor and, in many issues, the principal writer. We were very fortunate to have a core of regular contributors whom we tried to pay as often as we could. Working with the writers could be a challenge (my wife never got used to having the phone ring at all hours of the day and night), but it was immensely rewarding.

Three close friends of mine provided invaluable help. Gene Gumbs laid the magazine out for us and was dedicated to its success. Mark Martin, probably the single most talented artist working in American comics, provided great headers and a wonderful cover. Stephen R. Bissette, *Swamp*

One of the standard things to do at a convention is asking one of the stars to pose with you and your magazine. I was not above begging. Here I am with actor and gentleman James Karen.

Thing artist, *Taboo* publisher, *Tyrant* creator and film historian, became a regular writer for the two magazines. He also painted a beautiful cover.

The late Fleischer animator and director Myron Waldman and his wife Rosalie have not only been great friends for over 20 years, but they also provided much moral support for the magazines, as did my friend Richard Gordon, the veteran film producer.

Naturally, the greatest support came from my wife Mary and my mother, Sue.

During that time, *Animato* was the subject of a favorable review in *USA Today*, a nifty mention by Leonard Maltin – thanks Leonard! – on *Entertainment Tonight* and the subject of several newspaper articles in papers throughout the country.

Our partnership ended in the spring of 1997. Patrick retained control of *Animato* and I decided to start a new publication called *Animation Planet*.

I'm very proud of the magazine, although it lasted just three issues. The small distributors were going out of business or being bought out. I had fewer and fewer options.

One major distributor wanted to take 55% of my cover price, plus I would pay for shipping to its warehouse and to each store that carried *Animation Planet*.

As I was looking at a loan application in order to secure the additional capital I would need, my wife looked into my office and asked, "Do you really want to do that?"

I didn't. With the shake-up in distribution had come a dramatic deflation of the animation art bubble. The advertising base was much smaller.

And so I shut up shop in 1998.

I began posting a free on-line newsletter to anyone who wanted it and did so until the spring of 2000 when the demands of a new job prevented me from spending the time the newsletter required.

Then I "fell off the earth," as one writer recently described me on an animation chat group.

I recently "fell back" by beginning a blog on animation and other subjects at http://outoftheinkwell.blogspot.com.

This book is intended not just to represent my work from *Animato* and *Animation Planet*, but also to update it to show how animation has progressed from those heady days of the 1990s. There are also several pieces that will be new to readers outside of western Massachusetts as they appeared in the newspapers I edit.

In 2006, has animation finally reached its potential? Is it thoroughly accepted as a medium that can be used to tell a story, any story?

No, not yet. No one in Hollywood would green light an animated love story or western that didn't have songs or wasn't some sort of comedy. There is still the feeling that animation is best used for certain kinds of stories.

The days, though, of segregating animation as something just for children are over.

G. Michael Dobbs
December 2006

Chapter One: A New Industry

Let's look at the status of animation as the 1990s dawned. Thanks to the widespread acceptance of the VCR, Baby Boomers were buying animation both out of a sense of nostalgia and for their own children's entertainment. Animation collectibles were beginning to make their ascent as a hot item, as well.

The success of *The Simpsons* and *Ren & Stimpy* showed industry execs that animation was more than just a medium for children. Up until that time it's safe to say that most people in the film and television industry viewed animation as either Saturday morning fodder for kids or something Disney did for family audiences.

The television animation of the 1970s and '80s had reached mind-numbing lows with "high concept" shows that were anything but entertaining.

During this time, people such as Ralph Bakshi and Don Bluth, while finding mixed success with their own take on animation, were the exceptions to the rule.

The Simpsons and *Ren & Stimpy* were both an organic, almost underground phenomena. Both shows were simply in the right place at the right time to reach their audiences. They were obviously endorsed by network executives who decided to roll the dice.

And even more significantly, these shows were the product of an identifiable creator or creative team. Too often Saturday morning shows had been created in pitch meetings between producers and network executives with little more than an eye toward budget and a plot hook. Or Saturday morning cartoons had simply been part of a merchandising plan for a line of toys.

Both shows came from teams headed by a person with a well-defined original vision. These creators stayed with the show and continued to contribute to it.

The establishment of the WB and UPN also meant that there were two new networks interested in riding the animation wave. During this time both CBS and NBC changed its policies toward Saturday morning cartoons, but FOX not only pursued the kid audience on the weekends, but during the week as well.

What came about was a new attitude toward the medium and a willingness to experiment. It truly was a new era for the industry and the art form.

Animato #24 Fall 1992
The "Toon Age" is here
Turner Broadcasting launches a 24-hour cartoon channel

Here's a riddle: Let's say you're a television programming exec, and you notice the highest levels of television usage for children ages two through 11 are between 8:00 and 11:00 p.m., but you run your cartoon programming in the morning and in the 3:00 to 6:00 p.m. timeslot. What can you do to get both kids and adults to watch?

Well, if you were Ted Turner and his staff at Turner Broadcasting Systems, you'd buy the broadcast rights to a number of classic cartoons, and purchase lock, stock and inkwell the libraries of two studios. Then you'd develop a basic cable service to hook misty-eyed adults and animation fans who'd find it difficult to see these cartoons elsewhere. Oh yes, and kids will watch, too.

Welcome to the Cartoon Network, which will debut on cable systems throughout the country on October 1, 1992. Betty Cohen, Executive Vice President of the Cartoon Network, doesn't see the channel as another kids' network.

"A lot of these cartoons are not as meaningful to kids as to adults," she told ANIMATO. Turner Broadcasting did market surveys that showed "a large percentage of adults thought it [The Cartoon Network] was a good idea."

The approach for building up the network viewership is not unlike what Nickelodeon/Nick at Nite has done – hooking Baby Boomers to watch reruns of some classic and not-so-classic shows has resulted in building an audience of both adults and kids.

While Cohen is quick to point out, the Cartoon Network is not copying Nick at Nite's blueprint, the plan is similar; Mom and Dad will introduce their children to programming they enjoyed as kids.

"Our approach is to make the old feel fresh," explained Cohen. "We will give our audience a contemporary reason for viewing."

The Cartoon Network library is very impressive. The entire output of the Hanna-Barbera and MGM studios is owned outright by Turner Broadcasting, as well as the broadcasting rights to the Fleischer and Famous Popeye cartoons. The company also has control of a large number of the Warner Brothers shorts as well.

The only major characters not represented are the Lantz stars (Woody Woodpecker, Chilly Willy), Casper the Friendly Ghost, Betty Boop, the Terrytoon characters (Mighty Mouse, Gandy and Sourpuss) and the Disney stars. In total, 8,500 titles are available to air over the channel.

Considering many of these shorts are already being seen on the Turner channels of TNT and TBS, one might wonder how much overlap there will be. Cohen acknowledged some cartoons might air on all three, but never on the same day or the same time. Some of the more popular Hanna-Barbera titles, such as The Flintstones and The Jetsons, are currently committed to syndication deals that would prevent their immediate broadcast over the Turner network. The company is currently negotiating to retrieve those shows as soon as possible.

The Hanna-Barbera library is a major component of the network, and that fact might make some animation fans wince. After all, one can't really imagine many adult fans actually yearning to experience Touché Turtle again, much less Atom Ant or Magilla Gorilla.

Those fans should take heart, as Cohen notes the network will air *Toonheads* nightly at 11:00 p.m. This show will air the Popeye cartoons in their original glorious black and white, as well as many of the black-and-white Looney Tunes, World War II propaganda shorts and cartoons with ethnic humor. It's a show geared toward adults, and the controversial cartoons will be introduced in such a way as to place them in a historically accurate context.

Naturally, fans will wonder if original productions for the network are in the works, and Cohen assured the plans are there but not until the network has been on the air for three years. Cohen has been "heartened by the success of the Nicktoons. It has made me really happy, because they were not designed to sell toys. That's not their reason for being."

At a time when NBC is getting out of children's programming, one wonders about the wisdom of starting this cable service. Cohen assured that NBC's decision is "less of a statement if animation can work than it is if NBC can compete."

She notes that advertising dollars aimed at children have increased, and advertisers are looking for ways to reach young audiences. "There is a boom in animation. It's been 'here to stay' for 40 years on television," Cohen exclaimed.

Although advertiser support, a ready audience and available programming are not problems, getting onto cable systems is a challenge – a big one.

"Many systems have run out of space," said Cohen, adding that thankfully for the Cartoon Network and other new channels many cable systems are upgrading their technology that will allow for more choices. Turner Broadcasting is prepared, as it was for TNT, to weather a few lean years before the new network can be widely seen.

Just as music fans demanded their MTV, animation fans should contact their cable systems about the Cartoon Network. Cohen declined to say how many cable systems have signed up for the new service.

Cohen sees the Cartoon Network as "not just a channel, but a real force in broadcasting." Animation fans will see it as a paradise.

The Cartoon Network's programming has changed dramatically since its debut. Network officials developed new shows from a pilot program called "Cartoon! Cartoon!" Series from that effort included *The Powerpuff Girls*, *Johnny Bravo*, and *Courage the Cowardly Dog*.

Besides original programming, the network brought back Boomer favorites such as *Rocky and Bullwinkle* and *Speed Racer* and offered an updated version of *Jonny Quest*.

With the introduction of *Space Ghost Coast to Coast* in 1994, the network reached out to adults with a show that not only poked fun at the Saturday morning clichés of the original *Space Ghost* cartoon, but also to younger audiences who enjoyed the hip ironic humor.

The series made Space Ghost a talk show host with several of his former arch villains as his sidekicks. Recycling animation from the original series gave the series a rather numbing visual look, but one didn't watch *Space Ghost Coast to Coast* for the animation. Instead, the joy was watching a celebrity of some sort be interviewed in real time by George Lowe, the actor who provided the Space Ghost voice. Some guests understood the gag and played along, while others looked bewildered or angry.

The success of *Space Ghost Coast to Coast* fueled the creation of "Adult Swim," a late-night programming block with more off-center shows such as *Harvey Birdman, Attorney at Law* and *Aqua Team Hunger Force*.

The network also recognized the popularity of anime and imported series for that fan base.

The network created Boomerang, a spin-off channel that featured its older library. Regrettably, the black-and-white shorts of the 1930s owned by the network are still fairly difficult to see.

Both Nickelodeon and Disney followed with cartoon channels of their own.

In 2006, the network came under fire from animation fans as it started running non-animated programming.

Animato #29 Summer 1994
Returning to Cartoons
Hanna-Barbera's president is aggressively developing new talent the old-fashioned way

Fred Seibert wants people to understand there is a difference between "animation" and "cartoons," and that Hanna-Barbera is back in the "cartoon" business.

The president of Hanna-Barbera sees a cartoon as a one-reel animated film made by a cohesive team led by an animation director, and designed to make audiences laugh. While all "cartoons" are animation, not all "animation" is "cartoons."

"What had happened when Hanna-Barbera started television animation was they had people with 30 years experience making great cartoons," explained Seibert. "In their sleep, they could make funny cartoons. As those people left the industry, there was no way to replace them."

Without the vehicle of the one-reel cartoon, "the way of developing creative talent dried up," said Seibert, who has taken a very active step in reversing the trend.

Unlike many television productions of the past 30 years, units headed by a director made theatrical cartoons. At Warner Brothers, there were units led by directors such as Chuck Jones, Bob Clampett, and Friz Freleng. At MGM, Joe Hanna and Bill Barbera had a unit, as did Tex Avery. The director and his unit were responsible for producing a set number of cartoons a year. They developed their own stories and characters.

In March, Hanna-Barbera announced the company's Shorts Program with the goal of producing 48 six-to-seven-minute short subjects to air on the Cartoon Network beginning late this year and early 1995. Rather than employ the type of production techniques that have become standard in television animation today, the Hanna-Barbera Shorts Program is looking toward the past.

"Betty Cohen [president of the Cartoon Network] and I were talking, and we thought that the 'Golden Age of Animation' had less to do with theatrical releasing and full animation, and more with the fact that they were made one at a time," said Seibert.

Thirty years ago, advertising and network executives defined how television animation would be produced. With low budgets and fast schedules, television animation had to be made by committee with a realization that making animated drawings cost more money than recording a voice track. The result of these market demands was animation that was script-driven as opposed to image-driven.

With their Shorts Program, Hanna-Barbera wants to change all that, and has reinstated the unit form of production. "In the 'Golden Age,' writers filled the gaps between the pictures, while today's 'animation' fills the gaps between the words," Seibert said.

The new shorts will be returning animation back to a medium of images from being what's been called "illustrated radio." To get the strong visual and personal cartoons he wants, Seibert has invited a number of animators to head up their own unit, and direct their own short. Among the cartoons that have begun production are:

Look Out Below - Pat Ventura is re-interpreting two of Tex Avery's characters, George and Junior, in a new cartoon.

Hard Luck Duck - William Hanna's first solo effort since 1941 introduced a new character, Hard Luck Duck.

Johnny Bravo - Recent Loyola Marymount graduate Van Partible is using one of his student films as the basis of this short telling the story of a hip-swaying Fifties-esque rock 'n' roll idol.

Stay Out - Joe Barbera directs his own short starring Dino from *The Flintstones*, using the character design from the early 1960s.

Ralph Bakshi is also heading a unit. [See story in Chapter Three].

Although Seibert hasn't ruled out possibly piggybacking some of these shorts onto feature films released by Castle Rock or New Line (Hanna-Barbera, like the two feature film companies, are all part of the Turner Broadcasting group), he doesn't see theatrical release as the primary goal. His aim is to build a talent pool for the future of his company, and give The Cartoon Network a great publicity and programming boon.

Every two weeks animation fans (and hopefully, appreciative television writers and critics) can enjoy a brand-new raucous, kick-ass, old-fashioned funny cartoon.

Seibert isn't worried how "full" the animation is, but rather looks toward the bottom line. He said, concerning the "limited" versus "full animation" argument, that "the skill of the people to make you laugh" is the point.

"Do they have the resources to make you laugh? What issues are important here is what makes me laugh, what makes the world laugh," emphasized Seibert.

With that thought in mind, it's easy to understand why Seibert is willing to give both recent graduates from film schools and animators who have never directed before a chance to lead a unit and produce their own short.

"I'm looking for talent," he flatly declared. "The person has got to be an animator, not a writer, not a character designer, but someone who can run a film. The pictures are the boss."

With William Hanna and Joe Barbera themselves directing their own shorts, one wonders what these two men, who practically invented television animation, think about the new program. According to Seibert, they're "having a hoot."

By the end of his stay at the Cartoon Network, Siebert's *Cartoon! Cartoon!* effort had yielded 48 shorts, an Academy Award nomination, two Emmy nominations and seven half-hour series.

In 1997, Siebert took his *Cartoon! Cartoon!* format to Nickelodeon for the show *Oh Yeah! Cartoons!*, out of which came the series *The Chalk Zone*, *The Fairly OddParents* and *My Life as a Teenage Robot*.

A new season of *Oh Yeah! Cartoons!*, with 39 original cartoon shorts, was on Nickelodeon in 2006.

Animato #30 Fall 1994
Viva Las Vegas!

Animato's intrepid editor journeys to the land of casinos, slots and Wayne Newton to find out what's hot on home video this year.

Each year, thousands of video retailers from around North America go to Las Vegas, the site of the Video Software Dealers Association convention (VSDA). This year, *ANIMATO* was part of the press corps to find out what's new on home video and laserdiscs for animation fans, and it was appropriate that the animation fans' magazine was there. The two most anticipated video releases of this year are both animated!

I went out to the convention with a suitcase full of complimentary copies of the magazine, *ANIMATO* tee shirts, and flyers. I came back with even more brochures, tee shirts, key chains, posters, and review tapes! It takes days just to go through the material one has been given by the hundreds of companies represented at the show, and as a member of the press (we all wore highly visible name tags) we were expected to carry home everything! Luckily for me, a novice to both the VSDA and the city of Las Vegas, I had an expert guide in frequent *ANIMATO* contributor Christopher Kindred, who is both a native and resident of Las Vegas.

The convention is *the* trade show for the video industry, and the exhibitors make sure to remind video storeowners and employees that they are indeed part of "showbiz." The term "booth" doesn't do justice to the many very highly elaborate exhibit areas that are designed to dazzle the attendees.

What really dazzles people was star power itself. If you want to meet celebrities, the VSDA is one place to acquire an instant autograph collection. The various video companies brought the stars of their upcoming

Animation's role in the home video industry was plain to see at the annual Video
Software Distributors Association trade shows conducted in the 1980s and '90s.
These images are from 1994 and include my clowning with Ren and Stimpy.

releases to the VSDA in order to sign autographs and schmooze the folks.
The idea is, of course, if you actually meet these people, you just might
decide to buy a couple more copies of their video for your store.

I've been a journalist since 1975, and have interviewed dozens of show
business luminaries, but the VSDA certainly cracked any world-weary jaded
veneer I was wearing. I was constantly in awe of just the sheer number of
famous people attending the show.

Among the people I got to meet were: the voice of *Ren and Stimpy*
Billy West; Cameron Diaz, the female star of *The Mask*; Ricki Lake of John
Waters' *Serial Mom*; Hollywood legends Tony Curtis, Ann Miller and Cyd
Charisse; the voice of the Pink Panther, Matt Frewer; the great charac-
ter actor Lance Henriksen; Leslie Nielsen; adult film star legend Marilyn
Chambers; Fred Williamson; direct-to-video diva Shannon Whirry; Bill
Hanna and Joe Barbera; one of my favorite low-budget stars, Michelle
Bauer; black filmmaker Rudy Ray Moore; character great Don Stroud; star

of the shelved *Fantastic Four* film Alex Hyde-White; movie historian Leonard Maltin; and "Larry 'Bud' Melman" himself Calvert DeForest!

To drop a few more names, here's some of the people I saw, but did not get to meet: Debbie Reynolds; June Allyson; Chuck Norris; Fabio; Steven Seagal; Jerry Lewis; Shelley Duvall; Jean Stapleton; Angus Scrimm; Luke Perry; Dudley Moore; LaToya Jackson; the Barbi Twins; the Olson Twins; Stefanie Powers; C. Thomas Howell; Dana Plato; Richard Simmons; Deborah Shelton; Cynthia Rothrock; Roger Corman; Steve Railsback; Dan Haggerty; and Lassie!

The stars with the greatest perceived earning potential for the video industry, though, couldn't attend, although they were well represented. The most hyped films were *Jurassic Park* and *Snow White and the Seven Dwarfs*.

MCA/Universal proudly announced at the show the company was spending $65 million to publicize and market the video release of *Jurassic Park*, which has been for October 4. The film will be offered on video in standard and letterboxed forms with a suggested retail price of $24.98, and in a letterboxed laserdisc for $44.98 and a CAV-boxed letterboxed disc

VSDA attendees got a chance to see visit *Jurassic Park* through an elaborate exhibit. The lines were considerable around the bamboo-walled display, but Chris and I persevered. Inside were numerous production sketches, props, and photos, but the star was a life-size triceratops. By going through the exhibit, each person received a free *Jurassic Park* gift such as a sweatshirt or baseball hat.

At the Disney booth, *Snow White* was the focus of their marketing efforts. The animated classic will be available on Oct. 28, and will be priced at $26.99 on video and $29.99 on laserdisc. There will be also a limited edition boxed set (100,000 copies made) including the video, a "making of' video and book, and ten lithographs of original posters, and a CAV laserdisc release at $99.99.

Disney is also releasing *The Nightmare Before Christmas* this fall at the price of $19.99 for video, with apparently no laserdisc release set at this time. Jack Skellington was in attendance in the form of a 30-foot-tall balloon sculpture.

Riding on the wave of Disney's *The Lion King* is the release of *Leo the Lion: King of the Jungle* by Palm Beach Entertainment. This is the follow-up series to the venerated Japanese series *Kimba the White Lion*. The 25-minute tapes (recorded in Standard Play speed) will retail at $6.95. There are eight volumes planned at this time.

Fans mobbed animation patriarchs William Hanna and Joseph Barbera at their autograph session at the Turner Home Video area. During a brief lunch break, I got the chance to speak with both as they munched on sandwiches. Both men were happy to have participated in the Hanna-Barbera Shorts Program. Each had a chance to direct his own short, which marked the first time since 1940 that either man directed a cartoon without the other!

Barbera made the remark, though, that he "preferred the way we did them," referring to the two-director system the team perfected on their classic *Tom and Jerry* cartoons. When asked what the two men thought of today's cartoons, Hanna said he liked the work of people such as John Kricfalusi, but doubted that he could ever make shorts with that kind of no holds-barred humor!

ANIMATO advertisers AnimEigo had a cozy booth featuring Japanese cookies and a place to sit for weary attendees. The AnimEigo people handed out the first dubbed *Bubblegum Crisis* volume to all who wanted it.

The Library of Congress and Smithsonian Video is releasing a new collection of videos entitled *The Origins of American Film*, presenting rare films from the Library of Congress. The series includes an animation tape, *Origins of American Animation*; twenty-one complete films and fragments featuring the work of pioneers such as Tom Powers, J. Stuart Blackton, Wallace Carlson, and Winsor McCay.

Sony Wonder is continuing its Nickelodeon cartoon releases, and Charles Band's Full Moon and Moon Beam labels announced several new films, including productions which feature stop-motion animation. Included on the company's production slate is *Josh Kirby . . . Time Warrior*, a new serial described as in the "tradition of Buck Rogers, Flash Gordon and Captain Marvel." By the looks of the advertising material, there'll be plenty of story opportunities for David Allen's stop-motion animation.

Paramount is also making a large selection of animated television specials and one feature film featuring Charles Schulz's Peanuts gang. *Race for Your Life, Charlie Brown* will sell at $14.95, while the other tapes are either $9.95 or $12.95.

ABC Video has a Christmas sell-through promotion with *The Little Crooked Christmas Tree*, *P.J.'s Unfunnybunny Christmas* and *A Christmas Carol* all new to video and all priced at $9.95.

Manga Entertainment announced a number of Japanese animation releases for the upcoming year, including *Macross Plus*, *Appleseed*, *The Mighty Atom*, *Orguss 02*, *The Wings of Honneamis*, and *Giant Robo*.

While animation may not always get the respect or attention it deserves from the mainstream press, animation is clearly a mainstay of the video industry.

Animation Planet #2 Fall 1997
1997 VSDA Report

If the average animation fan had never realized just how important animated productions are in the home video market, then a stroll (more like a hike considering the size of the Las Vegas Convention Center) through the Video Software Dealer's Association Convention would open some eyes.

Actually, just walking into the cavernous lobby of the Convention Center might do the trick. It wasn't a live-action film promoted on a billboard-sized banner but rather the release of the direct-to-video animated production of *Hercules and Xena*.

The VSDA is the sales convention for the home video industry in North America. Thousands of independent video retailers from around the USA and Canada gathered in Sin City to find out what productions were coming out on video, to learn sales tips, and to get the scoop on upcoming technology and products that can help their business. Traditionally, this is the shmooze show to beat all shmooze shows. The studios want the retailers to buy many copies of their movies, so they give them a wide variety of souvenirs and bring stars to pose for photos and sign autographs. It's supposed to be an upbeat trade show with the studios thanking retailers for their continued support.

This year's VSDA, though, found the studios obviously cutting back, and the message received by too many retailers was that of a hearty raspberry. This was no lovefest. The independent North American video retailer has to contend with a number of problems, besides the major one of competing with giant chains such as Blockbuster. Video retailers are dealing with the major concern of a shorter window before a movie is released to pay-per-view. Traditionally, the studios gave the video industry a nice head start over pay-per-view by keeping their films out of pay-per-view suppliers for 90 days. Now the talk is shortening that window to just 30 days. With the proliferation of cable television channels and multiple premium services (just how many HBOs are there anyway?) the last thing the video industry needs is the removal of an edge they have over cable.

Many retailers walked around the convention floor wearing a pin protesting the pay-per-view move, but that was not their only concern. With the recent decision in Oklahoma to seize video store rental records in order for law enforcement officials to seek out people who had rented or purchased a film labeled kiddie porn (in this case the Oscar-winning foreign film *The Tin Drum*), retailers are also concerned about censorship problems and local legislation. There was even talk of releasing the censored versions of major films which are shown on airplanes to the home video market to avoid potential problems with over-zealous prosecutors!

The good news and bad news of the convention was DVD. Video rentals have been dropping and retailers were hoping there would be a solution to this problem. When I attended the convention three years ago, the savior was video game rental. This year, some touted DVD as a new tool the video industry could use to build rentals from higher end customers who want more for their rental buck than what VHS could give them.

If this was the good news, then the bad news was the lack of commitment to the new medium from Disney and several other studios. And to make matters more confused, there was discussion of a technology labeled "Zoom TV" which was going to offer more than DVD. Since the convention, Sony has pulled out of the DVD race to work on Zoom TV and

Disney just made an announcement they would release DVD titles, but has not said whether the new releases would be animated.

People were cranky, to say the least. Besides the real issues, the most common complaint of the retailers was a lack of star power and give-aways. The only studio that was actively giving away things was New Line, which distributed organizers, watches, vests, and other goodies to grasping crowds. Although many retailers just want the goodies for themselves, others use these items as promotional tools back home. This might seem petty, but video retailers are at the mercy of the studios when it comes to the pricing of the tapes they purchase, and have no control over which popular films are priced for rental and which are priced for sale.

Video retailers cannot count on significant rentals from blockbuster hits because so many of these films wind up in Wal-Mart priced under $15. Naturally, when the retailers come to the VSDA, they're looking for a few souvenirs, a Polaroid with a famous star, a little love, and a little respect.

The stars that were in attendance were mobbed. I managed to meet several and even had a chance to talk with a few. Jim Varney, famous for his Ernest P. Worrell character and a voice actor in *Toy Story*, was a delight with attendees as was director (*Clerks, Mallrats, Chasing Amy*) Kevin Smith. Veteran character actor Brion James was there to promote his *Pterodactyl Woman from Beverly Hills* and James Doohan of the original *Star Trek* was hawking a UFO documentary. The big guns included Linda Hamilton, Bill Pullman, Bill Paxton, Louis Gossett, Jr., Martin Sheen, Emilio Estevez, and Doug E. Doug. Fine performers all, but the number of stars was down considerably from previous years.

The interest in animation and its importance in the video marketplace was certainly evident with a number of productions being promoted. These included productions from:

Frontline Entertainment; *Dinosaur Valley Girls*, a stop-motion caveman comedy directed by Don Glut and starring Karen Black, William Marshall, a lot of semi-naked starlets and dinosaurs. Two versions are being sold; a director's cut with nudity and a "family" edition.

Goodtimes Home Video; *The Willows in Winter*, a British animated se-quel to *The Wind in the Willows*.

Plaza Entertainment Family Universal Network; a slate of sell-through titles including *The Treasure of Swamp Castle, The Elm-Chanted Forest, Nelvana's The Legend of the North Wind,* and *Treasure Island.*

Fox Home Entertainment; *The Simpsons.* Finally, the best of *The Simpsons* is coming to home video. Each tape has two uncut shows and the original *Simpsons* shorts that were broadcast as part of *The Tracey Ullman Show.* Also from Fox will be a direct-to-video Casper movie, *Casper: A Spirited Beginning,* featuring the same computer-animated spooks as seen in the theatrical feature.

Xenon Entertainment Group; Ralph Bakshi's *Street Fight (Coonskin).* Xenon is the company responsible for releasing much of the "Blaxploitation" cinema of the Sixties and Seventies to video. Bakshi's *Street Fight* is the animator's most searing commentary on this country and its culture. Both highly praised and damned when it was first released, it has been a difficult film to see.

MGM Home Entertainment; *The Pink Panther* Cartoon Collection. The company is releasing five 45-minute compilations priced at $12.95.

Liberty Home Video; *Davey and Goliath* Specials. The Tulsa, OK-based company is releasing the holiday specials featuring everyone's favorite animated Protestant.

Paramount Home Video; Christmas Specials; Christmas specials from *Hey Arnold!, Rocko's Modern Life,* and *Ren and Stimpy.* Joy!

Universal Studios Home Video; *Hercules and Xena - The Animated Movie: The Battle for Mount Olympus.* Take this direct-to-video home for just $20.

Lumivision, DVD Releases. Lumivision is releasing a number of its animated laserdisc titles in the new DVD format, including *Felix!, Animation Legend Winsor McCay, The Lost World* and *Animation Greats!*

Two true video phenomena were more than adequately represented at the show. The adult film industry provides the product that can mean the difference between profit and loss for the independent retailer when competing with the likes of Blockbuster, but this is not the venue for a detailed report of that part of the VSDA.

The other video phenomenon has been anime. Japanese animation has become extremely important to many video retailers, Because of its lack of television exposure and its handling of adult themes, anime is hip and is heavily rented by teens and young adults.

Central Park Media, Pioneer, A.D. Visions, and Urban Visions all had display areas and were attracting attention for the attendees. It may have a kiddie reputation among some people, but animation is a serious industry that a visit to the VSDA certainly proves.

Today, the trade show concept as a way to market to video stores has gone the way of the dinosaur. With national chains dominating the video rental industry, the studios no longer worry about marketing to the independent. It is far more important for them to make the sale to the purchasing departments at Blockbuster and Hollywood.

I attended my last video trade show in 2001 in Atlantic City and it was a sad little affair. Only the porn side of the show had any energy, largely due to the number of performers who were there to sign autographs for storeowners and employees.

A look around any decent-sized video store shows that animation remains a major category, thanks to productions aimed at families and anime.

Animato #31 Winter 1995
Women in Animation: Linda Simensky, Vanessa Coffey and Mary Harrington

Last year, the new organization Women in Animation was formed in Los Angeles to give women animation professionals a forum to discuss their craft and their gender's history in animation. Since J.R. Bray developed the organizational model that is the backbone of the modern animation studio, women have had a role in the creation of cartoons. Unfortunately, nearly all the positions women had were in the assembly-line jobs of ink-

Doug was one of the first group of Nicktoons developed by the
women executives of the company. © Nickelodeon

ing and painting. Women, for the most part, were silently banned from
creative positions.

There were very few exceptions. Laverne Harding's long tenure at
Walter Lantz's studio certainly proved that women had the ability to animate, as did Lillian Friedman's time at the Fleischer Studios.

Finally, after more than nearly a century of animation, women are in
positions of creative power in the industry, and if one needs evidence of
the success of women in animation one needs look no further than the cable box on top of your television set. The success of Nickelodeon's line-up
of cartoons can certainly be credited to the women broadcast executives
who chose those series, and worked with the creative teams to make them

a reality. Without their support, there would not have been Ren, Stimpy, Doug, a bunch of Rugrats, Rocko, and some Real Monsters cavorting on our television screens.

ANIMATO interviewed three of the women in positions of creative power at Nickelodeon: Vanessa Coffey and Mary Harrington in Los Angeles, and Linda Simensky in New York.

Linda Simensky

For a moment, I thought I had stumbled across a doppelganger of my AN-IMATO office. The walls are absolutely covered with comic strips, posters, and spot illustrations taken from magazines. The shelves are loaded with animation toys and figures. There are books, comic books and videotapes strewn about the flat surfaces of the office. Yes, this is an executive office. It looks out over Broadway onto Times Square. There is a receptionist area outside the door. But it looks like a fan lives here.

Linda Simensky has done what many readers of ANIMATO undoubtedly dream of doing. She's gone from being an animation fan to professional in her position as Director for Development of Nickelodeon. Simensky is the person responsible for finding the Nicktoons of the future.

"I basically look for the properties. I look at all sort of things. I look at comic books and comic strips. I look at short films, and the work of illustrators. I meet with animators doing work. I look at spot illustrations. I look for strong characters and really strong designs. I spearhead the process at Nick," explains Simensky.

Her responsibility ranges from the sketch presenting a character to the end of the first season the series is on the air.

"It's a long process; about two years until the end of the first season," said Simensky, who readily admits she becomes greatly attached to the people with whom she works and the series itself.

What is she looking for in a potential new series?

"There are two ways I divide it up. The first is the design and the character. The first thing that will reel me in is a great design, and that's a design that doesn't look like everything else that's out there. Basically it doesn't look like anything we've seen but still looks like an animated property," Simensky explains. "And then once I'm in with the design if the characters are interesting enough or funny enough, if there's an interesting hook to the show we're there. I can look at a sketch on a piece of paper and have a conversation with something, and have a sense if it should be developed."

Another of Simensky's tests is the "smart/ funny/fun gauntlet."

"It has to be one step beyond 'rad surfer dude.' It has to be smart. It has to be really funny. And fun: the super intangible. Does it feel like a fun property? Would I wear a tee shirt with that character embroidered on the pocket? Would I buy one for my younger cousin or would I cringe when I saw it?"

One of the criteria that certainly exists for other producers of television animation is whether or not a property is pre-sold; is it an adaptation of a popular comic strip, comic book, movie or live-action television show, and does it have considerable licensing potential? One can look at recent series such as *Sonic the Hedgehog, Problem Child* and *Beethoven*, for example, as examples of the pre-sold cartoon.

Simensky admits she doesn't know if she would be comfortable doing her job if she had to develop series out of toys or pre-sold properties. While Nickelodeon has an active licensing effort, the decision to air a series is not one dictated by the sales potential of PCV figures.

Simensky has had a long love affair with animation. She enjoyed it as a child, and found her appreciation for the medium grew when she was in college and discovered independent and foreign animation. Her favorite animated obsession? Vintage *Speed Racer* shows!

Simensky loves innovative cartoons, and wants the Nicktoons she develops to further animation's reputation.

"People aren't used to seeing innovation coming out of a television show. Innovation [in animation] traditionally comes from commercials and short films where people can take risks," says Simensky, who believes that innovation comes from "pushing the envelope." Pushing the envelope is something the network certainly has done with *The Ren and Stimpy Show*. While Simensky admits the show may go beyond the good taste barrier, she maintains that from the stretching of limits comes something new, fresh and funny.

Simensky is president of the New York chapter of ASIFA, and is very active in forming a New York chapter of Women in Animation. She beams when she recounts the initial meetings of the Women in Animation group in which women from the various animation studios in the New York area had the chance simply to connect with one another.

As an animation professional, Simensky is well aware of the sexism that exists in the industry, but says that at Nickelodeon conditions are different.

"Everyone has an equal chance of getting a job. There's no old boy network here. The best person is going to get the job. In the animation department there's no effort to skewer things one way or another," says Simensky. "The key thing about the people I work with," she says," is that we're animation fans."

Vanessa Coffey

The woman who is the executive producer of *The Ren and Stimpy Show* admits with a laugh that she "actually got involved in animation by accident."

Coffey began her career in animation at Marvel Productions in 1981 where she worked on the development of the long-running Saturday morning series, *Muppet Babies*.

"I worked at Marvel Productions for six years, and then left to go Murikami-Wolf –Swenson, where I worked on the development of the first five half-hour episodes *of The Teenage Mutant Ninja Turtles*, then I left for New York, and went to Nickelodeon and suggested they do an animated special, and have me produce it. I somehow sold them on that idea. It was the first animated special they would produce and own themselves," she recalls.

The success of the *Nick's Thanksgiving Fest* gave Coffey the credibility for thinking about developing series for the cable network. Nickelodeon asked her to find some ideas for series and Coffey went back to the west coast. She brought back three potential shows, *Rugrats, Ren and Stimpy* and *Weasel Patrol*, and picked up a fourth in New York when Jim Jenkins told her about *Doug*.

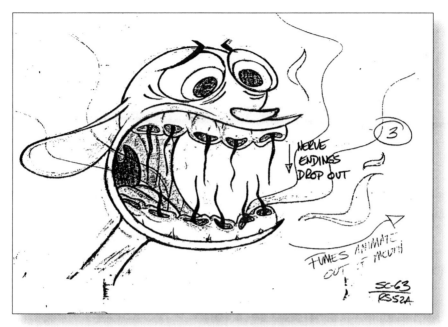

Clashes over the content of *Ren & Stimpy* were often presented in
interviews with John Kricfalusi as illustrative of the differences
between male and female senses of humor. © Nickelodeon

The network was impressed with the cartoons, allowed Coffey to produce pilot episodes that were then tested. All but *Weasel Patrol* were given
the go-ahead to be made into a series.

"And the rest is history," says Coffey with a laugh.

Being one of the few women executives in the animation business has
indeed often made Coffey feel like a stranger in a strange land.

"But I had a great mentor, and that was Margaret Loesch at Marvel
Productions. When I was there, she was president of Marvel, and she was
a shining example to me. She led me to believe that women in this business could succeed, could be smart and powerful. If it hadn't been for her, I
probably would have felt it was a dead end in this business. Then I went to
Nickelodeon and Gerry Laybourne and felt very optimistic about the possibilities. I felt very lucky to have been around Margaret and Gerry. In a lot

of studios and a lot of companies they're all run by men. If it hadn't been for Margaret I probably would have pursued another avenue in my career."

Some people in animation have made a point in the past several years of declaring that women cannot appreciate the kind of slapstick prevalent in animation. Has Coffey experienced that kind of prejudice?

"Yes, but I don't think that's an animation problem. I think that is a problem in general. I certainly don't think that it's men across the board who think that. I think that some men in this business feel that way, but I don't think all of them feel that way."

The Nicktoons were important to Coffey's career for more than one reason.

"After spending ten years in the animation business and after [being in] animation in television especially during the Eighties, which was horrifying, I didn't want to be in the animation business any longer if I couldn't make shows I couldn't watch and I couldn't be proud of. The idea was kids are so sophisticated and kids like unique styles in art and animation, and I felt it was important to give them a diverse style for each show as well as a diverse idea for each show.

"I wanted to be proud of my shows and I wanted to feel that I wasn't being condescending, and they were sophisticated. It was a very thought-out plan."

Doug was designed to present a role model with a positive point-of view, Coffey notes, while a show like *Ren and Stimpy* is "dessert."

What kind of impact has the success of Nicktoons made on the animation industry? Well, Coffey is not alone in her belief that the networks have recently shown more interest in developing original series rather than rely on adapting a comic book, a live-action television show or a movie. Nicktoons represents the notion that you can do animation that's not pre-sold.

"We didn't have to do characters based on a movie," declares Coffey. Coffey also thinks that more animation creators are seeing the possibility of success for original series, and have been pitching more ideas to the networks for different kinds of animated programming.

Besides her duties *on Ren and Stimpy,* Coffey is developing a feature film and several new series. Although she is strongly attracted to making the leap into live-action productions, she readily admits she "can't resist a good animation project."

Mary Harrington

Mary Harrington's introduction to animation was made when she was working for Steve Hahn, the co-producer of the 1987 *The Chipmunk Adventure* feature. Although hired to develop live-action projects, Harrington found herself fascinated by animation.

"It was really strange," she recalls. "I was doing live-action development at Bagdasarian [Productions], and became more and more interested in animation, and decided that's where I wanted to go with my career."

Harrington is now vice president and executive producer of Nicktoons. After her exposure to Alvin, Theodore and Simon, Harrington went to Nickelodeon in the fall of 1990. She had worked with Vanessa Coffey on the *Nick's Thanksgiving Fest* special and remembered the anxiety that production caused. The overseas animation studio was in the Philippines, and Nickelodeon had a difficult time getting the completed footage out of Manila after the military coup!

With the success of that special, Harrington began work on developing the first Nicktoons. The network started production on *Ren and Stimpy* in the fall of 1990 and on *Doug* in December of 1990. Harrington moved back to Los Angeles two years ago to work with Games Animation, and work with *Rocco's Modern Life*. While Harrington is very interested in finding a female creator to develop a new show, she's proud that the current Nicktoons "have proven that boys and girls can enjoy the same show."

The charge that animation humor is something women don't understand is something Harrington has faced, and discussed at length with Linda Simensky. The two have come up with a lighthearted theory that if some women don't care for slapstick, it's because they lack the "Three Stooges gene."

Harrington believes the Nickelodeon approach to developing a series incorporates the best elements of classic animation and live-action production. For many years in television animation, series were sold to the networks on the basis of a sales meeting in which a studio representative would present a series synopsis and a few key drawings to represent the production. Considering the quality of the overwhelming majority of Saturday morning series in the '60s, '70s and '80s, one can draw some damning conclusions on this way of developing a series.

Nickelodeon follows the live-action television model. It orders a pilot of a cartoon, and then tests it for audience reaction. Harrington also believes another difference is producing cartoons that are creator-driven. At Nickelodeon, the producer is part of a team along with the cartoon's creator, and the series' writers and directors.

"The creative vision is so much more dynamic when it's approached in this way," says Harrington.

The rest of the industry has indeed been influenced by the success of the Nicktoons and how they are made.

"Definitely, I feel we've been the leader of the pack. Following the launch of Nicktoons, there's been an increased energy in the animation business. The creator-driven process seems to be spreading to other studios. The animation artists seem to be more empowered within the industry since the launch of Nicktoons," asserts Harrington.

Harrington is proud of the number of women who are currently creating animation at Nickelodeon, and the mentoring effects the network is having. Two of the directors currently working at MTV's *Beavis and Butt-Head* are women who worked on *Doug*. She promises that Nickelodeon will be active in the new organization Women in Animation.

Harrington has two more goals for the network: to work with a female creator and to develop a show with a strong female character. Considering the success of the past few years, undoubtedly these goals will be met.

Nickelodeon's impact on animation was considerable during the 1990s. Its shows remained, for the most part, smart and cutting edge for children's programming.

Lightning did strike again with a property that crossed demographics with *SpongeBob SquarePants*. Although not as eccentric a show as *Ren & Stimpy*, it attracted a teen and young adult audience in a very similar fashion.

With the success of a magazine aimed at children as well as a motion picture division, Nickelodeon is still very much a leader in animation.

Linda Simensky left Nick in 1995 to become the director of programming at The Cartoon Network. In 2001, *The Hollywood Reporter* added her to its "Women in Entertainment Power 100 List."

In 2003 she was hired by PBS to be its senior vice president of children's programming.

Vanessa Coffey was hired by television syndication giant King World in 2001 as vice president of development.

Mary Harrington is an independent producer who came back to Nickelodeon in 2001 as the executive producer of the most outrageous animated series ever to appear on Nickelodeon to this date, *Invader Zim.*

Animato #32 Spring 1995
The studio best known for Woody Woodpecker is reinventing itself with the production of a variety of new shows

Quick! What comes to mind when you think of cartoons from Universal Pictures? Woody Woodpecker? That's right. But, come to think of it, there hasn't been much action from that character or the studio since the Seventies. That was the problem facing Jeff Segal five years ago. Segal is the president and founder of MCA Universal Family Entertainment and the Universal Cartoon Studios. He has been responsible for a new crop of cartoons bearing the Universal logo, including Saturday morning offerings *Back to the Future, Fievel's American Tails,* and *Beethoven* for CBS, *Problem Child* for USA Network and *Monster Force* and *Exosquad* for syndication.

Segal is no stranger to animation. He began his career in Japan working for Toei Animation Studios and Tsuburaya Productions on various animated productions. Once back in this country, he joined Hanna-Barbera as a writer/story editor/ producer for series such as *Super Ted, Fantastic Max, Midnight Patrol* and *Popeye and Son.*

"I started as a story editor and writer and worked on a lot of Hanna-

Barbera shows. From there I became involved with development and was elevated to the vice president of creative affairs and became involved with international co-venture projects that we were producing with partners in various parts of the world, Europe and Asia particularly. After I became the senior vice president, I came over to MCA," said Segal.

The entertainment giant recruited Segal to found and head a new animation division. His first task was to evaluate just what properties MCA had and to see if those properties could jump-start the operation. Segal made the decision to use some of Universal's hit films to spearhead his division's operations.

Segal's first series was an adaptation of the *Back to the Future* films. Next came a series based on other successful Universal movies and recently Segal added an effort to enter the direct-to-video market that has been trail blazed by Disney's *Return of Jafar*. MCA released earlier last December a sequel to *The Land Before Time,* which according to *Video Store* magazine has sold a very respectable 3.25 million units to date.

Universal's latest ventures are *Earthworm Jim* for the new WB Network, which is described proudly by Segal as "a subversive show," and a new Casper series for the Fox Children's Network.

"In the category of animation, we're a new company and we've tried to find a way of establishing ourselves," said Segal. He added that the company is now developing a computer-generated show in conjunction with a television network.

Segal has recently started the 1996-97 development season and reported that three-quarters of the projects the company is considering are creator-driven shows and one quarter being based on live-action feature films, although the shows finally green-lighted for production may not reflect this ratio.

One film Segal is actively considering for a series is the most expensive movie of all time, Kevin Costner's epic science-fiction adventure *Waterworld.* The goal of taking a successful live-action feature and turning into an animated series is building a franchise, Segal explained. *Beethoven*, a live-action comedy starring Charles Grodin as a harried husband and dad who has to cope with the problems caused by his family's Saint Bernard, did well enough theatrically to inspire a successful sequel. Both live-action films have done very well on home video, and now there is a cartoon series that keeps the *Beethoven* name and concept in front of its target audience.

With the animation industry buzzing over the concept of creator-driven shows, one might wonder if Universal has taken some critical lumps over its slate of cartoons adapted from hit live-action movies. Segal is quick to point out the commitment he has to the company's new creator-driven shows.

"Our agenda for animation is pretty broad. On one hand, we are really into creator-driven properties. For example, the *Earthworm Jim* property at WB is exactly that. The creator of the show is a brilliantly creative, wildly visionary guy who came up with this property. It became a video game, and he's working on the TV series and he's giving it a really interesting twist that only somebody with passion for a property can as opposed to somebody who's just doing it for a paycheck.

"Even on our TV series which we adapt from feature films we try to work with the original creative artists. The original writers for *Problem Child* were involved with the *Problem Child* TV series. On *Back to the Future* one of the original writers, Bob Gale, was the creative supervisor on the show and he worked daily with the writers to try to keep the consistency of what *Back to the Future* was all about."

One franchise Segal is working on to revive is Walter Lantz's Woody Woodpecker. The question Segal is trying to answer, though, is "how?"

There is the possibility of new theatrical shorts, a new television series and perhaps a feature film starring Woody and other Lantz characters, but Segal said the company wants to find a new approach to the characters which will ensure their acceptance by Nineties' audiences.

Of the two currently syndicated series one is an original, while one uses a very mighty Universal franchise. *Monster Force* is a reworking of the venerable Universal horror characters. In the new series, Dracula is an evil mastermind whose attempts to take control of the world are thwarted by a young scientist and his team who are aided by the Frankenstein monster. Universal is also producing the *Exosquad* science-fiction series for syndication. Segal noted that one challenge is finding suitable times for both shows. The competition for after-school broadcast time slots is stiff, not only from other animated series, but also from talk shows.

Segal is well aware of the almost daily changes in both the animation and broadcast industries, and stated that producing shows for just Saturday morning consumption does not supply enough revenue for an operation Universal's size. With the success of the direct-to-video sequel to *The Land Before Time* and Segal's intention to explore the possibilities of feature-length and theatrical cartoon production, no doubt one can expect some surprises from the relatively new company on the block.

Universal was a great example of a major corporate entity trying to hop on board the animation revival and not understanding the elements that made that revival work.

The studio did bring Woody Woodpecker back into production for a brief series on FOX in 1999. Directed and produced by *Ren & Stimpy* alumni Bob Jacques, the show featured Billy West as the voice of the woodpecker.

The principal output of the studio in recent years has been on making direct-to-video sequels to some of the company's animated feature film franchises. These include new installments to *The Land Before Time, An American Tail* and *Balto*.

Animato #34 Spring 1996

Sunbow Entertainment: The studio that brought you *My Little Pony* now has one of the hippest shows on TV. How did that happen?

Quick . . . what do *My Little Pony* and *The Tick* have in common? Well, would you believe they come from the same studio?

Sunbow Entertainment has attracted the interest of serious animation fans with the FOX show based on Ben Edlund's cult comic book. Those who might think Sunbow is a new player on the block just haven't noticed the company that was founded in 1978.

Sunbow series have include *GI Joe*, *The Transformers*, *Jem*, *My Little Pony 'n' Friends*, *Inhumanoids*, *Visionaries*, *Bucky O'Hare*, *Conan the Adventurer*, and *Conan and the Young Warriors*.

Sunbow has also produced two theatrically-released animated features, *My Little Pony – The Movie* and *The Transformers – The Movie*. Among its current line-up, Sunbow has two critical and popular hits, adaptations of *The Mask* and *The Tick*.

Sunbow has come into criticism in the past from advocates for children's television for producing animated series based on toy lines, and certainly there was reason to think that a show such as GI Joe really was a half-hour marketing tool for a toy line.

Today, though, Sunbow is pursuing two tracks. While production on the *GI Joe* and *My Little Pony* franchises continues, Sunbow has entered the creator-driven animation field with a bang. Ben Edlund's popular comic books featuring the incredibly stupid but well-meaning superhero The Tick provided the vehicle for Sunbow to break out of the kidvid ghetto.

Nina I. Hahn is the vice president of development at Sunbow and the executive in charge of finding new ideas for shows. Sunbow has two new shows in development: *Plex* at UPN and *Fat Dog Mendoza* at CBS.

Prior to coming to Sunbow, Hahn was development coordinator at Jim Henson productions and worked at HBO's Comedy Channel purchasing international animated shorts. She's been with Sunbow for four years and noted that when she came to the company its productions were "icon brand name properties." Her goal was for the company to grow in a new direction.

"What I tried to do is parallel paths. On one path maintaining the commercial side of what we do and revitalize those commercial properties so they have as much individuality within a comfortable formula," Hahn explained. "And on the other side, the other parallel course is to create a whole new division of properties that are very eclectic, niche, boutique one-offs."

Hahn described her mandate as "to create different shows for different reasons, different people." In an industry where animation studios strive to create a noticeable style, Sunbow management puts no priority on having a visual trademark.

The first niche show for Hahn has been *The Tick*. Hahn believed her first job was to establish Sunbow as a creator-friendly studio where creators could have a "hands-on experience with their own property."

"Ben Edlund has remained a central magnet to the property, and that was very clearly set up on my part. Not only do I think it's the right thing to do with the property, but because it's beneficial to Sunbow to establish as a place where creators could come and grow their concept into other means," she said.

Hahn emphasized her belief that if a company optioned a concept from a creator, the resulting show should be the concept and not an altered or watered-down one.

Sunbow's *The Mask* falls in between shows such as *My Little Pony* and *The Tick*, Hahn said. While *The Mask* is an adaptation of the popular film (which was in turn an adaptation of a comic book from Dark Horse), Hahn noted that Sunbow has worked very closely with Dark Horse and with the studio that produced the feature, New Line.

Hahn also tried applying a more creator-driven philosophy to establish shows such as *GI Joe*.

"How can I make this show [*GI Joe Extreme*] different from the other GI Joes?" asked Hahn. Her answer was to turn to comic book artist Bill Sienkiewicz, who created designs for the show and eventually developed a style guide to push the show into a different visual direction.

With its history of producing shows based on toy lines, the question of the importance of licensing might seem a bit obvious at Sunbow.

Hahn views licensing as a "natural progression of a concept."

"How it's handled is what everyone needs to be careful with, and how to get a concept up and running in the licensing world is no small challenge. The complaint 10 or 15 years ago, although on some level I see it, there's the exact mirror argument which is there are other companies out there where the show came first and then the toys and you're still selling the toys through the show. Which came first is not necessarily the issue. The issue is if the show is a good show and is the merchandising campaign a good campaign."

Hahn is excited about the shift in animated programming away from straight adventure and more toward comedy or comedy/adventure and how toy companies will interpret the new breed of programs into toys. Despite the explosion in interest in animation, independents such as Sunbow find the animation market a challenging one. Hahn noted that broadcast television is a changing marketplace. NBC no longer has any animated programs. The sale of ABC to Disney might impact on the number of non-Disney produced programming. The potential change in ownership at CBS makes that network also difficult to predict. The WB stations feature Warner Brothers productions (with the exception of Universal's *Earthworm Jim*), while UPN represents one network with potential for independents. Syndication is also highly competitive and difficult for an independent.

Hahn noted that while cable television has increased the possibilities for producers, the challenge is letting the viewer know where and when to find a show. One of Sunbow's strengths is its international sales division that sells the studio's product to 144 countries. By seeking international financing for animated series, Hahn believes animation companies will have to think "globally" more and more in the future.

One of Hahn's later projects at Sunbow certainly showed her willingness to pursue non-mainstream properties. Artist Bill Griffith relates on his Zippy the Pinhead website that Hahn approached him about a Zippy animated series and an initial deal was struck between Sunbow and Showtime cable network in 1998. When Sunbow pulled out of the deal because the studio could not agree on a budget with Showtime, Showtime turned to Film Roman. Unfortunately, financial problems at that studio led to the eventual cancellation of the proposed series.

In 1998, Sony Wonder, a division of Sony Music, bought Sunbow. Hahn joined MTV Networks in 2005 as its vice president of international development, Nickelodeon.

In 2006, *The Tick* cartoon series was brought out on DVD.

Chapter Two: The New Stars

With the animation boom came new studios and new names to the forefront. In years past some people knew who Walt Disney, Max Fleischer, Walter Lantz or Chuck Jones were, but generally people in the animation industry were routinely faceless.

That all changed in the 1990s as older fans began paying close attention to credits on cartoons and magazines such as the two I published. My magazines regularly interviewed directors, producers and voice actors. People wanted to know who did what on a show or a movie. Stripping away the curtain of anonymity was one of the most radical elements of the changes in animation.

Undoubtedly the element that pushed this movement was the success of the *Ren & Stimpy Show* in 1991-2. *Ren & Stimpy* creator John Kricfalusi gave provocative interviews decrying the state of animation and showed off his good looks in plenty of movie-star-like press photographs.

Kricfalusi was the first animator in years to court personal publicity and controversy. Since the fall of the Hollywood studio cartoon only one other animator had gone that route: his mentor, Ralph Bakshi.

Bakshi, though, didn't go as far in the short of length of time as Kricfalusi in establishing a public persona. Kricfalusi actively challenged the status quo of television animation, the medium that employed him.

Although thanks to the popularity of *The Simpsons*, millions of people

The *infant terrible* of 1990s animation, John Kricfalusi
is seen at a signing at an animation art gallery.

were seeing Matt Groening's name every week, Groening admittedly didn't
have as strong a control on his show as Kricfalusi did on *Ren & Stimpy*.

Kricfalusi also became the first martyr on the cross of creative-driven
cartoons. He had sold the series and characters to Nickelodeon and when
conflicts over delivery of episodes and content arose, he was kicked off his
own show.

Some of his production people went on to a new studio owned by
Nickelodeon to continuing making the show without him. To Kricfalusi
fans people such as Bob Camp (our first interview) were traitors to their
hero and to the show they loved.

Kricfalusi showed what could be done by recreating the idea of the production unit that had been used by studios such as Warners and Fleischers in
the heyday of the theatrical cartoon. A director who called the shots in story
development, character design and vocal performances headed the unit.

This method has been re-embraced by many studios and networks
and it's thanks to the success of *Ren & Stimpy*.

To this day, though, the economic model for an independent cartoonist to see his or her work on television requires the involvement of a corporate entity of some sort – a distributor or studio or network – and those organizations never want to simply be a vehicle. They want to be an owner.

Creators are always going to have to be partners with someone else and the best creators will have a very good attorney to protect as much of their rights as possible.

Animato #27 Fall/Winter 1993
Bob Camp: Continuing to Push the Envelope
with *Ren and Stimpy*

What does television's famed talking horse and *Ren and Stimpy* have in common?

After you've done magic nose goblins, what do you do for an encore?

Will there continue to be "Happy, Happy, Joy, Joy" after the departure of John Kricfalusi?

Director, producer and writer Bob Camp has the answers to these and other questions about what remains one of the hottest animated half-hours on television. It's easy to believe the hilarious and enthusiastic Camp that the best is yet to come for the show.

Camp has spent a large portion of his time in the last year defending his decision to stay with the show after the highly publicized departure of Kricfalusi, and while he is willing to continue discussing the conflict between Nickelodeon and Kricfalusi, he'd much rather discuss the new season.

"We're really pushing it this year," exclaims Camp. The shows are more outrageous, and new characters have been added. Here's a preview:

No Pants Today: Stimpy realized he's naked and goes on an epic quest for pants.

Jerry the Bellybutton Elf: Stimpy becomes so obsessed with his navel; he actually goes into his navel only to be enslaved making lint for Jerry the Bellybutton Elf.

Ren's Pecs: Ren decides to go for some pectoral implants made from some of Stimpy's butt fat.

Stimpy's Cartoon Show: An episode exploring a cartoon producer who doesn't do anything but gets all the credit.

It's difficult to give these short synopses credit as Camp just doesn't describe them to you during an interview, he practically performs them.

There will be 14 new half-hour shows, and despite the envelope-pushing Camp and his staff have done, he's not run into too many problems with the cable network censors.

"We've had a 95% approval [of scripts]. We're doing better than before," reported Camp.

The upcoming season will see the introduction of new characters, including a Scottish children's show host named Haggis McNaggis voiced by Alan Young (of *Mr. Ed* fame), and Wilbur Cobb, a "really big kinda muttering old showbiz guy" with stand-up comedy legend Jack Carter providing the voice. Another veteran performer, Charlie Callas, is also doing voice work.

"It's great to work with these guys," said Camp, who is trying to get other great older comedians involved with the show.

The voice actor Camp describes as the "key cornerstone" of the show, Billy West, will be providing the voices of both Ren and Stimpy.

"We always try to make it funnier in the recording session. Occasionally we do have a little Standards thing about something," Camp said.

This season, the show will be animated in a studio in Korea. The question naturally arises if the Korean artists will understand Ren and Stimpy.

"It's definitely alien [to them]," said Camp. "The owners of the studios understand the show quite well, and translate it easily." Camp plans to go to the studio to meet with the artists later this year.

"The better layouts you send, the better animation you get," explained Camp.

The use of a foreign studio is a necessity for Camp and his staff to produce *Ren and Stimpy* on time and on budget, which were major problems for Kricfalusi's Spumco Studio. Although tired of having to defend himself, Camp emphasizes that some media reports, which characterized him as a new-coming interloper, are simply not true.

"It's misconception. I was there from day one, from the very first drawing," he said. "If you like *Ren and Stimpy*, then watch the shows. If you're not happy, then switch the channel."

Camp added that "virtually the same crew is doing the show."

With two *Ren and Stimpy* CDs coming out as well as the video collections and a new group of merchandising, the pressure will be great on Camp to keep the *Ren and Stimpy* franchise on the cutting edge to maintain its great popularity. A conversation with him confirms he's certainly up for the challenge.

"We continue to get better," said Camp. "We try not to fall into a pattern, and are constantly looking for new ways to tell jokes and entertain."

Camp stayed with *Ren & Stimpy* for several more seasons. In 2004, he was a storyboard artist on Joe Dante's *Loony Tunes: Back in Action*.

Animato #27 Fall/Winter 1993
Joe Murray: The Independent Filmmaker Tries his Hand at Television with *Rocko's Modern Life*

The question facing any animation producer today is which road to travel . . . you can take the X-Men/Batman/Teenage Mutant Ninja Turtles route and produce a superhero adaptation, or you can take the *Ren and Stimpy* exit to an envelope-pushing half-hour, or you can go the way of Stephen Spielberg and re-tread some beloved animation stars.

Or you can travel like Joe Murray, the producer of *Rocko's Modern Life*. Murray is following in the tracks of the producers of such shows as *Doug*, *Rugrats*, *Eek! The Cat*, *The Simpsons*, and *Ren and Stimpy*. He's produced a very distinct show that is really nothing like anything else.

Murray, a veteran independent filmmaker, is making his television se-

Joe Murray's *Rocko's Modern Life* was one of the funniest early Nicktoons. © Nickelodeon

ries debut with Rocko, a cute little Generation X age wallaby a long way from home and on his own for the first time. While *Rocko's Modern Life* certainly has its share of gross-out moments, the series is genuinely clever and has a look all its own.

Murray said the move to television is a "big transition, to put it mildly."

No matter the problem, though, Murray is committed to produce a quality show.

"The style is more character- and visual-driven. The dialogue is not the focus. It's tailored more on the old Looney Tunes," said Murray. "We try to put more intellectual appeal to it."

Nickelodeon approached Murray after seeing some of his independent work, and apparently wanted a show with the feel of an independent production.

In the world of animated funny animals, the Australian wallaby hasn't had much exposure, and Murray chose that animal to be his star's model for several reasons. He believed the appropriate Australian accent would be appealing. Wallabies are cute. Most importantly, though, he envisioned Rocko to be "a stranger in a strange land."

Because Rocko *is* a little cute wallaby in a strange country, Murray and his writers can construct animated stories about the most mundane of activities. No epic battles or titanic struggles are necessary on *Rocko's Modern Life* when one has stories about . . . taking out the trash, going grocery shopping or accompanying a friend to his house for dinner.

Like so many of the shows now considered classics, *Rocko* definitely operates on both an adult and juvenile level. There are plenty of sight gags, but there is also the kind of characterization often missing today in animated shows aimed at kids.

The voice talent for *Rocko* comes largely from a cast of stand-up comedians, and Murray said, "The voice sessions turn out to be a lot of fun. The director is not afraid of ad libs."

Murray described the show's creative process: "The writers lay out each show in a written outline form, then the director does the storyboard, and then the dialogue is written by the show's director."

The show is animated in Korea by the same studio which was until recently used for some of the Disney television series. Murray is very concerned about quality, and had just finished viewing rushes for two days when interviewed.

"There are always some initial problems. It's too big a process," said Murray. He has two supervisors working in Korea, and tries to catch problems in the beginning. In an industry now dependent on using foreign labor, the problems of communication are common, and have plagued other animated half-hours. Murray has even used pencil tests, a relatively unheard-of practice for television, to make sure the show has the necessary quality.

"When you're running a small studio, you're on top of all the details. It's very hands-on," explained Murray. Producing a half-hour show for television means a lot of delegation. It's like trying to put a cage around Godzilla."

In 2005, Joe Murray was back on the air with *Camp Lazlo,* another "funny animal" show, on the Cartoon Network.

Animato #30 Fall 1994
AAAHHH! Real Monsters: Gross and yet artistic!

They don't look like vampires, mummies or werewolves, but The Gromble, Ickis, and Krumm are definitely monsters. Real Monsters. Debuting this fall on Nickelodeon is the latest project from Klasky-Csupo. Inc. *Aaahhhh! Real Monsters.*

The studio that has given the world *Rugrats* and *Duckman* now turns its creative eye to the shadowy forms under the bed, or in the dusty corner of a closet . . . you remember them from your childhood . . . monsters. Or, in this case, monsters in training.

Aaahhh! Real Monsters involves a group of student monsters attending the Monster Academy. Their goal is learn the fine art of scaring people, which is not as easy as it sounds despite their grotesque appearance. Anyone who might be reading this should know the new show is not a retread of *The Groovy Ghoulies* or *Beetlejuice.* The studio has brought its own unique vision to the production that is both sophisticated and sophomoric.

I can't help but love a show that is designed like a European animated short, but has armpit jokes.

Founded in 1981, Klasky-Csupo had built a solid, but fairly low key, reputation for doing animated credit sequences for motion pictures, commercials and music videos. In 1988, the studio went in a new direction when it was chosen to animate Matt Groening's *The Simpsons* for *The Tracey Ullman Show.* The short films were so popular (as practically everyone on the planet knows), a half-hour series was developed for the FOX network, and Klasky-Csupo animated the first three seasons of the show. A dispute with Fox and Gracie Films ended the association, and the studio received some bad press when the animation union made charges of unfair labor practices.

Gabor Csupo and Arlene Klasky are the producers behind some
of the biggest animated television hits of the 1990s.

The Simpsons was not the studio's creation, though, and Klasky-Csupo
didn't receive much attention for their work. Their new show for Nickelodeon changed that condition. *Rugrats* has won three Emmys and a CableACE Award, and that success led to two collaborations with Lily Tomlin
and Jane Wagner on the Edith Anne specials and the ongoing series, *Duckman.*

Besides the critical acclaim, *Rugrats* has been a big hit, ratings-wise.
People love the offbeat character design and the funny, clever stories of
a group of very young children and their parents. Despite all the success,
the studio has not been the recipient of the kind of rabid fan attention
bestowed upon others in contemporary animation. Winning Emmys unfortunately sometimes doesn't attract as much notice as a game of frog

baseball among the teenage fans that are the target audience for merchandisers. Frankly, I would have gladly bought a *Rugrats* tee shirt!

This situation may change with the debut of new episodes of *Duckman* and the faith Nickelodeon is showing *Aaahhh! Real Monsters*. The cable network has already committed to a second season. Behind the show are the studio's founders Gabor Csupo and Arlene Klasky, and producer/creative consultant Chuck Swenson, who are now all seasoned veterans of producing animation for television.

In an interview with *ANIMATO* Klasky and Swenson spoke about the new series.

"Nickelodeon came to us. Vanessa Coffey was the executive producer of animation at Nickelodeon, and she wanted us to pitch some more ideas because *Rugrats* was sort of winding down," explained Klasky.

"Gabor, the night before, put his thinking cap on and said, 'Well, no more dinosaurs, and we don't want to do babies anymore. What do kids really like?'

"And I think he thought back to what our boys really liked. The kids really loved monsters. So he did some very lovable characters on a sheet of paper. He just sort of whipped them out, and that was a germ of an idea. When he presented it to Vanessa, she absolutely flipped."

Swenson said the idea went through a number of changes, and that a lot of the look of the show can be attributed to the Russian artists and animators who work on the show, including director Igor Kovalyov. Turning to artists from Eastern Europe is natural for Csupo, who was born in Budapest, Hungary, and fled the country in 1975. The influences of different artistic traditions "really put a twist on the show," said Swenson.

Originally, the show was going to be set on a planet of monsters, but after developing the idea more with Nickelodeon, the show evolved into its present format. By having the monsters interact in the "real" world, Swenson noted the studio can show the humanity of the monsters and the monstrosity of we humans.

Klasky, Csupo, and Swenson have assembled an impressive vocal cast for the show. The star of *Aaahhh! Real Monsters* is Ickis, an insecure monster who resembles a cross between a bat and one of Santa's elves. Charles

Only *The Simpsons* had more influence over the 1990s
animation scene than *Ren & Stimpy*. © Nickelodeon

Adler, a veteran actor whose voice work has been heard in series such as *Tiny Toons, Tail Spin,* and *The Smurfs,* portrays Ickis.

Gregg Burger, who also is Cornfed on *Duckman,* plays the strict headmaster of the Monster Academy, The Gromble. Christine Cavanaugh, who was Chuckie in *Rugrats* and Gosalyn on *Darkwing Duck,* is Oblina, while first-time voice artist David S. Eccles is Krumm, the apprentice monster who holds his eyes in his hands, and never washes his armpits.

Guest voices will include Jonathan Winters, Tim Curry, John Astin, Elayne Boosler, John Byner, Eddie Deezen, Brock Peters, Billy Vera, and Jill Eikenberry.

Klasky and Swenson both emphasized that quality is vital to them. Respect for the intended audience is very important, according to Swenson.

"This place doesn't treat child audiences as 'mere children,'" said Swenson. "We knew we were children once, and we knew a great deal of what was going on. We lacked all the experience we now have, we weren't sophisticated, but we had innate knowledge, and we try to put that into all of our programming, out of respect for the audience, young and old."

"He [Csupo] loves making cartoons for children as well as for adults," added Klasky. "He and I and the general consensus of the studio is that we want to do something right for children, good for children. And we want adults to like it, too."

With others in animation raising the issue of the role of writers in animation, there's little argument about them at Klasky-Csupo.

"Obviously, animation is very close to our heart, but we learned a wonderful lesson working on *The Simpsons*, and that was how important a script is. Without a strong script, you don't have a strong blueprint. And so the way we work here as opposed to the way other studios or creators may work is that we always start from a script. We feel that works best for us. We have a very high regard for our writers, and we like to work in tandem with them. We find that's the best way to get the best of both worlds," explained Klasky.

After the script is written, the voices are recorded and a very detailed storyboard with hundreds and hundreds of drawings is created, said Swenson. The storyboard is photographed and digitized by computer and combined with the voices to create a real-time rough version of the short. This way the studio can make changes and tighten the film before sending the material to an overseas animation studio. Technological advances help the studio maintain a level of quality within the time and financial restraints of television animation.

While Klasky characterized the budget level of their shows as "very healthy," both she and Swenson readily admitted with a laugh that they're "never enough."

"We try to be adults about it, and say, 'Okay, this is what we got to deal with, and how can we push the envelope? How can we make this the best it can possibly be, and still remain on time and a budget?" said Swenson.

Both Swenson and Klasky agree, though, that no matter what amazing things computer animation can do, there is no substitute for hand-drawn illustrations in creating character animation, especially with their studios' funky, offbeat stars.

What's beyond the next two seasons of *Aaahhh! Real Monsters* and another season of *Duckman* for the studio? Klasky revealed that a feature may be in the works, but couldn't go into any detail. She and Swenson did say they wouldn't attempt to do a Disney-style feature. Instead they would bring the artistic sensibilities the studio has developed for their television work to a theatrical feature.

In an industry of trend followers and wannabes, that's great news.

No other animation studio in the 1990s achieved the kind of success that Klasky-Csupo did with its long-running series (*Rugrats, The Wild Thornberrys, As Told by Ginger,* etc.) and its string of most profitable theatrical features. In fact, the first *Rugrats* movie broke the $100 million barrier at the box office and became the only non-Disney feature up until that time to do so.

In 2005, Klasky-Csupo did not have as many shows on the air as they once did and there was one fan website concerned that the studio might go under.

In 2006, the official Klasky-Csupo website, however, listed a number of animated series currently in development and the announcement that Gabor Csupo had completed directing the live-action/CGI animated adventure movie *The Bridge to Terabithia*, which was released in February 2007.

Animato #29, Summer 1994
Writers Need Not Apply: An Interview with John Kricfalusi

The creator of *Ren and Stimpy* is passionate about returning animation to the control of animators

"Personally, I don't know why anyone would buy any of these cels," said John Kricfalusi with a loud laugh. "If they want them, we'll make them."

Perhaps only an artist such as Kricfalusi would go against conventional wisdom quite so blatantly by questioning his own limited edition cel program minutes before a signing at a major gallery. In a way, though, one might expect such an iconoclastic attitude from the creator of *Ren and Stimpy* who is now busy trying to launch a new series of cartoons.

While the American Royal Arts Gallery on Newberry Street in Boston filled up with eager Spumco fans, Kricfalusi took time to meet with myself and *ANIMATO* publisher Patrick Duquette to talk about his new projects and animation in general.

Talking with Kricfalusi is not unlike speaking to a religious fundamentalist. Animation for him is a very pure faith, and Kricfalusi sees a lot of barbarians running amok today in the temple. Showbiz corporate types and sitcom writers are among the worst infidels in Kricfalusi's book.

Foremost in the minds of his fans, however, is the status of a new Spumco cartoon. Kricfalusi reported reluctantly that the *He Hog the Atomic Pig* deal with USA Cable has fallen through. According to the recent issue of *Tease*, Kricfalusi is trying to interest the FOX Network in a George Liquor program.

A Spumco comic book from Marvel Comics, called *Comic Book*, is scheduled to begin appearing in the fall. Kricfalusi's heart, though, is in animation, and despite these frustrating set backs, he is very determined to get back into production.

"We're producing some Jimmy the Idiot [or Hapless] Boy shorts right now on our own, but that's kind of a long process. If we're going to complete them ourselves it will take longer than if we actually sell them to a distributor or a movie theater chain or a movie studio, which we're looking to do right now. We'd rather have a big distributor do that, but in the meanwhile we're not going to let that stop us," said Kricfalusi.

Kricfalusi has been attempting to develop strategies to revive the theatrical short, and spoke of either piggybacking the shorts with feature films (such as the *Roger Rabbit* cartoons) or of finding some other means of distribution. He acknowledged the difficulty of the talks, but believes theatrical distribution is vital.

Kricfalusi tried a comeback to Saturday morning
animation with *The Ripping Friends*. © John Kricfalusi

"I really believe the future of cartoons needs to be grounded on shorts like the past," said Kricfalusi. "There would have been no *Snow White*, no *Pinocchio*, no *Peter Pan*, no anything today if it wasn't for short cartoons. They built the industry. They built the animators . . . shorts are the greatest medium for practicing so then you can go on to features. I think the reason most animated features bomb is that there is no chance to practice, there's no chance to try out the art form before they go out and compete against live-action movies."

Kricfalusi has no shortage of ideas, either for these or other animation projects. Besides *He Hog and Jimmy*, there's a superhero send-up entitled *The Ripping Friends* and, of course, the character that made Nickelodeon very nervous, George Liquor. An educated guess would be that Kricfalusi has a soft spot for the hyper "manly" George, as he, much to our amusement, performed George for us with vein-popping intensity.

Kricfalusi is also intense about restoring the unit concept to animation. He is quick to criticize television animation that has been more controlled by scriptwriters than animators, and questions the role that any person who can't draw has in the creation of a story for animation. While he acknowledged the contributions of writers such as the late Michael Maltese, he wants to see animators and directors be the individuals responsible for the creation of the story and gags.

"We've got to get the animation back in the country, at least in North America, and generate the humor from the cartoonists themselves, not from writers, not from executives. We've got to give the cartoon industry back to the cartoonists," he said.

Ask him what he likes in current animation, and you get a quick reply. "Not much, some independent things, that's about all," he said. "I watched *Duckman* for about 10 minutes, and it didn't hold my attention."

As the time for the signing approached, I ventured a final question . . . with all of the critical statements he makes about the rather small animation industry, does he ever worry about his public opinions costing him a job?

Kricfalusi considered the question for a moment, and said thoughtfully, "Well, I don't think I'll ever again work on a Saturday morning show."

Kricfalusi did indeed work on a Saturday morning show in 2001. His *Ripping Friends* concept was brought to FOX and the misadventures of a group of arrested development superheroes was broadcast for one season.

Prior to that Kricfalusi had produced animation for several music videos, had created cartoons for his studio's website and in 1999 produced two Yogi the Bear cartoons for the Cartoon Network.

In 2003, he returned to cable television with a new *Ren & Stimpy* series for Spike, the self-described network for men. *Ren & Stimpy Adult Party Cartoon* was part of an adult animation block at the network that included a Stan Lee-Pamela Anderson collaboration about a stripper/superhero and a show starring the voice of Kelsey Grammar about a lawyer who wakes up one morning and discovers he has been turned into a six-foot-tall talking rat.

Kricfalusi pulled out the stops in these new cartoons. Ren & Stimpy could be gay lovers (in one short, Stimpy keeps repeating to himself, "I'm the catcher, he's the pitcher") or Ren could be happy washing the bare breasts of a top-heavy model. Scatological humor abounded.

In another short, Kricfalusi's mentor Ralph Bakshi not only provides a voice for a character named "Ralph Bakshi," but also appears in a live-action introduction and epilogue.

Six episodes were produced for Spike, before the network took the show off the schedule. Apparently there were three shorts that never broadcast and there was an effort by fans to re-instate the program.

In the summer of 2006, all of the new *Ren & Stimpy* shorts were released on DVD. I interviewed Kricfalusi for the newspapers I currently edit.

Talk to people in the animation industry today and ask them about their influences. You'll hear names such as Max and Dave Fleischer, Chuck Jones, Bob Clampett, Tex Avery and among the younger generation, John Kricfalusi.

Kricfalusi is the creator of *Ren & Stimpy*, a cartoon that was a phenomenon in the early 1990s. An outspoken advocate of creativity, Kricfalusi rejected the state of animation in the 1980s - television programs produced by committees that recycled tired gags and premises - and revived the concept of a strong director who worked with a team of artists and writers.

For the first time in many years, Kricfalusi established a style and look that was singular. Like them or not, there was no mistaking a Kricfalusi cartoon.

Conflicts with *Ren & Stimpy's* cable home, Nickelodeon, led to his being removed from his own series. His team of Ren, the psychotic Chihuahua, and his soul mate Stimpy, the affable but idiotic cat, maintained a loyal fan base and influenced a new generation of animation fans and professionals.

In 2003, Kricfalusi was asked by Spike, the cable channel devoted to programming for men, to bring the series back, only this time there would be no restrictions on content. The show would be part of an "adult" animation block that included *Stripperella* and *Gary the Rat*.

The network only aired a handful of the new *Ren & Stimpy* shows before cancellation and there were completed shows that never saw broadcast.

Now, however, *Ren & Stimpy* fans will get a chance to see what Spike didn't want them to see. The new two-disc *Ren & Stimpy: The Lost Episodes* has just been released by Paramount Home Video. The collection contains three episodes seen on Spike and three that were not aired. Kricfalusi, as well as some of his animators, introduce each cartoon.

The introductions are funny and pull no punches. Kricfalusi speaks his mind about the shows and about the status of animation today.

There are also some great extras that show Kricfalusi's animation process such as storyboards and pencil animation tests.

The cartoons themselves are a mixed bag. The strengths of the original *Ren & Stimpy* shorts rested in their outrageousness and liberal use of non-sequitor humor. Anything could happen in a *Ren & Stimpy* short.

Kricfalusi loves the Three Stooges and explained in one of the introductions he always liked how the lives and professions of the Stooges could change from short to short - something he adopted for his characters.

Kricfalusi didn't shy away from gross-out humor in his original shorts

- remember the Magic Nose Goblins? - and with the network's initial encouragement he pulled out the throttle on these type of gags in the new cartoons. From nudity to body functions, the new shorts have it all.

These *Ren & Stimpy* shorts were not designed for children, make no mistake.

If that kind of humor puts you off, then this collection is not your cup of tea. There are some great *Ren & Stimpy* moments in the collection, though, and "Firedogs 2" has the distinction of featuring another bad boy of animation, Kricfalusi's mentor Ralph Bakshi, as an animated character.

In an interview, Kricfalusi said that the very thing Spike executives wanted him to do caused the series to be cancelled.

"The executives told me to make them as outrageous as possible," he said.

He said that, unlike other networks with in-house censorship offices, Spike didn't offer him any parameters for content.

Their method of censorship, he added, was to pull the show off the air. That move surprised him as he pitched all of the story ideas to the network execs and "they laughed all through it."

Kricfalusi took many of the new cartoons from story ideas that had been rejected by Nickelodeon and produced them with no-holds-barred.

He's proud of the quality of animation in the series, some of which was done by Carbunkle Productions in Canada. A studio in Korea completed other animation. Kricfalusi said he had to have re-takes done, as the Korean studio animators didn't understand his method of animation.

Kricfalusi based his animation on "poses" - key drawings that begin and end an action that carry a lot of dramatic or comic impact. This technique mirrors how animators made cartoons in the 1930s and '40s, the height of theatrical animation.

The popularity of *Ren & Stimpy* cartoons in the 1990s spurred a revival in creator-driven animation but Kricfalusi sees a big change in the animation scene today.

"It's a lot worse the way I see it," he said.

He noted that "stars" - the creative people - used to have the power in the entertainment industry. Today, though, "the executives are in control."

"I see a lot of sad faces in animation today," he said.

Today he thinks that animated shows are "bland." He added that today the characters can swear, though.

"Bland characters telling immoral stories" is his conclusion.

He admitted with a laugh that probably this is "partly my fault."

While many people working in animation today have embraced trying to be outrageous, they've "left out characterization, good drawing and pleasant music," he said.

Will there be more *Ren & Stimpy*? Kricfalusi said he has at least 100 more story outlines and has done considerable work on a half-hour *Ren & Stimpy* special titled *Life Sucks*. He said that his production staff has told him the new special is the "best *Ren & Stimpy* ever."

Kricfalusi sees the future of the characters on direct-to-DVD productions. He noted that the previous collections have been "selling lots of DVDs."

"Yes, I'd like to make lots more," he said.

Animato #36, Fall 1996
Newbies at Nickelodeon
The Cable Network launches two new animated series in print time

A kid with a football-shaped head and animated kids; action figures with scuffed-up bodies and melted faces? You know this isn't Saturday morning, folks. Animation fans have grown to expect at least one new animated series each fall from Nickelodeon, but this year there will be two new series and they'll be in prime time.

Continuing their commitment to quality and quirky animated programming, the cable network premiered *Hey Arnold!* on Oct. 7 and

KABLAM! on Oct. 11, *Hey Arnold!* will be seen Monday and Wednesday at 8:00 p.m. and *KABLAM!* would air every Friday at 8:00 p.m.

Hey Arnold!

If *Rugrats* addressed the unseen concerns of babies and *Doug* looked at the angst of the suburban pre-teen, then *Hey Arnold!* squarely corners the urban fourth-grader demographic. While *Hey Arnold!* may continue the *Doug* tradition of exploring the not-so-little complexities of growing up, the show certainly has its own very distinctive style of doing it.

And that's exactly the way *Hey Arnold!* creator Craig Bartlett wants it. Bartlett is interested in producing a funny animated series, but also insists the show has something more than just humor as its focus.

"This is a kid who really feels something. It gives me something to latch onto and make sure that's what it's about. There's a lot of cartoon shows that are about wacky drawings and outrageous situations and we try to be entertaining in that way, try to be visually entertaining in the design of the worlds he lives in. We make sure it's a cartoon, but it turns out it's about emotions and feelings. I'm really glad about that because it really gives you something to write," Bartlett said.

Bartlett is enthusiastic about the show and its potential to mix a perceptive examination of childhood with fantasy.

Arnold lives with grandparents who have a boarding house in an inner-city neighborhood. Arnold's best friend is Gerald, and his biggest problem is Helga, a girl who secretly loves Arnold and shows her devotion by routinely torturing him. Arnold's life is filled with the stuff of childhood – pick-up games, school plays, homework, and inexplicable adults.

Arnold's edge, though, is his room. When Arnold steps into his room, he enters a place that will be the envy of every kid in America. Bartlett described it as a "Batcave" with gadgets and hide-away furniture.

"To the younger half of our Nickelodeon audience Arnold's inner life, that kind of fantasy, his own little inner sanctum he has up there, is really going to be important. For the older half of our audience – fourth, fifth, sixth grade – they're going to care about those relationships. Helga – she loves him yet she hates him. The constant threat of love or violence that's going on all

Craig Bartlett, the creator of *Hey Arnold!* and *Camp Lazlo*.

the time. I think that's the thing that will appeal to older kids," Bartlett said.

"The nice thing about the series is we had more time to stretch out and breathe," Bartlett continued. "Music drives the series. Whole episodes are devoted to something that's happened – Arnold's feeling bad and he thinks about it. He goes up to that room and lies on the power couch and listens. And I really like that."

Hey Arnold! may be thoughtful and introspective, but viewers shouldn't expect a cartoon version of an Ingmar Bergman film. Bartlett's show is also a hoot!

Fifty-two 11-minute episodes of *Hey Arnold!* have been ordered by the cable network to make up a first season of 26 half-hour shows. Nickelodeon will air two new shows every week.

Although no stranger to animation, this is Bartlett's first series. Bartlett started his career as an animator with Will Vinton productions and working as a stop-motion animator in clay. He fondly remembered his six years there as a "film making apprenticeship," because he learned all of the aspects of production, not just animation.

After leaving Vinton in 1987, Bartlett worked on the second and third season of *Pee-wee's Playhouse* producing the *Penny* cartoons. The *Penny* shorts were clay animations with storylines determined by a stream of consciousness narration by a young girl. The realistic soundtrack coupled with Bartlett's imaginative clay animation made the *Penny* shorts a standout in that innovative show.

Bartlett laughingly called his *Penny* shorts "2-D" animation since it was clay animation without armatures. The models didn't stand up on an animation table, but were animated lying on top of a glass plate that was suspended above the background art. Often working without a formal script or storyboard, the *Penny* shorts were produced "straight-ahead" from the beginning of the narrative to the end. Bartlett likened it to a "jazz performance captured on film."

After *Pee-wee's Playhouse*, Bartlett made three clay-animated shorts featuring his character, Arnold. They were featured in the 21st, 22nd and 23rd Tournee of Animation collections, and one, *Arnold Rides a Chair*, has been featured on *Sesame Street*.

In 1991, Paul Germain introduced Bartlett to Gabor Csupo of Klasky-Csupo, and Barlett began work as a story editor on *Rugrats*. It was his first introduction to cel animation, and German and Bartlett co-wrote the first season of *Rugrats*. He broke into the direction of cel animation on the 13th episode of that first season. He said he was happy to have made the switch from clay to cel animation.

"[The] key to my being able to succeed in Hollywood was being able to jump from one to another. If I had just done clay animation or special effects and stop-motion animation, I would have run out of work. I remember at the time thinking that this will be good developing a relationship with Klasky-Csupo and Nickelodeon because I had the sense I wouldn't have enough work to do if I stayed in clay."

Bartlett also did some direction work on *The Ren & Stimpy Show*, and worked with the Bob Rogers Company producing special venue films for Expos '90, '92, and '93 and the film *Mystery Lodge* for the popular southern California amusement park Knott's Berry Farm.

He's returned to television animation with *Hey Arnold!* and brought with him ideas to make his series different than those on which he worked. Besides the urban setting and the distinctive design, Bartlett decided to cast child actors for his voice performers rather than adult actors, a first for Nickelodeon and a rarity in animation.

Fourteen-year-old Toran Caudell plays Arnold, while 11-year-old Francesca Smith is Helga, and Jamil Walker Smith is Gerald. While Bartlett readily praised the adults who gave the voices to the kids in *Rugrats*, he wanted his show to be different. Adult actors were considered, but Bartlett said that once he cast Smith as Helga, he knew all of the performers had to be kids.

Bartlett knows that the changing voices of adolescence will be a challenge for him and his actors, but he's very pleased with their performances.

Bartlett called *Hey Arnold!* a "script-driven show," and said, "that's a real distinction today from a storyboard artist writing a show. We're coming from a tradition of writing a real detailed screenplay and going in to record it. This evolved over the last year. First, we experimented with boarding and recording at the same time. Then [we did a] storyboard first and recording the dialogue after."

Bartlett said that each show begins with a script that's recorded and then the voice track is given to the artist to help inspire the drawings.

"[This way it] gives the actors more ability to improvise to come up with stuff on the spot," he explained. There's plenty of ad-libbing among the adult actors with Dan Castellaneta as Arnold's grandfather, Tress Mac-Neille as his grandmother, and Maurice LaMarche as Helga's dad, Big Bob.

"They're wonderful improvisers," said Bartlett. His child actors may not improvise, but Bartlett and his staff listens carefully to the way they speak to incorporate their rhythms and sayings.

As an added comic twist, Bartlett has given his characters expressions that were popular thirty and forty years ago such as "Boy Howdy!" and "Criminy!"

Bartlett is hopeful the Nickelodeon audience will respond to *Hey Arnold!*

"I hope they like these characters because they have real feelings."

KABLAM!

What do you get when someone has the high concept idea of "live-action cartoons?" Well, eventually you get *KABLAM!* The new Nickelodeon show is a blend of cel animation, stop-motion, pixilation, and computer-generated imagery.

The show is set up as an animated comic book with cartoon hosts Henry and June introducing the various segments that include:

Sniz and Fondue; two young cats in search of trouble and adventure

Action League Now: stop-motion adventures of a group of well-used kid's action figures;

Life with Loopi: stories about an imaginative young girl told by her older brother Larry in paper cutout stop motion.

Patch Head: a live-action segment about the gear-jamming kid who lives in a watermelon patch and races his hot rod-like Big Wheel through country roads. This part of the show is easily what would have happened if the denizens of Mayberry had all dropped acid.

The creators of the show, Bob Mittenthal, Will McRobb, and Chris Viscardi, are no strangers to Nickelodeon. Mittenthal is the co-creator of the hugely popular *Double Dare* and created *Welcome Freshmen*. McRobb and Viscardi created the innovative *The Adventures of Pete and Pete*. McRobb had some animation experience by working on *The Ren & Stimpy Show*, but he and Mittenthal readily described themselves as animation novices in a recent interview.

Mittenthal characterized the genesis of *KABLAM!* with a laugh as an "anti-animation story." McRobb and Mittenthal were asked by an advertising agency to team up and create a "live-action cartoon show."

"We failed!" he laughed.

In their attempt to discover just what was a "live-action cartoon show" they discovered a lot of animation talent that didn't seem to fit into conventional television fare, some of which eventually fanned the core of *KABLAM!*

The individual segments of the show all have their own production units with Mittenthal, McRobb and Viscardi working with acclaimed cartoonist Mark Marek on the show's bridging sequences featuring the brother and sister team of Henry and June.

The team of three producers is also working closely with writer and director Tim Hill on the *Action League Now* segments. *Action League Now* is a combination of stop-motion animation and "chuck-a-mation," a technique in which a character is thrown by unseen hands into the action.

While *ALN* is certainly not stop-motion animation along the caliber of Ray Harryhausen, the idea was to replicate the kind of wild storylines and rough play kids themselves put their own toys through. A key aspect of the segment is the characters themselves: action figures that all have seen much better days. To give you an idea, one of the characters is Meltman, who must have been on the receiving end of a magnifying glass on a sunny summer day.

Greg Harrison, whose work has appeared on MTV's *Liquid Television*, is the man behind *Patch Head*, which combines live action with a variety of computer-generated imagery. More than any other segment, McRobb and Mittenthal believe this comes closest to a live-action cartoon.

There are a number of other segments to *KABLAM!*, some of which will appear more than others. McRobb, whose first exposure to animation was as a story editor on *The Ren & Stimpy Show*, said he didn't feel beholden to any particular style of animation. He wanted to present alternative material to the Nick audience. Both producers want to have the show to possess a genuine "underground" atmosphere to it. Their vision of *KABLAM!* is one of a "boutique," said Mittenthal. "*KABLAM!* is a place for independent artists who have a vision," he said.

The same attitude impacts the show's humor. By now, many people have commented on Nickelodeon's house style of pushing the envelope with gross-out humor. *The Ren & Stimpy Show, Ahhh! Real Monsters* and *Rocko's Modem Life* haven't shied away from wet, stinky jokes. McRobb notes that the production "had no mandate to include it [gross-out humor] or not to include it."

However, it's clear from the pilot that *KABLAM!* is the type of show that will present a more sophisticated entertainment. Through focus groups, the production team has learned about their audience, including the fact that kids are "aspirational." McRobb said that ten-year-olds want to be 12-year-olds, but not the other way around. Therefore, there's not been any effort to dumb down the content of *KABLAM!*

Ultimately, Mittenthal said, the production team wants to have a show with "funny pictures that move funny." For a cutting edge "live-action cartoon show" that's an admirable old-fashioned aspiration.

Bartlett had a chance to bring *Hey Arnold!* to the big screen with a feature film in 2002. In 2003 he worked as a story editor on the *Johnny Bravo* series and in 2004 he produced *Party Wagon*, a pilot for the Cartoon Network that was not picked up as a series. His new series, *Camp Lazlo*, is on the Cartoon Network.

Animation Planet #1 Summer 1997
Hercules Goes into Battle
Disney flexes its muscles with the release of its new summer animated feature

With the less-than-expected critical and fan reaction to the last two Disney animated features (*Pocahontas* and *Hunchback of Notre Dame*), film industry pundits might say The Mouse went back to the team who made *The Little Mermaid* and *Aladdin*.

Conspiracy theorists should rest easy here as *Hercules*, the newest film by the writing and directing team of John Musker and Ron Clements, has been in production for about four years and wasn't influenced by either of its predecessors and their serious themes.

All kidding aside, *Hercules* is a *very* important film for Disney. Not only notable for its return to a comedy with dramatic subplots, but its humor is described as "contemporary" by its creative team, which means it should be appealing to both children and adults. It is also clearly a franchise property that will lend itself to television series and movie sequels like *Aladdin*. Its mythological characters are perfect for licensing (the action figures will undoubtedly be in stores when this article appears).

Hercules is also an historic film for the company as it is the first Disney film in which the work of an inspirational artist can clearly be seen throughout the design of the movie.

Although there may be a platoon of guys in suits who would like to take responsibility for the revival of Disney feature animation, Musker and Clement's treatment of *The Little Mermaid*, and then *Aladdin*, set the stage for the successes of *Beauty and the Beast* and *The Lion King*. Speaking to *Animation Planet* from an editing suite at ILM's Skywalker Ranch, Clements and Musker took time from completing the final sound mix on this film to talk about their latest movie.

The Look
After *Aladdin* came out in November of 1992, Clements and Musker took some time off and began developing a science fiction project that even-

tually was put on the back burner by then Disney executive Jeffrey Kat-zenberg. Looking at the projects that the studio had in development, the team was attracted to *Hercules*.

"We looked at various ideas they had in developing and this idea of *Hercules* had been pitched by one of the animators in what they call 'Gong Shows.' They're meetings in which people in-house can bring ideas for possible future projects to management and if management likes them they can be put into development. This had been pitched a year or a year and half before we ever got involved with it by Joe Hadir, one of the animators," said Musker.

The idea of adapting classical mythology appealed to the team. "Mythology was such a ripe venue that hadn't been explored," explained Musker.

"It wasn't a stretch to find the contemporary in the ancient," added Clements. Since their artistic inclination is to do a humorous film, both men wanted to do the story as a comedy. Musker said that having watched the sword-and-sandals epics of the Fifties and Sixties he noticed Hercules and company were portrayed as a rather humorless lot. They wanted their story "not to take itself so seriously."

While the humorous approach works for them, they both emphasized the belief that not everything lends itself to comedy. The unspoken rule is that just because it's a cartoon doesn't mean it has to be funny.

"Every movie has its unique approach and there are many valid approaches," said Musker.

Hercules, according to Clements, is an "epic comedy." Musker added that while the production is funny, there are some serious themes to the picture, such as the responsibility of being a role model and hero.

Once Musker and Clements had settled on the idea of producing a film based on Greek mythology, they started doing research to produce a first-draft of the script. Early on in the development of the story British illustrator and designer Gerald Scarfe was brought in to do inspirational or concept drawings.

Rising to prominence in the Sixties for his brilliant and cutting caricatures, Scarfe is no stranger to animation. His work in the film adaptation of *Pink Floyd's The Wall* has become an underground favorite among many animation fans. Scarfe's interests have extended into theatre costume and set design that is how he and the production team connected. Musker is a long-time fan of Scarfe's work and had seen a production of Mozart's *The Magic Flute* that had been designed by Scarfe.

While Scarfe was in Los Angeles for *The Magic Flute*, Disney animator Rick Macki brought him by the Disney Studios for a tour that resulted in Scarfe doing some drawings of his ideas for some of the characters.

Having an artist provide artwork that acts as an inspiration to other artists is nothing new at the Disney studios. Walt Disney brought in noted illustrators, such as Kay Nielson, fifty years ago to provide his artists ideas they could develop.

"It was kind of experimental," explained Clements. "We had various artists doing early development stuff and you don't know what it could lead to. Possibly he could have done some preliminary drawings and that would have been it, but as we saw the work, everybody was really excited about it and we felt that we really wanted to get it into the movie. It had such a distinctive style to it."

What also aided the decision to involve Scarfe more and more in the production was the support of the executives assigned to the film, Peter Scheidner and Tom Schumacher, and that the animation team embraced Scarfe's style.

"We were really supported by management and that's why so much of what Gerald did got into the movie," said Musker.

In *Aladdin*, the influence of a famous illustrator was in evidence but to a far lesser extent. Animator Eric Goldberg used the style of legendary caricaturist Al Hirschfeld in his design of the Genie, but the deep involvement of Scarfe in the production was a first for Musker and Clements and for the Disney Studios. Musker and Clements arranged a retreat with Scarfe and the animation artists to work on adapting Scarfe's style. Thanks to fax machines, Scarfe and the production team kept in touch with drawings zipping between Burbank to Scarfe's home in Great Britain.

"I know there's a feeling among a lot of people at Disney that there's a stock style but that's not totally true. There's certainly a similarity between a lot of the movies. On the other hand if you compare the style of *101 Dalma-*

tians to *Pinocchio* those are totally different," said Clements. He emphasized that directors at Disney want their films to have a unique look.

"The style grows out of the story," Musker explained. "In our case, we were influenced by the [ancient Greek] vase paintings and it turns out in a way Gerald Scarfe's calligraphic style really complemented that."

"He synthesized Greek art with a combination of power and elegance," Musker continued. "He tried to capture that in the character drawings he did. When he did Zeus, for example, he was very monumental and yet he had this elegant filigree. There were details in his hair and his beard and his costume that gave this sort of delicacy."

"I think people think of Disney animation as a certain style, but Disney animation can be adapted into a number of styles," said Clement. "The main thing with Disney animation is a certain kind of acting and performing that is a hard skill to learn."

The Voices

Does the name of a well-known actor affect the box office success of an animated motion picture? With superstars such as Mel Gibson (John Smith in *Pocahontas*) finding their way into animation voice work, the question is whether people are being cast for their voices or for their names. Musker and Clements firmly deny they participate in this kind of stunt casting, and for them the only thing that matters is the ability of an actor to perform with his or her voice.

Both known and unknown actors read for the parts on *Hercules* with the final cast being composed of people of varying levels of recognition. Veteran actors James Woods, Rip Torn, and Danny DeVito perform the voices of Hades, Zeus and Hercules' sidekick, Philoctetes, respectively. Tate Donovan, an actor who has been seen in the movies *The Memphis Belle* and *Love Potion No. 9*, among others, plays Hercules, while Susan Egan is the female lead character, Meg. Egan has been playing the role of Belle in the Broadway production of *Beauty and the Beast*. British leading lady Samantha Eggar plays Hera.

"In our case I don't think we've ever done stunt casting," said Clements. "In *Mermaid* there were no real stars in that movie that were really well known. Buddy Hackett was probably the best known. With *Aladdin* the big star in that movie was Robin Williams, but I don't think we ever considered that 'stunt casting.' When we wrote the script, we thought of it early on with Robin Williams as the Genie and what we could do with that. It was still more 'this is the right guy for the part.'"

The rule for Clements and Musker is to select the actors "who are best for the role," regardless of their level of fame.

For Hades, the two had many actors read the role with screen bad guy supreme James Woods eventually winning the part. "James Woods wouldn't have come to our minds as the first person for the role," explained Clements, who said they were looking for an actor who can be a comic villain. Woods, while an excellent actor, has had relatively few forays into comedy.

"What we look for in voice actors are people who are very comfortable in front of a mic," said Clements. "People who like to play in front of a microphone. Where you get the best stuff is with actors who are very loose. If an actor becomes stiff in front of the mic you're in big trouble. James Woods just played and brought this spin on it."

Woods, like the other voice actors, adlibbed, which brought additional life to the character. "That's that you hope for," said Clements.

Unlike Hades, Danny DeVito's character of Philoctetes was written with the actor in mind. Musker and Clements wanted a voice to create a character that was a cross between a Brooklyn-born Yoda (!) and the wily and wheezy fight manager played by Burgess Meredith in the *Rocky* films.

Despite their casting DeVito in their minds, Musker and Clements still tested various actors before settling on DeVito, who was last heard on the animated screen as the head bad guy in *Space Jam*.

Rip Torn was also the team's imaginary casting choice when they wrote the character of Zeus. Torn's role as comic Larry Sanders' manager on HBO's *The Larry Sanders Show* inspired that choice. Musker and Clements wanted Hercules' father to have a certain amount of bombast, but also a lot of warmth.

"A fun Zeus," quipped Musker.

Broadway performer Susan Egan is Meg, and she was the second person to be tested for the role. At first Musker and Clements had reservations if the actress would play the role like Belle, whom she had been portraying in *Beauty and the Beast* in New York, but their fears were quickly allayed. Her characterization is "totally different from anything she's done on the stage," said Musker. She had the sarcasm, the wit and the vulnerability the team needed for Meg.

"It's hard to find good animation voices whether they're famous or not famous," explained Clements. "A lot of actors, even very well-known actors, when you take away the visual, what they bring physically to a part, and they just have a voice there's not as much left as one might think." Years ago when dramatic radio was in full bloom, Clements believed it must have been easier to find voice actors as there were dozens of performers who were trained to act with just their voice.

Bobcat Goldthwait and Matt Frewer, two comedic character actors who are not strangers to animation voice work (Goldthwait did Moxie on The Cartoon Network show, and Frewer did the voice on the latest incarnation of the Pink Panther), appear as Hades' two henchmen Pain and Panic.

"Voices are so important to the animators," explained Clements, "as the right voice makes the animators' job so much easier."

The Music

Although music has been an important part of animated features since Disney's *Snow White*, the art of writing music for an animated film went through a rebirth with the score by Alan Menken and the late Howard Ashman for *The Little Mermaid*. In too many animated features, song sequences seemed to be forced into the narrative of a film making the story grind to a halt.

The Little Mermaid used its music numbers to advance the plot or reveal something about the characters, and since that time the music has been not only an important creative aspect of the film, but also a crucial commercial consideration. The fact that Elton John's music in *The Lion King* spurred on CD sales to astonishing heights wasn't lost on the film industry either.

When Clements and Musker began writing the script for *Hercules*, they were not sure if Menken would be available as he had responsibilities on other films. "He had a really full plate," said Clements.

Menken was indeed available, and with lyricist David Zippel, began working on the film's music. "It's a very collaborative process; a real give-and-take," described Musker, who noted that Menken was willing to scrap a song if it didn't precisely fit the film.

"The last two movies Alan did, *Pocahontas* and *Hunchback*, were more classically-oriented and we thought the Hercules story would be more pop-oriented," said Clements. For instance, the Muses, the Greek goddesses of the arts, act as a Greek chorus (no pun intended) who sing gospel- and R&B-flavored songs.

Some people had suggested the filmmakers use an adaptation of traditional Greek music for the film, something Clements and Musker rejected as they believed the movie's "American sports hero / rags-to-riches" storyline needed a contemporary American score.

The Challenge of Hercules

Hercules' summer release will be a first for Musker and Clements. The team's past films were all released during the Thanksgiving season, and the shift in releasing strategy doesn't have the two worried, but certainly concerned.

"I think there's enough room to go around," said Musker. "I think one thing we had in the winter slot is that Disney had a corner on the market, but *Lion King* was released in the summer and carved out a huge part of the general audience."

In the past few years, the key summer releasing period has become an ever-increasing high-pressure time with studios banking on expensive special effects-laden films to attract audiences. While the Disney marketing department is no doubt one of the juggernauts of the motion picture business, the fact that audiences didn't respond to *Pocahontas* and *Hunchback of Notre Dame* in the same way as they had reacted to *Aladdin*, *The Lion King* and *Beauty and the Beast* hasn't gone unnoticed. The company launched a pre-release campaign centering around a traveling exhibit which toured large shopping malls, and a collection of *Hercules* merchandising (which is cleverly spoofed in the film) will be awaiting fans.

Clements noted that the competition between the event movies is intimidating, and said, "You never really know what's going to happen. Our goal is for the movie to work and we feel that it does."

If any studio had much to lose with the animation revolution of the 1990s, it was Disney. Their feature films just weren't capturing the audiences as they once did, until *The Little Mermaid* came along in 1989.

Clement and Musker have been credited as the team that re-invented the Disney feature for a new audience. With the surprise success of *The Little Mermaid*, the team established a musical comedy format that took the best elements of the Broadway musical and brought them to animation.

Although music had been a key element in animated films, Clement and Musker brought a new sensibility to it. Their next film, *Aladdin* (1992), was a huge hit and it spawned several--direct-to-video sequels and a television series.

Hercules did not make the level of money that *Aladdin* or *Lion King* did and some people viewed the film as a bit of a failure.

Treasure Planet (2002), their last film to date, was not a hit, critically or financially, and the team left the Disney organization for a while. As of this writing, they have established a new relationship with the studio.

Animation Planet #3, Spring/Summer 1998
Swimming Pools, Movie Stars . . . Bronco Fans

A limited-animated, bad taste comedy show on basic cable has propelled two young men into the entertainment mainstream. Here's what they think about their success with *South Park*.

Who could have known that an animated series on a basic cable

Matt Stone and Trey Parker are the creators of *South Park.*

network about foul-mouthed third-graders living in a screwed-up town would be a hit? Comedy Central has found itself placed on the pop culture map with its run-away hit show *South Park*. The cable execs are so pleased with the show they recently announced a new contract with creators Trey Parker and Matt Stone for an additional two seasons.

Not since John Kricfalusi found himself in the spotlight with *Ren and Stimpy* has the mainstream media paid so much attention to an animator. Unlike John K, though, Parker and Stone's stars are not just tied to a television series. Granted *South Park* received the highest rating for any entertainment series in basic cable history with "Cartman's Mom's Still a Dirty Slut" episode, but that just didn't make Parker and Stone hot entertainment news. Their new film *Orgazmo* made a splash at the Sundance Film Festival, and the pair is starring in the new comedy *BASEketball*.

South Park has won a CableACE Award for Best Animated Series and has also been nominated for the prestigious Environmental Media Award and the Gay and Lesbian Alliance Against Defamation Awards.

Earlier this year, the two met with television critics and writers at the Scribes annual convention for a news conference and the following is an extended excerpt of that gathering. A tip of the *Animation Planet* hat goes to Tony Fox of Comedy Central who made this transcript available.

TONY FOX: I'd like to bring Matt Stone and Trey Parker up, if I could have you gentlemen. They're going to show you a – set up a brief clip from the brand-new episode called "Damien." Give us just a minute and we'll get them miced. And then we'll have a question and answer session with Matt and Trey. They are Broncos fans.

All right, Trey Parker, Matt Stone, you want to set up the clip we're about to see?

TREY PARKER: Oh, this is from the episode we're showing called "Damien" and basically we're still working on it so we didn't have a lot of it done. But this was the – Damien is the son of Satan who is the new kid in school. (*laughter*) And he is, you know, tormented by the other kids because he's the new kid and he turns Kenny into a duck-billed platypus, and the reason he's in South Park is because his father wants to battle Jesus for the final domination of the world. So . . .

FOX: Let's roll that clip, please.

FOX: Questions for Matt and Trey.

MATT STONE: Oh, good. Let's go.

QUESTION: We talked to some animators throughout the press tour – (*inaudible*) – with some pretty heavy credentials. Fred Seibert and all. They really admire you guys. What does that mean to you?

TREY PARKER: It means a lot because, you know, when we first came out, we were really just kind of getting ripped on for how bad our animation was. And, you know–

QUESTION: They didn't say your animation was good. (*laughter*)

PARKER: Okay. That's cool. You know, I mean the thing is, we do try to have our own style, and we real – before the show ever – before we'd even made the first episode, we talked about how we really wanted to be able to – someone to watch it for three seconds, and say, "Oh, this is *"South Park."*

And I think that we've done that, and created our own look, and – it means a lot. I mean, having met these great animators – having met Mike

Judge and Bill Plympton and, you know, people that are fans – it's just awesome, because we so look up to them.

STONE: Yeah. I think it shows that the – I mean, we've gotten a lot of mileage out of the, you know – the one-dimensionality, or two-dimensionality of the animation and stuff. But I think, especially people that have like spent their lives in animation, and like seen so many different styles and everything – I mean, we do spend a lot of time on it. It's not just – it isn't just as simple as it looks, even though it is simple. I mean, we really do try to, you know –

PARKER: We try. (*laughter*)

STONE: Yeah. We try to do something unique, and I think that they – those people are starting to realize that we pack a lot of punch in that – the simplicity. So, it's cool that these guys that we admire notice.

QUESTION: And a short follow-up. Has success gone to your head, yet?

STONE: Oh, totally.

QUESTION: I mean, have you gone out to buy the Beamer–

PARKER: Oh yeah, totally.

QUESTION: –or, you know, improved your wardrobe.

STONE: We're totally different people now.

PARKER: Yeah, we have a stylist now. His name's Cosmo On Melrose and he's the gayest man in the world. (*laughter*) You know, he's our personal stylist. And it's great. It's awesome. Yeah. Our heads are huge.

QUESTION: I mean this is the nicest way because I love, but after watching the "Mr. Hankie" episode, I have to ask – how high are your therapy bills at this point? (*laughter*)

PARKER: *South Park* is our therapy. We don't need any.

QUESTION: Did you have to fight any battles to get that episode on the air?

STONE: No.

PARKER: No, in –

QUESTION: I mean, it really pushed the taste levels.

PARKER: As a matter of fact, when we were first getting sort of courted by, you know, all the networks, for people that wanted the show, I remember I sat down with Eileen Katz and Debbie Liebling at our first meeting, like two years ago, at dinner, I said, "You know, one thing I have to know before we really go any further. How do you feel about talking poo?"

And Eileen, I remember, just was like, "I love it." (*laughter*) And so that was part of when –

STONE: Little did she know it was going to become a reality.

PARKER: That was when we knew that Comedy Central was the right place.

QUESTION: So talking poo has been kind of a childhood dream for you?

PARKER: It was actually – Mr. Hankie was something – we had the idea for "The Mr. Hankie Show" even before *South Park*. And it's what we originally pitched to Brian Graden, like four years ago, at Fox – was *The Mr. Hankie Show*, and not *South Park*. And he was like, "Sounds great. Let's not do that." (*laughter*)

QUESTION: For both of you, talk briefly just about the genesis of the show. Just where did the idea come from?

PARKER: It really came from – I did – it was animation class, and I did this thing with all construction cutouts that was, you know, even worse animation-wise. And it won a student Academy Award, and I was flown here, and I was "All right, maybe there's something to this style," and so we said, "Let's try doing something with sync sound."

And it was actually when we were in college we did this first – the first *Spirit of Christmas*, which was Santa versus – or, no-no. Frosty the Snowman. And we did it, and it was – again, it was just something we sort of did for ourselves. And then that's what Brian Graden saw, and said, "Will you make me another one?" And that's when we made the spirit of Christmas with Jesus and Santa fighting each other.

STONE: We actually had the idea for *South Park* before we did the second *Spirit of Christmas*.

PARKER: Yeah.

STONE: We did the *Spirit of Christmas* that everyone's seen with Jesus fighting Santa, with a show in mind. You know, we wanted to do this show for quite a while. But, when we took the show around, before we'd done the "Spirit of Christmas," they kept saying, "Well, no one wants to watch kids. Kids want to watch kids animated. Adults want to watch adults animated. Why don't you make their families, like *The Simpsons* or something like that?"

And then after we did the *Spirit of Christmas* of course – and then that became a huge, underground hit – then everyone's tunes changed, which was pretty cool.

QUESTION: Two questions for you guys. First thing is, you know, when the show first started out I think we all realized that it would be controversial. I don't think that we thought it would cover the ownership of talking poo. And I'm wondering if you guys could comment on the controversy, and where it's –

PARKER: Yeah, what he's talking about is the John-somebody, John –

STONE: Just call him John K. [Kricfalusi]

PARKER: His last name is really hard to pronounce, but the guy who created *Ren & Stimpy*. After – we'd – the Christmas show had aired and we came back to find out that he was making some big stink about – (*laughter*) – he was making a lot of noise about the fact that "Mr. Hankie" was a rip-off of some character he'd created on his website, called like – poo – it was a talking poo, too.

And so I quickly – he went to the press himself, apparently, and called a bunch of people himself. And so it really pissed me off just because – and I actually wrote him specifically saying, look, just so you know, "Mr. Hankie has actually appeared on the opening sequence of *South Park* since it aired in August, and even before that when we made the pilot a year before that, Mr. Hankie's always through the frame.

And that is because that's sort of a grassroots of *South Park*. Like I said, we pitched that to Brian years ago, and before that, "Mr. Hankie was something I did in college. And so, you know, Brian Graden, who is now the president of MTV, was the first one to come out and say, you know, "I was pitched 'Mr. Hankie' four or five years ago."

So as soon as this John guy got that letter, he wrote a letter back saying, oh, okay, I see how it could just be a coincidence. But you should just admit to the press that you're a big *Ren & Stimpy* fan.

STONE: So admit it, Trey.

PARKER: I'm not a *Ren & Stimpy* fan.

FOX: And never will be.

PARKER: Yeah, I mean, I have nothing against it. I never – I saw an episode or two, but that's about that.

QUESTION: Is there anything that the two of you have ever rejected as being too gross or too outrageous? And taking it beyond that, is there anything on TV that you find offensive, or in the movies or anywhere in the universe?

PARKER: I find *Full House* offensive. (*laughter*)

STONE: *Contact.*

PARKER: *Contact.*

STONE: *Contact* with Jodie Foster just made me so angry I just –

PARKER: It seriously made us not ever want to see a movie again.

STONE: I was so angry.

QUESTION: Why?

PARKER: It was just so bad. (*laughter*)

STONE: That movie was just horrible. And just to see someone waste that kind of money and waste my time made me so angry.

QUESTION: How about the first question? Do you ever have an idea and then you say, nah, we can't do that, it's just too –

STONE: Yeah, we've done that a couple times. I don't know if we'd want to talk about   what –

QUESTION: Yeah, you would.

PARKER: No, I mean, I think because it's not – it's more, you know, what – we've seen things, more like short films because we were big into the underground stuff, you see things where people try to be really offensive. But then that's just offensive, period. And there's no – you know, we try to have – it's not like we sit down and go, okay, what should the message of this show be – but we try to have a point and a story, and something that people can go, yeah, I remember that, I remember something like that happening or I remember being eight years old now.

And so, we're not – that's the thing – we're not in the business of offending people. We're in the business of making people laugh. And people are going to get offended in the process.

STONE: I think the reason why so many people are talking about the talking poo is because there was a story there. There was a spine to that show. It wasn't just a dancing piece of poo, like, dancing across the screen for half an hour.

PARKER: Like the *Ren & Stimpy* guy's was.

STONE: Yeah, which is probably – (*overlapping laughter*) But it was a story about Kyle and being Jewish on Christmas, which is something I can totally sympathize with. And it wasn't like – what it was – it wasn't an intense – like everyone in the neighborhood making fun of me. We kind of heightened that.

But it was on Christmas day for my entire life, I've been completely bored, because I have nothing to do. And there's – no malls are open, all my friends are busy. So that was the push of that story. And the talking poo was in that story. And that's why I think people grab onto it. Not just – without a story, it's not very subversive, it's just annoying.

QUESTION: Following up on the Kyle character, what for you, Trey, was it like growing up? Were there any Jews in South Park? And Matt, as well, talk more about that.

PARKER: It was like the show. I mean, that's part of where the idea came from. I think there was one Jewish person in our entire town,

And this poor girl had to – you know, every year at school, we'd have the big Christmas pageant and she had to come out by herself and do a Chanukah song. And she was always really bummed about it, you know, because she was really singled out, you know. "And here's the Jewish person, let's accept them."

But she didn't want to be so pointed out. And so that's just what it was in this small town.

STONE: I grew up more in the suburbs of Denver, and so it was just all my friends. We were all just white. (*laughter*) And I think that's another part of Kyle's character in that whole thing in the show is that it's kind of a mixture of where like Trey grew up and having that loneliness and kind of feeling like I don't belong.

But at the same time, at the end of the day, all the kids are just friends. And do you know what I mean? And it doesn't matter that Cartman's fat and probably the lamest person on the face of the earth, and Kyle's Jewish, and Kenny's poor. At the end of the day, they're all friends. And the next morning they're at the bus stop. And that's the most important thing. There's kind of both elements there.

QUESTION: Matt and Trey, was it hard for you to decide to let Kenny live in the Christmas special?

PARKER: It wasn't hard. (*laughter*) I mean it's Christmas, you know. You just can't kill people on Christmas. I just couldn't. But it's the same thing. We just – as soon as, and hopefully we're going to keep doing – you know, as soon as people really start to expect something from us, we want to give them something else. And that became such a huge thing. You know, Kenny dies. Kenny dies. Kenny dies. That it starts to become like, "Okay, well, Kenny died again."

So we try to do other things like letting him live and turning him into a duck-billed platypus.

STONE: He'll be dying more, though. But he'll be dying more, oh yeah.

QUESTION: I have a quick two-parter. First of all, how did you get Robert Smith involved? And as well it's Satan. I've seen the parts where they say "Satan Celebrity Ego Maniacs and Robert Smith." Does that mean he's a pretty nice guy or –?

PARKER: Oh, it was really just sort of – when we – when the show hit, we kept getting calls. All these celebrities that wanted to do voices. And we thought, "All right, either there's a lot of fans or these celebrities just want to do voices before we rip on them in the show." So we kind of realized it's like, "Whoa, we could probably meet kind of whoever we wanted."

And so the first person we wanted to meet was the chick from *Species*. (*laughter*) And so we put the call out. And her name is Natasha Hendrick? Hendrick? Henstridge. Yeah. That she's the chick from *Species*. And we called her, and she came in and did a voice that's the second new episode in February, of the "Substitute Teacher."

And so that was great meeting her. But then I've been a huge Cure fan since I was about ten. And so we sent some new shows to Robert Smith, and like a week later, I'm on the phone, and he's in the studio about to do – he plays Robert Smith in *South Park*.

And I'm just on the phone literally just, like, shaking, sweating palms, looking like a total nerd. [*In nerd voice*] "It's nice to talk to you." And it was – it's great. It's really cool.

QUESTION: There's a lot of merchandising coming out now: T-shirts, hats here and everything. How involved are you with the merchandising producing and what decisions?

STONE: Well, they – on one hand, we want to be as involved as possible, because we want to keep the integrity of the show together and everything. On the other hand, it's a huge animal. It's a huge – we couldn't – we can't be involved with every little part of it, so generally the way it is they come up – whoever's they.

I don't even know who they are. They come up with designs and they send it to us, and we basically approve or give notes. And then it goes back and forth for the T-shirts and mugs.

It works out pretty good. But as I said, we can't have our – we can't be there 100% of the time. It's just too much. I came up with a good T-shirt the other day. I want to do one that's Kenny just going like this, and it says "Viva Kenny!" on it. (*laughter*) So they probably won't make that either.

EILEEN KATZ (*Comedy Central exec*): Actually, it's out in the stores –

QUESTION: Is *The Spirit of Christmas* going to be available in any kind of legitimate form?

STONE: We have been trying to do that for about six months now. We said, "Wow. A lot of people want –" And it came less from a place of like, "We should just go out and make a million dollars to – oh, that'd be cool." So many people want a fresh copy of it, and we see this stuff on the Internet where people are like, "Where can I get a VHS copy?"

And the problem is all the music we used in *The Spirit of Christmas* – because we just threw it together, and we never thought anybody would really see it outside of our friends.

We used this Mel Torme Christmas disc. And we can't clear any of the music.

PARKER: And we can't – we only have it on this mixed video version. We have to go find the negative and everything. We don't know what we did with it.

STONE: We don't know where all the elements are. So *The Spirit of Christmas* exists like it does, and we can't clear the music. So I don't think we'll ever be able to – we're still looking into trying to figure out a way, but – then the other thing is, do we want to re-do the music and change what everyone's called like a classic. Then we're going to come out with a new version. So it's kind of a weird thing. So it's kind of our contribution to –

QUESTION: I have two questions. One is, when do we see the soundtrack for the memorable Christmas songs like "Kyle's Mother's a Big Fat Bitch?" And the second question is who does which voices?

PARKER: We'll answer the second one first. I do Cartman and Mr. Garrison and Bar Brady. Matt does Kyle, Kenny, Jesus, Jimbo. And there all the others – we just sort of split it all up. We do them all. Matt and I do them all. But male voices or boys' voices. And then – I don't know – pretty soon we're gonna run out, and they'll all start sounding the same, if they don't already.

QUESTION: Oh, I'm sorry, second question. Forgive me, we didn't finish.

PARKER: What was it again? Oh, the soundtrack. We're actually – what we're working on now is the Chef's soundtrack. We're doing the Chef album. And it's really cool, because everybody from Ozzie Osbourne to Fiona Apple want to be on it. So we're getting Isaac to do this whole Chef album, and that's going to be just – I can't imagine a more fun thing to do for the next few months.

And so that's our big focus and then, you know, we have more albums coming after that. And maybe one would be a Christmas one. But for now, we're just focusing on Chef's album.

QUESTION: How did you guys get together, and how old are you?

STONE: I'm 26.

PARKER: I'm 28.

STONE: He's 28. And we met in college, basically in Super8 class.

PARKER: Yeah, we met in beginning filmmaking class.

QUESTION: Where?

PARKER: At the University of Colorado in Boulder. We're both natives and –

STONE: – And Broncos fans.

PARKER: Yeah. We met there in school and we sort of got – kept getting paired together to make films. And we were – Matt and I were always the guys that were sort of making short films every weekend, you know, for like $100 instead of like saving up a bunch of money to make really beautiful films like other people were. We were making little crappy ones, but a lot of them. We care more about quantity than quality.

QUESTION: Can you guys talk a little more about Cartman? I mean, you called him before the lamest guy on the planet. But he's also pretty evil the last few shows, between the Hitler costume on Halloween and the *Big Fat Bitch* song at Christmas.

PARKER: Yeah, and see the thing that I love about Cartman is he's not really evil, because he doesn't really understand what he's doing. He just doesn't get it. And that's the beauty of it is that these boys can say these things and do these things, and it's okay, because they don't even know what they're doing.

And that's what – that's to me what's so cool about Cartman is that – you know, Cartman will probably grow up to be a fairly normal guy once he figures out that he really shouldn't dress in Hitler costumes.

STONE: He's just a product of his environment, I think.

PARKER: But, you know, it's just that's the thing. When you're eight years old, you don't – you're told what's not cool and what's not correct, but you don't really understand why. And that's what's so fun about writing these guys.

QUESTION: And is Stan just there to be the straight man?

PARKER: Somewhat, but, you know, Stan's got his quirks too. But Stan is sort of the – he's sort of the centerpiece and the holding force of the most normal eight-year-old. Which you need. You can't just have four really bizarre kids. But I think it really – to me, anyway, and to Matt when we came up with it, it really –

The bus stop sort of dictated who your friends were. It wasn't like, you know, you picked your friends. It was who was at your bus stop. And there was always sort of the two best friends, a fat kid and a poor kid. And it seemed like no matter what group it was, there was always that.

STONE: Because we didn't grow up together. But when we start talking about shows – "There was this fat guy." "Yeah, we had a fat guy in our group." (*laughter*) "We had this really porker we made eat worms." "Yeah, we did, too."   So it was kind of like we realized that maybe every single person in the whole world grew up the same way.

PARKER: Yeah, it was like I knew this guy that died every week. And he was like, "Yeah, we did too." (*laughter*)

QUESTION: How much has success bred more tolerance? I mean, the things you do are really far out. You can't do that but all of a sudden now the popularity it seems like they're letting you do anything. And how – I've heard that advertisers are beginning to really – who just avoided the show in the beginning – have really begun to try and get in there.

PARKER: Shows are going to be shorter. They're going to be like three minutes long. Show's going to be three minutes.

STONE: With 18 minutes of commercials.

QUESTION: Well, I guess the first part of that you guys can answer, but –

PARKER: I think that – I don't know, I mean consciously anyway, it doesn't feel any different to us. I mean, we don't feel more or less free than we did with the pilot. In a lot of ways, I think the pilot's more outrageous than a lot of shows.

But we're not – we don't think consciously of, oh, we need to tone it down or we need to go even further. We just sort of – what this has always been about since Matt and I started is making each other laugh. And so that's all we kind of do, is we make each other laugh. And then that's what we put on the show.

And, you know, I don't know – we just sort of take it as a show-by-show thing. Like I said, we don't think in terms of, okay, how outrageous can we be? We just think in terms of humor.

QUESTION: Has there been any kind of an organized protest at all?

FOX: There has not.

KATZ: No, none at all.

FOX: We've gotten some letters, but no organizations have begun any lobbying type effort against us.

KATZ: Except for that one episode.

PARKER: My grandma is kind of pissed off.

QUESTION: Trey, ever since *South Park* came on, I've been dying to see what you look like when you do the voice of Cartman.

PARKER: Oh, geez.

QUESTION: *(overlapping)* – just a little?

PARKER: I just had to do this at Sundance about 40 times. *(laughter)* *(as Cartman:)* "You sonofabitch. I'd kick you in the nuts." [*laughter/applause*]

QUESTION: What are you going to do when the show gets older? Are you going to age the kids or keep them eternally young?

STONE: That's a good question.

PARKER: We talked about having just Ike get older. *(laughter)*

STONE: We were just talking about that.

PARKER: But yeah, we were talking. You know, it's funny, I don't know that we ever thought of having this problem of having to think this far ahead. Matt and I were so used to thinking in terms of, okay, we'll do this and then we'll do that and we'll do this. And now all of a sudden, we have this thing that we're going to be doing for a while.

And so I don't think the boys will get older. I mean, it's kind of – that's the beauty – I love the kids so much I just want to keep them the way they are. And as soon as – and that's the thing, as soon as it stops being funny to us, then that's when we're going to change stuff, you know, because that is what it's all about.

So as long as it's funny to us, which will probably be a real long time, we'll just keep doing it the way it is.

QUESTION: Matt and Trey, can I just ask you a question about – this is getting really large ratings for Comedy Central relative to the fact of Comedy Central ratings. But in Canada, it's airing on a main broadcaster, but it's airing at midnight. And it's actually getting ratings – some weeks, it beats things like *Friends*. It's on midnight on Friday nights, and it's actually a top-10 or top-12 show of all shows.

PARKER: Wow, that's cool.

QUESTION: Do you have any theories why it would be so much more popular in Canada?

STONE: Well, I think it says something about Canadians. *(laughter)*

QUESTION: What does it say?

PARKER: And that's actually – what's about to come out is that Terrence and Phillip are actually Canadian. And that show is from Canada.

But I don't know. And I know that when I was talking to Robert Smith of The Cure [*laughter*] – Bob said to me, he said [*laughter*] –he said that he thought it was going to be huge in England. And because he thought it was a very British sense of humor. Which makes sense because Matt and I were both huge Monty Python fans. I mean, that's absolutely undoubtedly where our sense of humor comes from.

STONE: And no one ever puts that in any articles for some reason. I don't know why people are afraid of that.

QUESTION: Has it played in England yet?

PARKER: No.

FOX: It's been sold. I don't know whether it's actually aired there yet.

KATZ: It hasn't started airing yet, no.

FOX: But it has been sold, I believe.

PARKER: I think it's like June or something.

KATZ: In June.

FOX: To two places.

QUESTION: Which channel?

FOX: I believe Channel Four –

KATZ: And Sky, that's right. That's correct.

QUESTION: Do you have some favorite episodes?

STONE: I think for me, "Damien" – God, "Damien" could be. Watching last night. But for me, probably "Sparky" and/or "Christmas."

PARKER: I think, yeah, I mean, "Big Al's Big Gay Boat Ride" is just, you know, it was –

STONE: It just has such a good story. People think we're joking, but that's when we've got an episode and we're like, that really told a good story with a good character, then that's like – that's the hardest kind of –

PARKER: We've been using "Big Al's Big Gay Boat Ride" as a model, really, you know, in our own writing. I'm saying this is the best thing we've done, structurally. So we use that as a model.

QUESTION: Trey, are you going to be doing any more live-action work like the Mr. Hankie Play Set?

PARKER: We just shot yesterday, we just shot live-action promos for the show, which were fun. They were fun to do. But we're actually, Matt and I right now are starring in a new Universal movie, so we're like actors all of a sudden. We're starring in a movie called *BASEketball*, which is the Zucker brothers' new movie. David Zucker is directing. And it's me and Matt. And our opposites are Yasmine Bleeth and Jenny McCarthy. So it kicks a lot of ass. (*laughter*)

STONE: We come from a live-action background, so live-action is totally fun.

PARKER: We did two features before we did *South Park*, and that's – we were just in Sundance with our features. And, of course, you know, the audience was *South Park* fans, but –

QUESTION: What were the features?

PARKER: Our first feature we did when we were in college is called *Cannibal: The Musical*. And it was released by Troma. And it's a 90-minute musical about Alfred Packer, who was a notorious cannibal in Colorado. And then right before *South Park* got picked up, we did a film called *Orgazmo*, which is about a Mormon missionary who ends up in the porn business. [*laughter*]

QUESTION: Do you have any plans for a *South Park* feature and/or a spin-off from *South Park* for another series?

PARKER: We're young for a spin-off. I mean, I would love to see *The Terrence and Phillip Show*. But I think we've definitely been talking about a feature. We were psyched to do it, and it's sort of a weird thing, because Paramount and Warner Bros. owns Comedy Central, so they're going to have to duke it out themselves.

STONE: And after the *Beavis and Butt-Head* movie did so well, that was, like, you know, everyone wants to do one.

PARKER: But, yeah, we definitely want to. But the only way we'll do it is if we can have it be a rated-R movie. Because we don't want to do – you know, *Beavis and Butt-Head*, as big a fans as we are of that show, you know, we went to the movie and it was kind of just like an hour-and-a-half version of the series.

And there's no reason to really do that. But if we can go and do more of a *Spirit of Christmas* type of thing and have it be rated-R, then we'd be into it.

STONE: Because like, I think a lot of critics loved – I mean, the *Beavis and Butt-Head* movie was good, but if you were a fan of the show and had seen like the hundreds of episodes we've seen, it didn't really seem that great. So we want to do something that just takes it to another level.

That there's a reason we have to do a movie, this couldn't be on TV.

QUESTION: Two quick questions. Number one, does Kenny actually have dialogue? And number two, is it getting harder at all, I mean, you've talked about this a little bit, but as you go on, do you find that you're stretching the limits of your own imagination at all, or are there untapped recesses of your mind that we'll discover?

PARKER: There's totally. I mean, we have writers' retreats about every three weeks, which is really just me, Matt and a couple other people. And we just sort of sit there and – there's so many ways you can go in this show. I mean, in animation, you know, but – and there's a two-part of that. You know it's like because of this world we've created we can go in so many direction, it's so limitless.

On the other hand to answer the other question, you know, I don't feel – I feel like, you know, rather than feeling tapped out, I'm feeling like as every episode progresses, like I definitely get a bigger handle on Cartman as a character, you know, and he gets easier to write because now I start to really know him and I know what he's going to say and he's really starting to have a personality, as well as the other boys, you know.

And, oh yeah, Kenny says real stuff and if we told you what he said they'd take it off the air.

QUESTION: How do you guys feel about the fact that so many kids are fans of the show and they may not get the joke and think that it's really cool that Cartman's dressed as Hitler?

STONE: We have said from the beginning that we thought that – because I assume that the next question we expected to be asked about the TV-MA and stuff like that and how that ties into kids.

We don't find any problem with this show with kids. Personally, on a personal level. And I mean kids being like 10 years old, 11, 12, I'm not talking about younger that that. Because we think the show's smart. We don't think that kids are going to do anything but learn words that they already know, that they already say in school like 800 times a day when they're on the playground.

So we find most of – a lot of other TV that's on networks, like the stuff that's on Fox – the world's, you know, worst road kill (*laughter*) and worst – we find that much more offensive. There's episodes –

PARKER: I mean, yeah, there are people getting stabbed and shot on *Cops*.

STONE: It's just so much worse for a kid to see.

PARKER: And it's real, it's not construction paper, you know.

STONE: I go to sleep, like knowing that kids watch the show, to me is like when me and Trey were growing up and we were watching *Monty Python* and we were watching *Stripes* and *Animal House* and seeing humor that was like so much more sophisticated than what was presented to us.

It was like, okay here's what you can laugh at and now we're all over here in the closed room laughing at this good stuff. And you're just sitting there going –

PARKER: But the bottom line is, I mean, we're not making the show for kids, that's why we're fine with the TV-MA, we're making it for us, we're making it for our friends, for people our age, and you know kids tap into it just like we tapped into *Python*. We didn't the – *Python* was doing Hitler jokes way before we were. And it's not like it made me –

STONE: I'm not Hitler.

PARKER: Yeah, it's not like, you know, it made Matt hate Jews, or anything. It's like we saw a lot of stuff we didn't get but I think kids are smarter than people credit them with. And because they see Cartman dressed up like Hitler they're not suddenly going to go out and become Nazis. It's just not going to happen.

STONE: The other thing is, I think a lot of kids are watching the show but that doesn't mean that – I think in a lot of cases I think the parents have tuned in and seen the show and said, oh this is – I mean we meet so many parents who, much more than kids, a lot of the people in the industry and stuff and like, oh my son loves the show, we watch it every week.

So there's a lot of kids who watch the show with their parents and their parents have like okayed it. It's not a lot of kids who are doing it behind their parents' back or whatever.

South Park has remained a huge success for Comedy Central and its envelope-pushing ways have inspired other animated series to go in their direction of outrageousness.

South Park: The Movie was also a success and earned its creators an Academy Award nomination for Best Song. Parker and Stone dressed in drag to attend the ceremony and much to the Academy's relief they did not win that year.

BASEketball was modest hit at the box-office and probably the first time that a team of creators so identified with animation actually were actually sought after to star in a mainstream film.

The team's latest feature *Team America: World Police* (2004) featured puppets in a Gerry Anderson *Thunderbirds* style. The film was a political scattershot that hit both conservative and liberal targets. Once again the team pushed the envelope and the Motion Pictures Producers Association ratings board threatened the film with an NC-17 rating for one sex act between the puppet leads.

The Nightmare Before Christmas: An Old Style Returns

Somewhere, I hope George Pal is smiling.

The success of *Tim Burton's The Nightmare Before Christmas* has brought the kind of animation made popular by Pal over 50 years ago back into the spotlight.

Just a few months ago, the smash success of *Jurassic Park* led many people to believe that stop-motion animation as most of us know it was now as dead as . . . well . . . a dinosaur. I have to admit the effects of *Jurassic Park* gave me pause. Could moviegoers accept something less than what they saw there . . . a high-tech combination of computer animation, puppetry, and life-size automations?

Well, perhaps what *Jurassic Park* did do was to kill the low-budget dino movie (one of my guiltiest pleasures), but thankfully not destroy the continuing potential of "old-fashioned" stop-motion animation.

But why all this affection for stop-motion? Animation is the "purest" form of cinema because it *can* be indeed the work of a single artist. Economically speaking, though, it's not practical for cel animation to have that kind of artistic "purity" in the mass market.

The very nature of stop-motion allows itself to continue to be identified as the achievement of one person. We describe a film as a "Willis O'Brien picture" or a "Ray Harryhausen movie." Even though some animators used assistants, the animation in stop-motion pictures has been historically the work of primarily a single artist.

The Nightmare Before Christmas, because it is completely stop-motion, does break with this precedent. Economics dictated a veritable platoon of animators be used in order to create the film on schedule. More importantly, though, *Nightmare* also breaks with the overall stop-motion tradition of creating something to look "real." Audiences thrilled to King Kong because he was made to look like an actual living entity. Ray Harryhausen, Jim Danforth and Phil Tippet have all been celebrated for their ability to give obviously unreal entities the illusion of life.

The only stop-motion animator in America to make a career of presenting highly stylized films was the late George Pal. The *Nightmare* crew owes much to both Pal and the pioneering Russian animator Wladislaw Starewicz. Both men frequently used models that were less articulated than the models of Harryhausen and O'Brien. Their point was not to make their subjects look real, but to fulfill a stylized artistic vision.

George Pal brought his type of animation from his native Europe, and he perfected a kind of stop-motion animation that was unique in this country. Supplementing his articulated models, Pal would also create a series of stiff models representing a sequence of movements. To animate facial expressions, Pal would fashion a series of heads with varying expressions that would be replaced in sequences to create mouth and eye movements. Pal's crew would create intricate sets for his shorts, and the films would also boast of outstanding musical scores.

His short subjects were dubbed "Puppetoons," and were released by Paramount during the late 1930s and into the 1940s. Every year from 1941 to 1947, one of Pal's Puppetoons received an Academy Award nomination, but unfortunately he was never honored with an Oscar. *Tubby the Tuba, Tulips Shall Grow, Rhythm in the Ranks, And to Think I Saw it on Mulberry Street* are among his best shorts.

Besides his musical fantasies, Pal worked with the legendary children's author Dr. Seuss on adaptations of several of Seuss' books. The closest Pal got to creating a star from his shorts was the character of "Jasper," an African-American caricature that some people might find offensive today.

When Pal made his move into features in the late 1940s, live-action science-fiction and fantasy became his trademark. Sadly, many fantasy film fans familiar with *War of the Worlds, 7 Faces of Dr. Lao,* and *The Time Machine,* among others, aren't aware of Pal's great contribution to animation.

Pal's techniques were used by the Rankin-Bass team in a series of animated feature films, and, more memorably, a number of television specials that are still broadcast after more than 25 years, and now sold on home video. Technique is the only element shared by *Nightmare* and the Rankin-Bass productions. Made strictly to a general formula (a sentimental holiday theme, possible tie-in with an existing song, "hosted" by an established media personality), these shows were never as well animated as the Pal productions nor were they ever as imaginatively conceived. The irony is that until the release of *Nightmare* on home video, the Rankin-Bass productions, such as *Rudolph the Red-Nosed Reindeer,* are the easiest examples to find of this kind of animation. Some of Pal's shorts are contained on the *Puppetoon Movie* video release (I.V.E., 1986) that can still be found in larger video rental outlets. One hopes the success of *Nightmare* persuades the owner of the Pal shorts to strike a deal for their release.

Tim Burton used some of Pal's techniques when he animated *Vincent,* his acclaimed Disney short subject that has never been officially released.

A wonderful tribute to the late Vincent Price, *Vincent* told the story of a young boy who wanted to be just like the horror film star. Shot in moody black and white, and featuring a narration by Price, *Vincent* was a film the Disney management obviously did not understand and believed they could not market. Hopefully, they understand there is *now* a very large market for this film.

While at Disney, Burton developed the idea and characters for *Nightmare*, which sat in a file cabinet until his string of box-office successes happened, convinced the Disney powers-that-be to resurrect the concept.

And thank goodness. With fellow superstar director Steven Spielberg producing pseudo-Disney syrupy drivel, Burton is carrying on a tradition of individual style and expression that is both wonderfully refreshing and vital to the animation industry.

One of the most interesting aspects to what happened in animation during the 1990s was as soon as one pundit declared a style of animation had been supplanted by a new one, there would be a great example of an old style resurface.

Despite the success of pictures such as *Jurassic Park* and *Toy Story*, each using state-of-the-art computer animation, films such as *Nightmare Before Christmas* and the *Wallace & Gromit* shorts showed that traditional forms of stop-motion animation were still relevant. When in the hands of artists, they were also popular and profitable.

What critics failed to understand is that animation is indeed an art form with many media. No art critics would declare that watercolors were dead, so why did some people write off cel animation or clay or puppet stop motion?

Writing this in an era in which cel animation has finally been supplanted by computer animation for feature films, one wonders if the older methods have finally been abandoned. I don't think so. All audiences care about is whether or not something is good.

At the Academy Awards in March 2006, there were no computer-animated features nominated and the clay-animated *Wallace and Gromit* feature, *The Curse of the Were-Rabbit*, walked away with the Oscar.

From *The Journal/Bravo,* Dec. 11, 2004

Warner cartoon stars shine thanks to the right director

You know them and you love them. They taught you the great themes of classical music. They showed you that anything marked "Acme" wouldn't work. They even introduced you to your first cross-dresser.

The Warner Brothers cartoon characters - Bugs Bunny, Daffy Duck, and Elmer Fudd, Wile E. Coyote and company - are finally back in a vehicle that matches their happily subversive personalities.

The irony about the Warner Brothers cartoon stars is that they are among the most popular animated figures in the world, but until *Looney Tunes: Back in Action* was released, no one really understood how to show-case them in a new movie.

The classic WB cartoons have entertained three generations of kids and adults, but until now efforts to create new cartoons worthy of carrying the torch of the classics have been disappointing. *Space Jam*? It was nothing but a glorified sneaker commercial starring a basketball player with Bugs and Daffy as support.

Sure this new movie features plenty of flesh and blood stars such as Brendan Fraser, Jenna Elfman and Steve Martin, but the animated characters have someone in their corner, a director who is as subversive as they are.

And that evil genius is Joe Dante.

Dante's newest film shows that even when assigned to shepherding the prize moneymakers of the Warner Brothers merchandising machine, the director brings the same sensibilities as seen in the two *Gremlins* movies, *Small Soldiers*, and *Matinee* among others.

If you haven't seen the film, then run out and see it pronto. The plot brings many of the characterizations and situations created by classical cartoon directors Chuck Jones, Friz Freleng and Bob Clampett up to date. Like those three directors, the humor is for both adults and kids and Dante doesn't mind sending up the most sacred cows of today's film industry.

The plot involves Warner Brothers security guard DJ (Brendan Fraser) stumbling upon the fact that his movie star father Damien Drake (Timothy Dalton), who is renowned for playing a James Bond-like hero, is actually a spy. This revelation takes place on the day he is fired from his job by a Warner VP Kate Houghton (Jenna Elfman) who blames him for not escorting Daffy Duck off the premises whom she has also fired. When the Warner Brothers decide they need Daffy back, they tell her to find him, but Daffy has already taken off with DJ to Las Vegas to find out what has happened to DJ's father.

It seems that Drake was trying to secure a gemstone known as the Blue Monkey that can change people into a monkey and back. It is coveted by the chairman of the evil Acme Corporation (Steve Martin), who plans to turn humanity into monkeys to work in his factories and then back to humans to buy the goods they just made.

Along the way we are treated to a barrage of gags that demands repeated viewings. You have to love a scene in which Porky Pig and Speedy Gonzales discuss their lack of political correctness.

Dante is a rarity in the business. He's a movie nut fan boy who went from seeing as many movies as he could to writing about them to working in the business. Landing a job with legendary low-budget movie producer Roger Corman in the 1970s, Dante created many of the trailers for Corman's New World Pictures. He got his chance to direct when fellow Corman-ite Jon Davison made a bet with Corman that Davison couldn't produce a feature-length film in a week for a reported $50,000.

Davison tagged Dante and Allan Arkush to direct *Hollywood Boulevard*, a very entertaining drive-in picture. Dante's first solo effort, *Piranha* - a film Corman described as his version of *Jaws* - followed and was a huge hit for Corman. Dante's next film, *The Howling,* a landmark werewolf movie, got the attention of audiences and critics.

Perhaps best known for his two *Gremlins* films, Dante told *The Journal/ Bravo* in a telephone interview that he has been typecast a bit by the success of his "family fantasies," which is how he became associated with his new film.

Besides his sense of humor, Dante said he brought a technical proficiency to the director's chair because so many of his films featured various special effects. The ability to understand the latest film technology was crucial with this film. Dante explained that within the year and a half production period, technology that they had used at the beginning of the shoot had been supplanted by newer hardware and software by the end.

Script went through many changes

He explained that *Looney Tunes: Back in Action* is the culmination of much effort to develop a follow-up film to *Space Jam*, which was released in 1996. Dante said that one script even had Bugs teaming up with action star Jackie Chan.

Finally, writer Larry Doyle sold Warner brass on a script in which the characters are going around the world and was broken down into a series of interrelated seven-minute shorts.

Once the production was approved, though, there were still many changes made to the script and Dante said that over the year and a half it took to make the movie, there were a "couple of drafts."

He readily admitted that because the script wasn't finished the production became "a little scary."

He explained that in the case of this film, Warner Brothers had an open hole on his fall release schedule that had been the place of the next *Harry Potter* film. Studio execs told Dante that the film had to be finished by that date and so he said they "worked backwards."

The result was an intensive year of filmmaking with six months of shooting the live-action scenes and a year of creating the animation. Dante noted that for the amount of animation and the level of quality that had to be met the work normally would have taken two years.

"They [the animation crew] did a great job," he said. "Everyone worked seven days a week."

Dante worked with animation director Eric Goldberg, a Disney veteran who animated the Genie in *Aladdin* among other accomplishments.

Although in most films that marry animation and live action the live action is shot well before the animation begins, in this film the live-action production overlapped with the animation because of the film's quick production schedule.

Both Dante and Goldberg directed the vocal performers. Joe Alaskey performed most of the roles originated by the late Mel Blanc, including Bugs and Daffy. Billy West, the lead vocal performer on the *Futurama* series and the original *Ren & Stimpy* shorts, performed Elmer Fudd. Springfield native June Foray reprised the role of Granny that she has been performing since the 1940s. Dante had high praise for all of the voice performers, especially Alaskey.

"It's a very tedious process," Dante explained of the voice recording and said that Alaskey had to do some takes 10 to 12 times to make sure he sounded as much like Mel Blanc as he could.

Performing the voices took talent and patience, as did acting in front of the cameras with characters that weren't on the set.

"It takes a specific talent to look into space," said Dante of his live-action cast. Dante added that "actors like to get something back" and that a lack of reaction from a co-star who is yet to be drawn makes the job tougher.

He said male lead Brendan Fraser was a "standalone candidate" for his role because he has had experience acting in special effects-heavy films such as *The Mummy* movies and *Monkeybone*. His being attractive to women and a good actor didn't hurt either.

The cast also includes many performers who are members of the Dante stock company, including Mary Woronov, Robert Picardo, and naturally Dick Miller. Miller, a highly recognizable character actor who has appeared literally in hundreds of movies and television shows, has been in every one of Dante's films and there's a rumor that Dante will rejects scripts if there isn't a part for Miller in it.

He rejected that notion with a laugh and explained that he grew up watching Miller in films and when he started with Corman he was introduced to him and started using him in his films whenever possible.

Movie lampoons corporate filmmaking

The irony about the film is that it satirizes the corporate mindset of the motion picture industry - a mindset that was quite apparent in this production. There was a lot riding on this film - it was the studio's Thanksgiving family release with a reported $100 million budget and starred characters that has generated millions of dollars in licensing money.

Dante said there were "many many voices" from studio executives on the film's story and gags.

"This was a difficult production," he admitted.

With this kind of film, Dante didn't have the luxury of reviewing complete sequences as they were made because the animation wasn't complete.

"You can't even look at what you have," he said.

Studio execs and test audiences were shown cuts of the film that lacked finished animation that didn't result in truly informed opinions.

"When all the animation was done, it was a revelation," he said.

Because the film was post-production for a year, there were many alterations to it. Dante said he would second-guess himself on whether a gag was funny enough to make a final cut and said there was actually "a tremendous amount of improv" resulting from the editing.

The result is that Dante and company crammed as many gags into the film as they could. Dante explained that as a "child of Mad Magazine, who read the jokes in the margins," he has been "over-stuffing" his movies for years.

Originally the film was two hours in length and Dante had to cut it down to a more reasonable running time for a family film and to pick up the pace.

One part of the film, which has thrilled horror and science-fiction fans, almost didn't make the final cut. Bugs, Daffy, DJ and Kate are taken to Area 52 where various alien monsters are kept. Area 51, by the way, is just for the tourists!

There, Mother (played by Joan Cusack) oversees the internment of infamous creatures from B-movies of the past, including the mutant from

This Island Earth, the brain from *Fiend Without a Face*, the Ro-Man from *Robot Monster* and the Daleks from the *Dr. Who* television series. Marvin the Martian is among those being kept in over-sized Mason jars.

The sequence is funny and nostalgic, but Dante said that some people viewing the test prints thought the monsters were "corny" and instead an animated sequence with Pepe Le Pew was used.

Thankfully, Dante prevailed and the witty scene was restored to the film, although some of the footage did remain out of the film. Dante has just completed working on the supplemental materials for the DVD release and said that 28 minutes of unseen footage will be featured on the disc, although more could have been included.

What's up, Joe?
With the film completed, Dante stood back and watched how the production was promoted and released. For reasons he couldn't fathom, the studio did not push the film, and it has not been the box office smash it could have been.

Dante said that he usually is thinking about his next picture while he is finishing a film, but because this shoot took so long and was so involved, he paid complete attention to *Looney Tunes*. He is not sure what the next project will be but he is sure it won't be another fantasy film for families.

In 2005, Dante was among the directors chosen by Showtime to participate in their *Masters of Horror* series. His installment, *Homecoming*, received rave reviews.

Chapter Three: Maintaining Independence

While new animation stars worked within the redesigned studio and network systems, there were some who maintained an element of independence. These were people who wanted to have as much creator control and ownership over their creations.

Creator control is as huge an issue in animation as it is in comic strips and comic books. While the economic models do allow the possibility for creator ownership in comic books – one can still self-publish and distribute to comic book shops – animators don't have that option. One needs a means of financing and distribution to make animated production self-sustaining, if not profitable.

Various independents have taken different approaches to the issue. There are wily veterans such as Ralph Bakshi, who redefined what "mainstream" meant in animation. Bill Plympton has found an economic model that allowed him to make both highly personal films and a living.

Then there was Don Bluth, the former Disney animator, who attempted to compete with Disney with family-oriented features but without the same financial resources.

All of these creators walked along a tightrope of finding financing and distribution for their films.

The Internet age does allow an independent animator to self-distribute animation to a large market, but the question remains how does one make money from web-based cartoons?

Animato #29 Summer 1994
Ralph Bakshi: Back to Basics and Loving It

Ralph Bakshi is a happy man.

The original enfant terrible of animation; the man who pushed animation into an X rating with *Fritz the Cat*; the man who managed to make perhaps the most personal and politically-charged animated features to this date is once again doing short subjects, and he is loving it.

This isn't a comedown for the man who shouldered the blame for the multi-million *Cool World* debacle.

"I'm the happiest I've been in 25 years," he said proudly.

"They [Hanna-Barbera] asked me to do shorts, and the budgets are not enormous (they're about $200,000 a short) and what's spectacular for me about it is I'm allowed to create my own characters, do my own drawings, and get back to where I started in the business because I'm pretty disgusted where I am today. In other words, it allows me to go all the way back home and reminds me how I got to *Fritz the Cat* and *Heavy Traffic*. For me, it's been a personal renaissance," said Bakshi.

Bakshi's deal with Hanna-Barbera is to produce five shorts within the next two years, with an option to produce five more. He feels so strongly about participating in the Shorts Program that he recently turned down directing an animated children's movie.

There's no executive parking space for Bakshi at his new studio. The man who was running his own studio in California with hundreds of employees is now very happy to be in a casual, almost make-shift two-room studio in Manhattan with a very small staff. When *ANIMATO* publisher Patrick Duquette and I visited him, his assistant was covering the phone and taking care of logistics, while another staffer was working with an Amiga computer set-up, which delivers instant pencil tests. The sounds of New York from open windows attempted to compete with Bakshi's confident voice colored with a hearty Brooklyn accent.

This limited edition cel has much more of the Bakshi feeling in it than the finished *Cool World* did.

Around Bakshi's work area literally dozens of drawings of characters and gags are pinned up on the wall. Some are in color; some are finished drawings, while others are rough sketches. There's another overflowing pile of drawings near his desk. For anyone who ever imagined what Bakshi's studio would be like based on viewing his early features . . . well, this is it.

Rather than just produce cartoons, such as the late and lamented *Mighty Mouse* series, or fight the kind of studio politics he faced with *Cool World*, Bakshi is back to basics . . . writing, directing and producing his own material. He's also going to animate, something of which he admits to having done too little in the past few years.

With his early features, Bakshi did as many drawings as he could to turn over to animators, but as his career went from *Fritz the Cat* and *Heavy Traffic* to films such as *Lord of the Rings* and *American Pop*, his role changed.

"As the studio grew, more people started to do work. I became a producer more than a director, and I had all these other responsibilities, and my whole tone changed. In other words, the kind of stuff I wanted to do, the kind of stuff I was trying to do suddenly shifted," said Bakshi. "And I had no idea it had shifted. I was very proud of the studio. I was very proud of having 400 people work for me. I was a big-time Hollywood director. I was very proud of what they were paying me. I don't know if it was ego, but basically what happened to me was I became another man without really realizing it. And I wasn't happy with my work. I wasn't happy at all. And I didn't know why I wasn't happy."

Getting back to basics means that Bakshi has two other animators besides himself and just three assistants. With the exception of inking and painting, all of the production work will be done in New York.

"From here, I want to build back, and create a small feature film unit that will do the kind of animation that I gave up after *Coonskin* was thrown out of the theaters," said Bakshi.

Only since beginning work on these new shorts has Bakshi realized something about himself. With the encouragement of his wife, the help of a therapist and considerable soul-searching, he said he now sees how lucky he was to create three features – *Fritz the Cat, Heavy Traffic,* and *Coonskin* (known on video as *Streetfight*) – which were highly personal artistic and political expressions.

"My wife said they let me get away with murder," he said.

"Hollywood forced me to change and said if you want to continue to do animation you have to clean up your act. [Go from R-rated material to PG] and make sure there are no ideas in the PG. I was very political," said Bakshi.

Ask him about his films, and Bakshi is quick to respond with frank and surprising answers.

"I love *Wizards*, but I don't love *Lord of the Rings*. I appreciate *American Pop*, but I don't love it. And I appreciate *Fire and Ice*, but I don't love it."

Bakshi prides himself on being a cartoonist, and for him the title has a very particular meaning.

"A cartoonist is an observer of life, and he puts down what he observes. And that was very important to me . . . Goya taught me that, Daumier taught me that, Rolandson taught me that; the artists I love, the guys I used to look at as a kid taught me that. I didn't think there was any way else to cartoon. That's cartooning. The rest is illustration. What Disney does is illustration, not cartooning. They illustrate the script very well, but they don't cartoon. *Mutt and Jeff* is cartooning; Herriman is cartooning. The essence of cartooning is underground. It's graffiti on the wall. It's a jab in a face. It's not agreeing with. And that's what I was doing without intellectualizing it."

For a man who was blamed for the failure of the high-profile animated release *Cool World*, Bakshi is extremely forthcoming and candid in discussing the production. Settling back into his chair and puffing on what seems to be a never-ending series of cigarettes, Bakshi opened the discussion with the revelation that *Cool World* started out as an almost completely different story.

"I wanted to do a horror film. I went to work [writing the script] and Paramount bought it. The original concept was that a live-action character gets into the cartoon world (it makes sense how he got there) and goes to bed with this girl who wanted to be real. And they had a baby and the baby was a monster. And the baby happened in 30 seconds. The whole thing was about the father and son relationship. It really was a strange story. I think it was a potentially good film."

Bakshi admits he was enthusiastic at the time to be working with a $30 million budget (up until then *Lord of the Rings*, at $4 million, was his most expensive production), but that elation wore off when on the first day of shooting the live action, a second script arrived.

"I should have quit. That's where I made my mistake," said Bakshi. "I should have walked off the set, but they were paying me a fortune, and I rationalized it and said 'who cares?'"

Paramount convinced Bakshi that their script was better, and despite numerous misgivings over serious plot holes, Bakshi stayed on.

Bakshi worked on the film for the better part of two years when studio politics deposed Frank Mancuso, Sr. as head of production and installed former NBC television honcho Brandon Tartikoff. Tartikoff told Bakshi he no longer wanted *Cool World* to be an "R"-rated film, but rather a "PG-13." Bakshi was just days away from finishing the production.

Adding to his woes was Paramount's decision to hire a company to run previews showing audiences filmed storyboards rather than finished animation. The reports from the survey company recommended numerous cuts, as did Tartikoff. Bakshi fought against the cuts, and was fired from the production.

Now, though, the *Cool World* experience is definitely water over the dam, and Bakshi believes its failure prevented him from being involved with other "work-for-hire" productions.

"*Cool World* was the luckiest thing that could have happened to me, although at the time it was the worst thing that had happened to me," Bakshi declared. "I don't care if I ever make another Hollywood film. I'll find a way to finance my own feature films. I'll do it myself."

Bakshi is certainly not brooding about the past, and said he'd be a happy man if what he did the rest of his life was making shorts, as long as the shorts were done on his artistic terms. He described his contract with the Hanna-Barbera Shorts Program as being "an honest deal," and is ecstatic over the creative freedom he has.

Using "full" animation, Bakshi's team for the shorts involves both young artists starting out in animation and veterans. He is using the talent of a former UPA artist for the backgrounds of his shorts, and is also hiring an editor who worked for UPA.

Bakshi has completed the storyboard for his first short, a hilarious tale of life in the big city, fame, and music. If there was any doubt of Bakshi's enthusiasm for making shorts, it was completely forgotten as he performed the cartoon for us.

Waking back and forth in front of the dozens of drawings hung on a wall, Bakshi did more than just explain the action, and perform the voices, the sound effects, and part of the music . . . he *became* the cartoon!

Laughing along with us, his joy of creating something he loves was indeed easy to see.

Bakshi completed two cartoons for the Hanna-Barbera Shorts Program in 1995. There was apparently some disagreement between H-B brass and Bakshi on content issues and the other two productions were never made.

In 1996, he became involved with producing an animated HBO series *Spicy City* that didn't make too much of an impression with viewers or critics.

He moved to Silver City, New Mexico in 2003, where his son has established the Bakshi School of Animation.

According to his website, Bakshi is working on a book based on *Wizards* and a new feature film *Last Days of Coney Island.*

Animato Spring 1994
An Animato Preview: *Thumbelina*

After producing films with talking dinosaurs, immigrating mice and a rock 'n' roll rooster, Don Bluth and his partners Gary Goldman and John Pomeroy are offering movie audiences a new idea for them . . . a classic fairy tale.

Thumbelina will be in theaters nationwide as this issue of *ANIMATO* first hits the newsstands, and according to Goldman, the film is a departure from the partners' other productions.

"This is our first classic fairy tale. The style is no different than our other films, but I think it is our prettiest picture since *The Secret of NIMH*. There's a lot of detail in it," said Goldman. "It's our first picture, you might say, which is more of a 'female picture' along the lines of *The Little Mermaid*."

Thumbelina does indeed share one important link to that blockbuster Disney film. Jodi Benson, who performed the voice of Ariel, is also Thumbelina's voice.

Based on the famous fairy tale, *Thumbelina* tells the story of a tiny girl born to a lonely woman, and, as a teenager, searches for true love

This production drawing shows the Rotoscoping process
used by Bluth's animators on *Thumbelina*.

and acceptance. Along the way to the happy ending, Thumbelina must overcome a troupe of singing toads, villainous beetles and amorous moles before she can be united with her prince.

The film has traveled a long road to reach theater audiences. Goldman explained that he and his partners started looking at fairy tales six or seven years ago for source material. Specifically, they looked at stories that Disney had not adapted. *Thumbelina* appealed to them because the partners felt children would identify with a heroine who shares their concern with height.

Bluth is credited with the screenplay that Goldman noted is faithful to the original Hans Christian Andersen fairy tale. Produced at the Bluth studio in Dublin, Ireland, the film was the creation of the studio's almost 500 artists. Although, Goldman and his partners are firmly committed to producing traditional hand-painted cel animation, state-of-the-art computer techniques were also used on *Thumbelina*.

Like the use of computer-generated animation in recent Disney releases, Bluth and his colleagues used computers to help create backgrounds, such as the streets of Paris in *Thumbelina*.

The voices were recorded before Disney's release of *Aladdin*, and besides Benson include Charo as Mrs. Delores Toad, Gilbert Gottfried as Berkely Beetle, Carol Channing as Ms. Fieldmouse, and John Hurt as Mr. Mole. Like

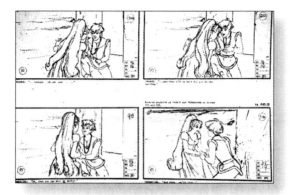

These storyboards portray the action of *Thumbelina*.

other Bluth productions, the design team incorporated elements of the actors' features or mannerisms into their animated counterparts.

Thumbelina should have released well before now, but, as Goldman points out, such are the hazards of independent production. Goldman, Pomeroy and Bluth are not aligned with any one studio for financing of their projects. They must seek out not only financial partners for the production of their films, but distributors as well.

"There's no difference between independent production of live-action films and animation," noted Goldman. But the quality and the box-office success of Disney animated features sets the pace for the rest of the industry, and Goldman admits that "Disney finances their films with deep pockets."

Goldman, who worked at Disney with Bluth and Pomeroy, said that Disney spent $12.5 million on *The Fox and the Hound* while the fledging Bluth Studio spent only $6.5 million on their first feature, *The Secret of NIHM*.

"Today, Disney spends between $20 and $45 million on a feature," said Goldman, "and no one can keep up with that."

The individuals and institutions that back independent animated features want the kind of production values the Disney films have, but, according to Goldman, they naturally want the filmmaker to accomplish that with far less money.

Depending on outside financing means possible delays in the produc-

Seen in a Disney-esque publicity shot for *The Secret of NIHM*,
Don Bluth has had a prolific career in feature animation.

tion of a film if there is a change in the backing, which is exactly what happened to *Thumbelina*, said Goldman. But once a film is finished, and delivered for distribution, the problems awaiting an independent producer are not yet over. Frequently a distribution deal is set up with the financing as well as the choice of laboratories to produce prints of the film.

Goldman can remember with horror when he and Bluth saw a release print of *All Dogs Go to Heaven* at a theater in Dublin, and were devastated by the job the lab had done.

"It looked terrible," remembered Goldman. "We were afraid what audiences were going to see. It was soupy green."

How the prints look, and how the film is marketed are decisions that that many independents have little or no control. Bad choices can "deflate all your work to nothing," said Goldman.

Thankfully, Goldman and Bluth are happy with *Thumbelina*. Warner Brothers is distributing the film, and prepared a "great" trailer. Goldman is also happy with the prints prepared by Technicolor.

What's up next for the partners? The studio is now working on a new feature tentatively titled *The Penguin and the Pebble* with James Belushi and Martin Short, among others, supplying voices.

Of all of the independents Don Bluth has had in many ways the oddest career in that his films often resemble the work of the very studio he left.

Quitting Disney to work on his own style of animated film, his first movie, *The Secret of NIHM*, was a surprise hit. However, his output has had severe ups and downs. Hits such as *The Land Before Time* and *An American Tale* – both of which inspired several direct-to-video features that Bluth did not produce – are balanced with almost unwatchable movies such as *The Pebble and the Penguin, A Troll in Central Park, Rock-A-Doodle* and *All Dogs Go to Heaven*.

Bluth's films often have suffered from weak stories, although the animation is always quite good.

Bluth did score another hit with *Anastasia* in 1997, which marked a departure from the kiddie stories that were his trademark. Critics were not all impressed with his retelling of the story of a woman who thought she was the daughter of the last Czar of Russia.

Perhaps sensing he should go into a new direction and attempt to appeal to an older audience, Bluth made the science-fiction tale *Titan A.E.*, which was released in 2000. It was a handsome film to watch, but once again the story was not compelling and the film flopped.

Since then, Bluth produced his third video game, a new version of *Dragon's Lair*, in 2002.

Animato **#32 Spring 1995**
The Clayboy Makes It to the Big Screen
Gumby's feature film is set to debut this summer

He's lean, green and, now, is going to be a star on the movie screen. Art Clokey's Gumby has been a staple on television since the character's debut in 1956 on the *Howdy Doody Show*. Now, the clay-animated character is on his way to theaters for the first time in *Gumby: The Movie*.

The movie's release capitalizes on Gumby's newest success in television, a show on Nickelodeon featuring both older episodes and ones produced in the mid-Eighties.

"Years ago, they thought Gumby had had it. It would just come and go like fads. Fortunately, we got a chance to make a new series back in 1986 and '87. They combine that with the old ones on the present Nickelodeon show," explained Clokey. The Nickelodeon show has received solid ratings from both new and older fans.

Indeed, Gumby has maintained his place in the American pop culture for almost 40 years. The original episodes were widely syndicated after their network run, and then enjoyed distribution on home video. Gumby merchandising has almost been a constant in the marketplace for years. Clokey, more than any other animator, has popularized the medium of clay animation.

The Gumby feature proved to be disappointing at the box office.

Clokey, who had wanted to produce a feature, took the profits from the television deal to underwrite the feature, which he and his wife Gloria produced in their Marin County, CA studio.

"We did the movie in 1988, '89 and '91. We just finished some of the post-production a few months ago," said Clokey. Since the Clokeys were financing the feature themselves, Clokey reported with pleasure that they could work "like humans" on the film with a schedule of eight-hour days, instead of the 14 hours demanded by the new television work.

The movie was a family affair with Art Clokey co-writing, directing, and storyboarding the film while his wife Gloria also co-wrote the script, did the set breakdowns and wrote some of the songs. Art performed three voices, including that of Pokey, while Gloria was the voice for Goo, one of Gumby's friends.

Those looking for another animated musical fairy tale will be disappointed. *Gumby: The Movie* is indeed animated, and has music, but follows the style long established by Clokey. As anyone who has watched

Gumby can tell you, Gumby is . . . well . . . different than other animated characters. Clokey's sense of the abstract and surreal and his strong religious and moral beliefs produce a singularly individual animated film.

In this case, when was the last time you saw an animated film in which cloning, rock 'n' roll and low interest loans were key plot points?

Producing the new television episodes provided the Clokeys with a way to find the talent necessary for a feature film.

"We were able to train animators on the new series we did in 1986-88. We had 18 animators. We found them from all over the country and trained them," explained Clokey. "That's why the new series is uneven in its quality. Some episodes have good animation and some don't. Lorimar [the company] who was financing the series wanted to have it done in 18 months. Well, we did it in 20 months. If you realize the 99 episodes we did was equal to six to eight feature films, you see we couldn't be very perfectionistic in our shooting."

The feature film was made under different conditions.

"We picked out some of the best animators to do the movie after we did the series. We had all the equipment, studio, and artists and so on to do the movie. The first version was completed in 1992, and since then we've made changes and the last changes were made about six months ago. We improved the soundtrack and got a new composer, and did some editing and so on. We added a song over the end credits so people won't want to get up out of their seats."

Gumby: The Movie is an independent production which is being released by a small New York-based distributor, Arrow Releasing, Inc. Clokey could have gone with a larger distributor, but decided against it.

"Warner Brothers and Universal both registered some interest in distributing it. Warner Brothers wanted to put Eddie Murphy in it, and Universal wanted to change the script too much. So we passed them by and decided to do it ourselves."

In this time of computer-generated animation, Gumby is comfortably and reassuringly low-tech in many ways. Gumby and his co-stars are still wire-reinforced models made of the clay-like modeling compound plastocene. While Gumby the character has proven to be durable, Gumby the model is not. Eighty to ninety Gumby figures are used to make a single television episode.

While much remains the same, Clokey noted there have been changes to the production techniques.

"The big changes were in the new materials, the new plastics that came out in the time between we were making the old series and the new, like Styrofoam and Foamcore board and various types of tape. One of the things we used that we never used before was a motion-controlled camera. We had the camera mounted on a device that was controlled by the computer. We could program in exact movements we wanted the camera to make."

Something else new for Gumby is a girlfriend named Tara, which Clokey points out means "star" in Sanskrit. This kind of detail and a strong moral core are some of the most appealing aspects of Clokey's work. His background and interests are reflected in his films, but Clokey said it's not deliberate.

"It comes out of my subconscious when I'm writing a script, it's almost like daydreaming. The subconscious is a very spiritual place sometimes," Clokey explained.

"No, we don't set out to make a moral issue. It just happens spontaneously. I was brought up going to be an Episcopal minister. After graduating from the university, I went to seminary in Connecticut, but after the first year I decided I didn't want to be a minister in the Episcopal or any church. I, what you might say, fled to Hollywood where I could make religious films. I couldn't make religious films there because I had to be a member of the union to get into any of the production companies."

Calling himself "an idealist," Clokey recalled that for the first seven years of Gumby's run, he would not allow any merchandising because he wanted the character to be "a gift to children and not exploit children." Clokey also produced the religious animated children's show *Davey and Goliath*, underwritten by the Lutheran Church, for a decade.

Clokey has maintained a deep interest in the world's religions, and has been particularly involved with the teachings of Sri Sathya Sai Baba, a guru from India. In fact, Clokey attributes much of the new interest in Gumby to an event that happened in 1979 when Clokey went to India to meet

Sri Sathya Sai Baba, and the religious leader blessed Gumby. *Gumby - The Movie* is dedicated to this teacher.

What's next? Arrow Releasing has announced an October date for the distribution of the video of *Gumby: The Movie*, and Clokey has already completed the script for the next Gumby feature, *Gumby II*.

As of 2006, *Gumby: The Movie* was Clokey's last production.

Animation Planet #2 Fall 1997
Beating the Odds:
Bill Plympton Doesn't Need $85 Million to Make a Movie

Combative nosehairs.

Mutant brain lobes with super powers.

Don't look now, you've entered *Mondo Plympton*.

Since 1983, when he was asked to work on the animated adaptation of Jules Feiffer's song *Boomtown*, Bill Plympton has turned out an amazing body of work including short subjects, commercials, and, now, a total of three animated and two live-action feature films.

Few animators today have styles as distinctive. If you've seen Plympton's work once or twice, it's easy to recognize it anytime after that. His use of colored pencils, his fondness for exaggerated takes, his gleeful use of violence, and an obvious fascination for body parts above the waist all typify a Plympton film.

Plympton finds himself in the enviable position of having two animated features currently beginning to make the festival rounds. *Mondo Plympton* is a hilarious collection of both early and current work with animated bridging sequences featuring Plympton answering questions about his films.

His other feature, *I Married a Strange Person*, is the most audacious American feature animation since Ralph Bakshi's *Coonskin*. Sexually and politically charged, *I Married a Strange Person* has something that will offend just about everyone, and I say that as a compliment. (See accompanying reviews.)

Plympton sat down for a leisurely interview with *Animation Planet* earlier this year in his mid-town Manhattan apartment. His apartment seems to be a good visual metaphor for his career. Located in a distinctly unflashy wholesale district, Plympton's large warehouse-style space is neatly divided into his living quarters, his mail order operation, office, and animation studio. There is a clear focus and a rigorous economy of resources which matches Plympton's on-screen style.

The focus is always on the work itself. His career in animation is even more impressive when you realize that Plympton animates every inch of film himself.

Perhaps his focus is clear because being an animator is something he has wanted to do for nearly his entire life. At age 14, he sent off a collection of his drawings to Walt Disney himself in the hopes of landing an animating gig at the studio. While the Mouse Company turned him down then, years later after the success of *Your Face*, they offered Plympton a chance to join up.

"At one point they [Disney] wanted to hire me and offered me a million bucks. Then I saw their contract and I [*breaks into laughter*] . . ." The highly restrictive contract gave Plympton all the reason he needed to stay independent.

"[It] is too bad because Disney was *it*. I would have killed to work for Disney."

After his youthful interaction with Disney, Plympton made one more attempt to enter animation. While at Portland State University (he's a native of Oregon) he made an animated promo for the yearbook that was accidentally shot upside-down, making it less than useful.

Discouraged with animation, Plympton turned his sights to illustration and cartooning, and moved from the northwest to New York City in 1968, where he studied for a year at the School of Visual Arts. He began contributing cartoons and illustrations to such publications as *The*

New York Times, Vogue, House Beautiful, The Village Voice, and *Rolling Stone.* He also contributed to men's magazines such as *Screw* and *Penthouse,* and has recently collected those cartoons in the book *The Sleazy Cartoons of Bill Plympton.* A long-time film fan, he designed three film magazines, *Cineaste, Filmmakers Newsletter,* and *Film Society Review.*

He also entered the comic strip field with *Plymptoons* first appearing in *The Soho Weekly News* and then syndicated by Universal Press.

Despite his busy career in illustration, when he had another opportunity to attempt animation with *Boomtown,* he eagerly took it and credits producer Connie D'Autuono for helping him through the learning process. A short five years later in 1988, he received an Academy Award nomination for *Your Face.*

After working on *Boomtown* he was inspired by filmmakers such as Spike Lee and Jim Jarmusch to pursue a career making movies outside of the mainstream. Then he discovered animation festivals, which "blew my mind." Not only would the festivals fly Plympton out to exciting cities where he was wined and dined, but he also received an opportunity to see how audiences reacted to his films.

"The neatest thing was to hear people laugh at my drawings. I was totally hooked and I think that's why I'm such a maniac because I'm trying to make up for lost time, all these years I was doing these print cartoons. In the back of my mind I was writing little scenarios and I was wondering how I would make a film about this [cartoon]."

Now Plympton has produced two new features – the first, which will be seen by audiences, is *Mondo Plympton.* What inspired this film were Plympton's experiences working in comedy clubs. He would show his short films, introduce them with funny stories, and take questions from the audience.

"It's a throwback to the Winsor McCay days when he was doing vaudeville, showing his films and talking," he said. The effect of *Mondo Plympton* is that of spending an evening with a very funny friend.

One of the highlights of *Mondo* is Plympton's recent short, *Nosehair,* and its production history seems to sum up a lot of what's wrong currently with the animation industry.

The highly publicized World Premiere Toon program from Hanna-Barbera's program asked him to participate in their development program which has since resulted in *Dexter's Laboratory* and *Johnny Bravo* series and the Academy Award nominee *The Chicken from Outer Space*. Although supposedly the program was to give both veteran and new animators a chance to produce a funny five-minute short, the real goal of developing series concepts became quickly apparent.

Plympton was offered a budget of $100,000 and was excited over the prospect. "They flew me out to L.A. for a big meeting at a big conference table. I went through the storyboards and told them how funny it would be. They just sat there with blank faces," he said.

Their reaction was telling Plympton that "maybe we could get some Hanna-Barbera writers to help you fix this up. They apparently missed the whole point of the humor. Afterwards I started to think that the reason they didn't go for it was that were no merchandising possibilities in *Nosehair* and there was no character they could hang a series around. That's what they were looking for, a *Ren and Stimpy* kind-of thing."

Nosehair tells the story of man who wants to get rid of a wild nose hair and the nose hair's reaction to its eviction. While funny and surreal, it's not the stuff of action figures.

Plympton elected to finance the film himself, and reports "it made a lot of money. It did all right." Despite what happened to him, Plympton is glad the company had the program and said, "It's a healthy sign they're going to independents and are trying to get away from *Yogi Bear* and *The Flintstones*."

While Plympton wants to produce his own animated films his own way, he understands the other side of the coin. One of his long-time friends is Matt Groening, creator of *The Simpsons*.

"I understand that [the trade-off for working in television]. I have no complaint about that. If a TV network is going to spend $5 million, $10 million for something they should get back [something] on their investment," he noted, and added that his friend Groening has become wealthy from his involvement in mainstream animation.

"I just like creating my own characters, doing my own ideas. Creating the characters is the fun part; having them do what I want them to do without worrying about censorship. And that's why I continue to do theatrical shorts and theatrical features."

The only censorship Plympton believes in is whether or not something is funny. "I've gone beyond embarrassing my folks. They've given up on me. It's basically whether or not the audience will sit still and laugh at it. That's my censor."

Despite being friends with both Mike Judge and Groening, Plympton doesn't watch *The Simpsons* or *King of the Hill*.

"I like the physical, the visual, and the surreal of Warner Brothers and the early Fleischer stuff and what I find lacking in today's animation is that visual humor, except maybe for *Duckman*. It comes pretty close. I do enjoy watching *Duckman*. I feel bad about that [not watching other shows] but I'm totally happy that *Simpsons* and *King of the Hill* are getting such great ratings."

"I think you can have physical humor without increasing the budget that much," he continued. Animation is a visual medium and "television executives are missing the point of animation. Most TV executives come from a verbal background and they just don't understand animation."

For Plympton, creating animation is the easy part. Distributing the films is the most difficult chore. His eye-opening experience with his first animated feature, *The Tune*, prompted Plympton to maintain ownership of all his subsequent work. Being a businessman is not a role he relishes.

"I'm not good with money," he admits, and while making deals with theaters for play dates takes a lot of time, that's "the price you have to pay for independence."

"I'm making some money, but none of my features have really broken even. I'm hoping *Mondo Plympton* will because it wasn't an expensive film to put together. Most of my income comes from the shorts; TV sales, foreign sales. I do very well in Europe, and, of course, my commercials. I do well on video sales."

Despite his critical and commercial success, the various distributors who specialized in independent films haven't pursued Plympton. He believes the reason is that "animation is an odd duck" and while a distributor such as Miramax understands the commercial possibilities of a film such as *Pulp Fiction*, they don't see those possibilities with animation.

Along with self-distribution, Plympton also finances his own films. It's a big risk, but one Plympton is willing to take as he observed that "*Snow*

White is making 10 times the money that it did when it first came out. Animation is timeless. I keep selling them [his short films] over and over every two years to a different channel. It's almost impossible to lose money on these films. So I prefer to finance them myself."

In an era when budgets for studio-animated features begin at $15 million (*The Rugrats Movie*) and can go up to $85 million for *Hercules*, it's amazing to realize that *I Married a Strange Person* cost only $200,000. Of course, Michael Eisner isn't putting his own savings on the line!

The independent distributors might have really missed the boat with *I Married a Strange Person*, Plympton's other new feature. Inspired by the outrageousness of anime such as *Beast of the City*, *Strange Person* is filled with surreal, explicit imagery that is both hilarious and shocking.

"It's basically a love story," said Plympton with a straight face. Well, it *is* a Plympton-esque love story between newlyweds Grant and Kelly and how they cope with a recently developed lobe in his brain that allows him unlimited powers to make his fantasies become reality.

When Grant makes love with his wife and imagines another woman, she becomes that woman. After a television appearance at which he demonstrates his power, he attracts the unsavory attention of the giant SmileCorp Corporation that naturally wants his lobe.

Plympton further describes his new film as "over the top stuff . . . almost a parody of Japanese animation with organs flying around and body functions."

Strange Person marks a difference in production techniques for Plympton. His pencil drawings were photocopied onto cels and inked and painted. Previously his pencil drawings were cut out and pasted onto cels. The backgrounds are also different. Plympton took extreme wide-angle photographs of models and then painted them with watercolors.

While other cel animators have turned to computerized ink and paint systems, Plympton is dead-set against using the new technology. He doesn't like "the feel. It's de-humanized . . . if I had a nickel for every time someone asked me if I did this with a computer I'd have the money for another film."

If he has strong reservations about computers, he has even stronger concerns about shooting live-action films. Plympton produced and directed two live-action comedies, *J. Lyle* (1994) and *Guns on the Clackamas* (1995).

He described live-action film making as "very difficult, very expensive. It burns my brain out. There are so many variables that can go wrong. With animation the chances of things going wrong are much smaller. A million things can go wrong on a live-action set."

This is an understatement considering that on the first day of shooting *J. Lyle*, a naked transvestite stabbed him on the streets of New York! Shooting continued after he was released from the hospital.

"I shot *J. Lyle* on the streets of New York and it was such a nightmare I promised myself to do the next film out in Oregon in the country, in the woods, where there was no one attacking me [*laughs*]. It [*Guns on the Clackamas*] was a 20-day shoot and it's a better film I think. It's a cross between *Blazing Saddles* and *Spinal Tap* about a mythical Hollywood Western in which everything goes wrong during the shooting of the film."

Plympton gives the impression that he is sincerely happy to be back in the animation fold. He is elated about the role of video in furthering the careers of independent filmmakers.

"I didn't realize when I put out the *Plymptoon* cassette that it would be such a moneymaker. Everywhere I go people want it. Video is the great democratic marketplace. Anyone can put their films out on video and there are a lot of stores now that will buy independent video. It's not so much the power of MGM or Paramount, it's what the people want to see . . . Every time I meet an animator I tell them to put their collected works out on video, because people want to see them, people want to buy them," he said, adding a prediction that the Internet will be the next big means of distributing film.

Unlike most people, Plympton has only one misgiving. "My only regret is that I didn't start in animation earlier because that was my first love."

Reviews
Mondo Plympton (1997)

Mondo Plympton is more of a landmark than one would originally surmise.

True, it's a very funny look at one animator's career with some cheaply done, but still clever, bridging sequences holding this compilation together. My only half-hearted gripe would be that, for long-time Plympton fans, there is too much familiar material in the first half of the movie. We've all seen *Your Face, Twenty-five Ways to Quit Smoking, Boomtown,* and *Draw* before. While that really doesn't diminish my own enjoyment, the real treat is roughly the second half of the film in which Plympton presents material I haven't seen before.

Plympton includes censored commercials that were deemed too violent for television, clips from his two live-action films, and the shorts, *Smell the Flowers* and *How to Make Love to a Woman*.

But for me, this film is significant for another reason. With all of the talk of creator-driven animation on television and the importance of creator rights these days, the bottom line still hasn't changed much. If you want to work in commercial mainstream animation, the route you take is to come up with a good idea and sell it to a producer. If you have a good lawyer or if the producer is benevolent, you might retain certain rights to your concepts or characters. Perhaps you will own your intellectual property in total after a certain number of years or perhaps you receive a percentage of the merchandising.

But you still can't do what Plympton has done. You can't put together a collection of your own material, distribute it, and make money from it.

Think of all of the recent bright lights in the industry: the Nickelodeon crew of John Kricfalusi, Jim Jenkins, Klasky-Csupo, Craig Barlett; wily vets such as Ralph Bakshi; the folks behind *Animaniacs* and *Pinky and the Brain*. None of these fine talents could put together an 80-90-minute compilation feature of their best work because they don't own their best work.

With the exception of *The Tune*, Plympton has carefully maintained the rights to his work and has put forth an example with *Mondo Plympton* that I hope other animators will follow.

I Married a Strange Person (1998)

Bill Plympton cautioned me that the version of *I Married a Strange Person* should not be considered the final cut of the film, so this is less a review than it is a preview of what I consider to be one of the most outrageous animated films ever produced. When *Strange Person* hits the festivals and art houses next year, be prepared for just about anything.

Strange Person is another version of the venerable "What if I could do anything I want" premise, but done with Plympton's typical off-center approach. There's no genie here, nor a supernatural or science-fiction reason explaining how newlywed accountant Grant gets his special powers. Instead we see how fornicating ducks cause some sort of short circuit when they crash into Grant's television dish and the shock causes Grant to grow a lobe that gives him the power to make any idea into reality.

Grant's wife Kelly isn't too pleased with the change in her husband, although it does make their sex life more interesting. Grant's life gets more complicated when the evil head of the giant SmileCorp Corporation spots Grant demonstrating his power on a television talk show. Coveting the lobe, he sends out his private army to retrieve Grant and get the lobe grafted onto his own brain.

Plympton has said that this film was inspired by anime, and it's easy to see that the excesses of Japanese animation simply convinced him to allow his imagination completely free reign. Seldom in recent years has an animated features been exclusively a vehicle for artistic expression as opposed to a marketing device.

The sheer purity of this film, as well as its bawdy humor, should make it a hit, although its explicitness will not be appealing to everyone.

I look forward to seeing the final cut of this incredible film.

As of this writing, Bill Plympton's most lavish feature, *Hair High*,
has yet to be distributed outside of the film festival circuit. © Bill Plympton

From *The Journal/Bravo*
2004

NEW YORK CITY – Independent animator Bill Plympton would certainly
take a call from Disney or DreamWorks if e ther of the two animation giants wanted him to head a project.

"I'd jump at the chance," he admitted, while seated at his drawing
table and working on his new feature *Hair High*, scheduled for release next
year.

But he isn't holding his breath for a call and is continuing on the career path that has won him an Academy Award nomination, status as a
cult filmmaker, and, as unlikely as it might seem, success as a television
commercial producer.

The same career has landed him in the record books as well – no other cel animator has done all of the animation work on a single feature, much less four features.

While Plympton was finishing up the animation on *Hair High* – 90% of the animation was done at the time of our interview in mid-June – his previous feature *Mutant Aliens* was about to receive its release on home video from Indie DVD, a small label specializing in working with independent filmmakers.

If you've not seen a Plympton short or feature, be prepared to laugh, to be surprised and to be shocked. Plympton has seldom gone through the trouble and expense of getting his films rated – although *Mutant Aliens* is rated R – and his films are definitely for adults.

Because of the rating, *Mutant Aliens* was actually picked up by Blockbuster, which will undoubtedly contribute to the film's financial success. The success of anime – Japanese animation – has changed many people's minds about adult animation, he explained. Anime has helped make his films more commercial.

Now available, *Mutant Aliens* is about an American astronaut who is marooned in space to serve the political agenda of the head of the federal space department. Fast-forward 20 years and now he is back with a deceptively innocent looking group of animals who have a little agenda of their own.

The film is amazingly sad and poignant at times while outrageously funny and wild at others. For anyone who is willing to strap himself or herself into a very different kind of cartoon, Plympton provides one hell of an animated rollercoaster ride.

The DVD features a cute "make your own mutation" game and a great documentary on Plympton and how he works. For anyone who seriously likes animation, *Mutant Aliens* is a must see.

Plympton is a native of Oregon who had always loved animation. He turned his sights to illustration and cartooning when he moved to New York City in 1968 to study at the School of Visual Arts. He began contributing cartoons and illustrations to such publications as *The New York*

Times, Vogue, House Beautiful, The Village Voice, and *Rolling Stone.* He also contributed to men's magazines such as *Screw* and *Penthouse,* and collected those cartoons in the book, *The Sleazy Cartoons of Bill Plympton.* A long-time film fan, he designed three film magazines, *Cineaste, Filmmakers Newsletter,* and *Film Society Review.*

He also entered the comic strip field with *Plymptoons,* which first appeared in *The Soho Weekly News* and then syndicated by Universal Press.

Despite his busy career in illustration, when he had an opportunity to attempt animation with *Boomtown* – an animated adaptation of one of cartoonist Jules Feiffer's songs – he eagerly took it. He credited producer Connie D'Autuono for helping him through the learning process. A short five years later in 1988, he received an Academy Award nomination for *Your Face.*

After working on *Boomtown,* he was inspired by filmmakers such as Spike Lee and Jim Jarmusch to pursue a career making movies outside of the mainstream.

Plympton is quite unique among independent animators. He maintains complete control over his film from start to finish. He develops the story, does all of the animation, and supervises the voice work, the music and other elements of postproduction.

He then hits the film festival circuit marketing the film, seeking attention from critics and distributors. He maintains the rights to his films in order to insure how they are presented.

He goes against all of the conventional wisdom of today's animation industry, a business that is aimed at developing characters and stories with mass-market appeal and potential for licensing.

Plympton is no snob, though, and once considered taking a contract from Disney, but ultimately rejected it for being too restrictive. He's happy to produce animation for such crassly capitalistic efforts such as television commercials. He recently completed a pilot for a proposed series for MTV. The network tested the film at a mall in New Jersey and came up with the damning conclusion that it wasn't appropriate for 14-year-old girls.

In many ways he is a throwback to the earliest of motion picture cartoonists.

When animation was first developed by pioneers such as Emil Cohl and J. Stuart Blackton at the end of the 1800s, the medium seemed to be one that was executed by a single artist. The task, though, was making separate drawings for each frame of film (24 frames equal a second of screen time) quickly made any sort of elaborate animation too costly for commercial cinema.

That's until an enterprising producer named J. R. Bray studied how cars and other consumer products were made and created an assembly line for cartoons, which could turn out short films at a profit.

Plympton is a rarity in the field today, as he has turned the clock back to being the one guy who does nearly everything.

How much work is it to animate your own feature film? Plympton said that for *Hair High*, his newest production, he has completed 30,000 drawings so far. That averages to 100 drawings a day for 300 days. To help attract people to his website (www.plymptoons.com), Plympton set up a camera that allowed visitors watch him draw.

Visiting his studio, one could see that while Plympton does indeed draw all the animation, he employs a group of talented artists who paint the cels for his films. These young people quietly and meticulously paint each of Plympton's completed drawings that have now been photocopied onto a transparent cel. They paint the cel from behind the drawing – as opposed to on top of it – to avoid any brush strokes.

In the creative process that became *Mutant Aliens*, Plympton explained that he found a photo in a book of one of the dogs that the former Soviet regime had launched into space prior to a manned flight. He wondered just how many animals had been shot up to die in space by both sides, and what would have happened to them. This formed the concept behind the new film.

While other animators write a script and break down scenes visually with a storyboard, Plympton takes the unusual, but commercially sound, move of combining those two ways of polishing his story into creating a graphic novel. The graphic novel allows him to make some money and publicize the upcoming film. The *Mutant Aliens* graphic novel is now in its

A self-portrait of Bill Plympton.

second printing and was translated into three languages. There is also a graphic novel version of *Hair High* as well.

Looking for ways to maximize your investment of time is a key activity for independent filmmakers such as Plympton. He spends a fair amount of his time presenting his productions at film festivals and making personal appearances. Just this summer, Plympton traveled to the Annecy Animation Festival in France, the Newport (RI) International Film Festival and then to the San Diego ComicCon.

Appearing at festivals is "absolutely essential," he said.

Hair High is the most lavish Plympton production to date, he said. First, he has been refining the animation and making it smoother. Second, he is using a voice cast with some name actors such as Dermot Mulroney, Keith and David Carradine, Beverly D'Angelo and Martha Plimpton. It was his friendship with Plimpton that led him to the rest of the cast members.

Plympton pushed himself for this film to be better looking than his previous films. *Hair High* tells a comic horror story set in the 1950s in which two high school students who have been murdered come back one year later on prom night for revenge and the king and queen of the prom crowns they had earned that night.

The film's preview looks great and Plympton is trying to get the film into the Sundance Film Festival and the Cannes festival.

It's not easy, though, and Plympton's investment in his work is always a risk.

Even though all of his features have taken years to turn a profit, Plympton admits with a smile that he "is willing to take that chance because I'm hooked on this freedom of expression thing."

In 2006, Bill Plympton still is touring *Hair High* to festivals around the world. His short film *Guard Dog* was nominated for an Academy Award in 2005 and as of this writing he is working on an animated sequence on Shay's Rebellion for a new series on the History Channel, *Ten Days that Unexpectedly Changed America*.

His latest short, *The Fan and the Flower* is touring festivals as well and he has released several new DVDs that collect his work from 1997 to 2002.

Animato #34 Spring 1996
"Breaking the templates":
Academy Award nominee John R Dilworth remains an independent despite the honor

The building's custodian brings in two huge bouquets of flowers, and the recipient offers one to me to bring home for my wife.

"What am I going to do with these?" he said with a laugh.

It's still a month away from the Academy Awards, but John Dilworth is already feeling the effects of being nominated. The phone rings and rings throughout this interview, but he isn't the least bit interested in answering. He knows what the calls are all about. The New York-based independent animator is so matter-of-fact about his Academy Award nomination for Animated Short Subject that he hands the official letter from the Academy over to me to open.

This isn't a show of calculated nonchalance or a case of elitist snobbery. Dilworth is happy and impressed with his nomination for Courage the Cowardly Dog in *The Chicken from Outer Space*, but he just won't let the success of his latest short change his personal or professional life as much as it could. Dilworth is a passionate thinking animator who has managed to walk the line between commercial animation jobs and personal projects.

Work from his Stretch Films Inc. has appeared on MTV, Nickelodeon, Fox, CBS, HBO, Showtime, Random House Home Video and Children's Television Workshop. *The Chicken from Outer Space* made its television debut as one of the Hanna-Barbera's *World Premiere Toons* (WPT) on the Cartoon Network. Dilworth acted on his instincts as an independent animator and qualified his film for Oscar consideration, receiving a nomination.

Dilworth's work on *The Chicken from Outer Space* received the Best Direction Award from the 1995 ASIFA-East Animation Awards and Festival, and won first place in the animation category at BACA's New York Annual Film and Video Festival.

Before I start taking notes or turn on my recorder, Dilworth suggests we get to know each other better. Over fruit juice and spring water, we conduct a far-ranging and philosophical pre-interview. Dilworth always has his feet firmly planted on the ground, but he is willing to discuss things one usually doesn't speak about in an interview about commercial animation. That is, of course, the point.

While Dilworth is a talented, savvy artist, he is also a man with an agenda, and opinions that are too interesting to be off-the-record. With his permission, I start scribbling and turn on the recorder.

John R. Dilworth (right seen with fellow animator Michael Sporn) made
the leap from being an independent animator to working with
The Cartoon Network with his *Courage the Cowardly Dog.*

Dilworth's background in animation is not one of working for studios
on Saturday morning series. He's an independent filmmaker whose early
works include *Pierre* (1985), *The Limited Bird* (1989) and *When Lilly Laney
Moved In* (1991).

Developing as an animator outside of the mainstream has given him
an opportunity to look at the animation industry with a different perspective. A theme Dilworth returns to is "breaking the templates." Too much of
animation is dominated by formula, and Dilworth, while he doesn't mind
working within a program such as WPT, wants to do something different.

Dilworth wants "to promote the revolution of the individual accept-
ing diversity." He chuckled after saying it, and noted he doesn't want

to sound pompous or too far out. He's serious, though, about people questioning the status quo and bringing individuality and originality to animation.

Chicken from Outer Space is one of the few WPT entries that is not a self-conscious pilot for a series. Dilworth's short sets up characters and their relationship to each other, and then tells a story. He certainly broke the WPT template with his short.

"Customizing" is another Dilworth idea. He understands the business conventions of commercial animation, but believes an individual artist would take those conventions and alter them to fit his or her project or style.

At a point in his career in which the brass ring is being held out for him to grab, Dilworth is exercising caution.

"Artists should think about what it is they are doing. You should really ask yourself where you are going," he explained. "Just because somebody mentions something doesn't mean you've got to do it."

Dilworth is referring to offers that are now floating his way since the announcement of his nomination. His phone has been ringing off the hook with people who are suddenly interested in meeting with him. Dilworth is certainly no stranger to the ins and outs of commercial animation. He was a storyboard artist on *Doug*, produced a Christmas video for *Ren & Stimpy*, and produced the animation for the Nickelodeon Fruit Roll-Ups commercial. Remember the *Beavis and Butt-Head* music video with Cher? He worked on the video with director Yvette Kaplan, and he was given a platinum album in appreciation of his effort as conceptual director.

His more personal work has also been seen, though. *Smart Talk with Raisin*, a bizarre film that aired on MTV's *Liquid Television*, drew a lot of attention. Dilworth had high hopes for *Angry Cabaret*, a pilot he made for MTV in 1994. *Angry Cabaret* provided a unique animated framing device for music videos, but unfortunately the series did not come to fruition.

His short *Dirdy Birdy* explored the relationship between a bird insisting on mooning and the cat insisting on disposing of the bird in truly hideous ways. The short is funny, and is obviously more than just grotesque slapstick. It's also about the relationship between the two characters and says something about a co-dependent couple that *Tom and Jerry* never did.

Dirdy Birdy literally took Dilworth around the world as the short appeared in festivals and competitions in Canada, Norway, France, Russia, Australia and Portugal. The 1994 film is currently touring in *Spike & Mike's Festival of Animation* and their *Sick and Twisted* collection as well. The film also toured with the 1995 Lollapalooza Musical Festival and opened the feature documentary *Crumb* in Montreal.

Networks in Finland, Germany, Spain, France and Belgium have purchased broadcast rights for *Dirdy Birdy*.

Dilworth also directed the pilot of Michael Pearlstein's *Psyched for Snuppa* in 1992, which has been included in the new Nickelodeon series *KABLAM*, which, will be seen in October.

Chicken from Outer Space is a cartoon that Dilworth admits he wasn't sure he even wanted to make. He had originally hoped that *Dirdy Birdy* would be the film that would be accepted into the WPT program. While the powers-that-be at Hanna-Barbera passed on the former film, they were interested in Dilworth.

He had begun *Chicken from Outer Space* as an independent film that the Sci-Fi Network expressed interest in purchasing the broadcast rights. Hanna-Barbera offered complete production funding, and Dilworth decided to forego funding the film himself and happily accepted their deal. He enjoyed being part of WPT, which he sees as having a very positive impact on the animation industry. The working relationship was so smooth that when he submitted the storyboard for Hanna-Barbera's consideration, only one change was made – one that Dilworth readily admitted made the film better. The short was completed last November and Dilworth began pondering his next project.

While Dilworth isn't sure what's he going to do for his next film, he's willing to consider what offers come his way. Currently he is in "serious negotiations with Hanna-Barbera to bring Courage to a series on the Cartoon Network.

One thing on which he is sure is that he's taking his mother to the Academy Awards with him.

Courage the Cowardly Dog was a hit for the Cartoon Network and Dilworth acted as executive producer, director and a writer on all 104 shows. He also supplied the voices for a number of characters. The show stopped production in 2003.

Since then he has returned to producing shorts and his film *The Mousochist*, from 2001, has been screened in festival around the world,

He recently completed his latest independent film *Life in Transition*.

Animato #35 – Summer 1996
An Arabian Knight-mare. The story of Richard Williams' epic film *The Thief and the Cobbler* is a cautionary tale for all creators

The recent cancellation of plans to release the 1995 Miramax film *Arabian Knight* on home video is the latest sad twist in the history of Richard Williams' *The Thief and the Cobbler*. The award-winning Canadian animator had been working on his dream project for almost 30 years only to see the film completed and substantially altered by others. Now animation fans won't even have the opportunity to see what did remain of Williams's vision. At a time when almost every G-rated animated film priced at $20 or less is snapped up by parents, the decision to indefinitely postpone the video release makes no economic sense for Miramax and its parent company, Disney. But, then, much about this production makes little sense.

The history of live-action motion pictures is filled with examples of films that have been abandoned before completion (Van Sternberg's *I Claudius*, Welles's *It's All True*) and films that were severely altered by distributors (Gilliam's *Brazil*, Welles's *The Magnificent Ambersons*). Animation, though, has seldom had these kinds of stories. The nature of the process of producing commercial animation is one of careful planning. Commercial animation has seldom ever had the kind of wheeling and dealing that has characterized live-action film production. *The Thief and the Cobbler* is an exception.

In Williams's original concept, there was to be no romance and no music in his film.

Miramax Films released the animated feature *Arabian Knight* with little fanfare last summer. There was no mention that the film was the brainchild of the man who directed the animation in *Who Framed Roger Rabbit* and one easily could conclude the film was some sort of cheap knock-off of Disney's *Aladdin*. Hardcore animation fans recognized the film for what it really was, the much-delayed *The Thief and the Cobbler*.

This is a story with no winners, as the outcome is that Williams's prize project will never be seen as he intended, the reputation of an animation professional has been shredded and another non-Disney animated feature has died at the box-office.

Richard Williams is a bit of a conundrum. His work has won an Oscar and an Emmy, and although he was the animation director for *Who Framed Roger Rabbit*, he has little name value to the general public. A Canadian who went to Great Britain with animation producer George Dunning in the mid-Fifties, Williams set up his own studio in 1958 and produced animation for commercials and independent shorts.

His big break came when he was selected to produce animated titles for *The Charge of the Light Brigade* in 1968. His production of *A Christmas Carol* received the Academy Award in 1972. Williams became better known to American audiences through the fantastic shorts that made up the titles for the revived *Pink Panther* series in the mid-1970s.

Williams began work on *T&C* in 1964 when he planned to do a film about a children's book character named "Mulla Nasruddin." Williams had already provided the illustrations for the book. An early reference to the project came in the *1968 International Film Guide*. Williams received great praise that year for his title animation work in films such as *A Funny Thing Happened on the Way to the Forum* and *The Charge of the Light Brigade*. The book notes that Williams was about to begin work on "the first of several films based on the stories featuring Mulla Nasruddin."

Like director Orson Welles, Williams would take on an outside assignment in order to put money into his own project, so work went slowly on his film as reflected by subsequent editions of the *International Film Guide*. In 1969, the *Guide* noted that animation legend Ken Harris was now working on the project, which now was entitled *Mulla Nasruddin*. The illustrations from the film show impressive Indian and Persian designs.

In 1970, the project was re-titled *The Majestic Fool* and for the first time, a distributor for the independent film was mentioned, British Lion. *The International Film Guide* noted that due to the increase in production for the small studio, the staff had increased to 40 people.

The Academy Award Williams won for *A Christmas Carol* undoubtedly strengthened his position in completing his feature, which was now being referred to as *Nasruddin!*

He began recording the dialogue tracks for the film and hired Vincent Price to perform the voice of the villain, Anwar (later remained Zigzag).

The whole focus of the film, though, was about to be changed. In a promotional booklet released in 1973, it was announced that Williams apparently decided that "Nasruddin was found to be too verbal and not suitable for animation, therefore Nasruddin as a character and the Nasruddin stories were dropped as project.

"However, the many years work spent on painstaking research into the beauty of Oriental art has been retained. Loosely based on elements in the Arabian Nights stories, an entirely and original film entitled *The Thief and the Cobbler* is now the main project of the Williams Studio. Therefore any publicity references to the old characters of Nasruddin are now obsolete."

Like many publicity releases, this one didn't tell the whole story. The writer failed to mention that while Nasruddin was out, "old" footage and characters were indeed being retained. Price's Anwar/Zigzag, the Thief himself, and the elderly nurse to the princess were all being carried over to the "new" film, which Williams was promising would be a "100-minute Panavision animated epic feature film with a hand drawn cast of thousands."

Sequences from the old film, which made it into Williams's new film, included the camel laughing at the Thief at the waterhole, the wounded soldier riding to tell the Golden City of the news of the One-Eyes, and the princess's nanny beating the Thief up when he tried to steal her bananas.

For the next several years, Williams continued to work on the film while completing commercial assignments. He recorded a number of British actors performing various voices during this period.

In an effort to become "bankable" (his word), Williams took on what was supposed to be the part-time job of supervising a new feature film based on the Raggedy Ann and Andy stories. Originally, Williams' contract called on him to work two weeks out of every month, an arrangement he later described to animation historian Milt Gray in *Funnyworld* as "silly."

The Raggedy Ann film proved to be a nightmare for Williams. While he was being made responsible for the film, he had little control over the production, which was being bankrolled by the publishers of the original stories and its parent company ITT. He was later removed from the final stages of production, but received most of the blame for the film's box office failure.

During the production of *Raggedy Ann*, Williams received a fair amount of publicity and in an interview with John Canemaker in the Feb. 1976 issue of *Millimeter*, he gave a hint about his vision for *T&C*.

"*The Thief* is not following the Disney route. It's to my knowledge the first animated film with a real plot that locks together like a detective story at the end. It has no sentiment and the two main characters don't speak. It's like a silent movie with a lot of sound."

A radical approach, to be sure, but one must consider the animation scene at the time. The Disney Studio was still floundering from the loss of its founder, and the studio's animated films that had stirred the imagination of the critics and audiences were definitely not Disney.

Williams' old boss George Dunning had directed *The Yellow Submarine* to acclaim and Ralph Bakshi's violent, profane and highly personal film *Heavy Traffic* hadn't just made money, it was accepted with a fair bit of hoopla into the collection of the Museum of Modern Art. This indeed was the time for yet another approach.

For the time, though, the pattern continued of Williams funding his film with outside jobs, while he refined his vision of the project. A little light was seen at the end of the tunnel when trade ads appeared announcing that veteran Hollywood producer Gary Kurtz had teamed up with Williams to complete the film. The ads announced that *The Thief Who Never Gave Up* would be released in Christmas 1986, but, of course, it wasn't.

Williams did meet the man in 1986, though, who would bring the film to the screen. Producer Jake Eberts, whose company had financed films such as *Dances with Wolves* and *City of Joy*, met with Williams and began funding the production. According to an article in the August 30, 1995 edition of *The Los Angeles Times,* Eberts eventually put in $10 million of the film's $28 million budget. Eberts wasn't exactly a stranger to animation as he had co-produced *Watership Down.*

Williams continued to work on *T &C*, and reported in a 1988 interview with Jerry Beck that he had 2 ½ hours of pencil tests for *T &C*, and that he hadn't used the storyboard method to make the film. Williams felt the storyboard method of production was too controlling.

For a filmmaker who was producing this feature with his own financing, this approach was certainly daring and allowed animators to push themselves into creating remarkable scenes. It is not, though, the best way to estimate costs.

Williams's bad experience on *Raggedy Ann* was compounded with his experience with *Ziggy's Gift,* a Christmas special featuring the comic strip character created by Tom Wilson. Williams also told Beck that, even though the production won an Emmy, he didn't want to be a hired hand again on a project.

Of course, he was just that on the film which brought him more attention than anything else he's done to date, *Who Framed Roger Rabbit*. Williams's supervision on the animation of *Roger Rabbit* gave him the chance he needed to complete *T &C*. Footage of *T &C* helped secure the job on the Disney/Spielberg collaboration, and the overwhelming success of the film certainly reassured people of Williams's abilities. The success of *Roger Rabbit* proved that Williams could work within a studio structure and turn out wonderful animation on time and within budget.

Following the 1988 release of *Roger Rabbit*, Williams concentrated on *T &C*. Charles Champlin profiled Eberts in his April 11, 1991 column in *The Los Angeles Times* and noted that "one of the projects under his wing *is The Thief and the Cobbler* . . . Williams should be able to finish it at long last."

With money coming in from Eberts's Allied Filmmakers and a distribution deal with Warner Brothers, Williams settled back into his London studio to finish the film.

It was not to be, though.

The production of *The Thief and the Cobbler* had been insured by the Completion Bond Company in order to protect the film's investors and guarantee the film would actually be finished according to a pre-determined deadline. For today's independent filmmakers, completion insurance is a necessity in order to line up outside investors.

Williams's deal with Warner Brothers was to deliver his film so Warners could beat Disney's *Aladdin* to the box office in 1992. When Williams missed that deadline, the Completion Bond Company took the film from him in May 1992. His part in the project that had occupied nearly thirty years of his professional life was over.

The Thief, however, had a life of its own.

The Completion Bond Company now had to finish the film in order to get it released and make back the company's money. With the announcement that the insurance company had taken over the film, the distribution deal previously set up with Warner Brothers fell apart.

Enter Fred Calvert.

Calvert is an animation veteran who had been hired by the Completion Bond Co. as a consultant. He had started his career on the animation staff at Disney in 1956, and left the studio after *101 Dalmatians* to work for the legendary animator Bill Tytla. Calvert subsequently had stints at Format Films and Hanna-Barbera before forming his own company. Working with the Children's Television Workshop, Calvert created 300 to 400 animated films for *Sesame Street*, and later entered the Saturday morning scene producing several series.

He traveled to Williams's London studio several times to check on the progress of the film, and was finally asked by the insurance company to do a detailed analysis of the production status. His conclusion was that Williams was "woefully behind schedule and way over budget," he recalled in an interview for *ANIMATO*.

Williams did indeed have a script, according to Calvert, but "he wasn't following it faithfully." The Completion Bond Company did insist that Williams construct a storyboard in order to establish the film's narrative, but Calvert said Williams resisted this request.

"He sort of worked spontaneously," said Calvert. "It led him down some futile paths, I think, and he wasn't getting the footage done."

The Completion Bond Company wanted Calvert to finish the film, an assignment he tried to avoid. When the arrangements with another producer fell through, he took the job "somewhat under protest." His job was to take the completed footage and literally fill in the narrative gaps in order to make it a commercially viable film.

"We took it and re-structured it as best we could and brought in a couple of writers and went back into all of Richard Williams' work, some that he wasn't using and found it marvelous . . . we tried to use as much of his footage as possible," he said.

Of the footage Williams completed, Calvert was only able to use about 50 percent of it, because of the repetitive nature of the scenes.

"We hated to see of all this beautiful animation hit the cutting room floor, but that was the only way we could make a story out of it.

"One of the problems, there were a number of these situations in the script, there might be two or three sentences describing the Thief going up a drain pipe. But what he animated on the screen was five minutes up and down that pipe which would ordinarily be five pages of script . . . These were the kind of imbalances that were happening. He was kind of Rube Goldberg-ing his way through. I don't think he was able to step back and look at the whole thing as a story.

"[He's] an incredible animator, though. Incredible. One of the biggest problems we had was trying our desperate best, where we had brand-new footage, to come up to the level of quality that he had set," said Calvert.

Inserting several song sequences and giving the film's hero, Tack, a voice were commercial decisions that flew in the face of Williams's concept. While having a speaking hero wasn't Calvert's choice, he felt it was a logical decision in order to tell the story.

To get the film produced in a timely manner and within budget, Calvert sub-contracted certain sequences out to other producers. The Don Bluth Studio produced the first song sequence and the second song was by the Kroyer Studio. Calvert produced the third song, sung by the desert brigands.

Most of the footage Calvert produced was with animators who had been working on the film under Williams, and he was finished with the film in about a year and a half. By the time Calvert had completed the film The Completion Bond Co. was out of business, largely because of the loss it had sustained on T&C.

"I don't know why they [Miramax] did what they did to it domestically, but it was a sad mistake. If Richard had been able to finish it with a strong story, it would have been magnificent. I think we did our best and delivered a releasable picture," Calvert said.

Once Calvert finished the film, he went to other projects, and was surprised when he learned his version of the film had played in two foreign markets, South Africa and Australia. Known as The Princess and the Cobbler, the film is a revelation for those who saw the Miramax cut.

It is radically different in both content and tone from the Miramax release. It seems clear that Calvert had indeed made an earnest attempt to preserve as much of Williams's vision, while adding elements that would heighten the conventional commercial appeal of the film.

This shot of Zig Zag shows the intricate visual detail Williams built into the character.

The changes Calvert made include a voice for the Cobbler (who has about 10 short lines in the film), three song sequences, and adding a romance for the Cobbler and Princess. What Calvert maintained is more important to the film – many of the original voices, has far less narration, more footage of the film's climax concerning the War Machine, and the Mad Holy Witch sequence.

To show off even more of Williams's footage, Calvert used outtakes as the images under the end credits. There is more footage from the War Machine sequence (the Thief in the air in an accidental airplane); a scene at the Thief falling from the minaret attempting to steal the golden balls; more footage of the Thief tempting to steal the gem from the statue at the base of the Holy Mountain; and a scene in which the Thief is about to steal something from the Princess's bedroom, but discovers the "carpet" on which he is walking is actually a pack of vicious white dog-like beasts.

The longest of the end credit sequences shows the Thief tempting to steal green gems out of a bottle, getting caught and having his hands cut off in Islamic justice, only to hobble away to a safe place to reveal his hands hadn't been cut at all!

As animation fan Luke Menichelli pointed out to this writer, the Calvert version of the film does have some loose ends. Tack is carrying a mouse in his pocket after his jailbreak, but we never see what happens to it. What character is in the sedan chair that is carried into the king's court and is seated next to the king during the polo game?

Even with its additions and cuts, the Williams/Calvert *The Princess and the Cobbler* is a dazzling film, but it is not for all tastes. It is not a film that pulls at the heartstrings, or goes for big obvious laughs. It is an adult film in many ways, and its strengths are not necessarily commercial.

In the 30 years in which Williams worked on the film, theatrical animation had seen several downturns and rebounds. Twenty years ago when a director like Ralph Bakshi was making news with *Heavy Traffic*, the farthest thing from the mind of an artist is whether or not his film could inspire a line of action figures.

Today, from the point of view of distributors and theater owners, an animated feature ideally has elements for children that can be exploited by a potentially lucrative merchandising campaign, yet have an edge that adults can enjoy. *The Princess and the Cobbler* does not fit into this definition. Williams's idea for his film is one that substitutes emotional content for visual splendor.

There are more than a few instances to suggest that Williams wanted to do a film more for adults than for children. After all, the chief of the One-Eyes doesn't sit on a throne, but rather on a group of women who are forced to pose in the shape of a throne! Later, these women kill the One-Eye chief by throwing him off a cliff. There is a Benny Hill-like urination joke, and Zigzag will probably go down in cartoon history as the first villain who is eaten alive on screen.

There have been a number of reports on how Williams pushed his animators to the breaking point by having them constantly revise sequences and by editing the story of the film by eliminating completed animation. For instance, in the January/February 1975 edition of *Film Comment*, a profile on animator Grim Natwick includes a cel from the Mad Holy Witch sequence with another character, the Enchanted Prince. This scene isn't in the completed sequences and neither is a scene in which the witch is pointing at a castle which was reproduced in a late Seventies edition of the *International Film Guide*. Did Williams actually edit out finished animation by Natwick whom he had lured out of retirement? How much animation was eliminated because Williams's vision of the story changed? Interestingly, Natwick (and another animation vet, the late Ken Harris) aren't included in the credits of the Miramax version.

Williams obviously wanted to make a film that was based on a noncommercial production model; a film that was born more out of spontaneous creativity than careful planning. His manner truly tested the limits of hand-drawn animation. Williams's designs certainly tested the skill of his staff. For instance, look at the character design for the film. Zigzag simply doesn't have hands; he has long fingers which each have three large rings. What an incredible pain that must have been to animate! Tack doesn't have a mouth, per se; the cobbling nails he holds by his teeth define his mouth. The animators must always draw the mouth to allude to this stylistic joke.

The background designs are almost hypnotic, and all of the years of studying Near Eastern art certainly paid off. The palace scenes are amazing, but the War Machine sequence with its obvious M.C. Escher look surpasses even those set at the palace.

The problem with the film, though, lies in its strength. By subjugating character development and emotion to the animation, the film's moment of triumph rings a little hollow.

The War Machine sequence is the climax of the film. The Cobbler confronts Zigzag who is leading the vanguard of the unstoppable One-Eyes, a barbarian warrior nation on its way to sack the Golden City. The Cobbler, following the advice of the Mad Holy Witch, flings a tack at Zigzag. This tack sets off a chain of events that destroys the War Machine and defeats the One-Eyes. Erected over the middle of the War Machine are the three Golden Balls stolen from the Golden City by Zigzag, and the objects of the fanatical efforts of the Thief. In the middle of the destruction, the Thief goes about attempting to reach the balls in order to steal them once again.

Every frame of the sequence is crammed with action and reaction. Clearly based on the Buster Keaton school of comedy, the Thief is an "innocent" whose survival is based on simply being in the right place at the right time as the War Machine falls apart. Unlike Keaton, though, whose unsmiling heroes were always sympathetic, there has been no effort to build any sort of emotional attachment between the audience and the Thief, and, therefore, the sequence has surprisingly little suspense.

The lack of an emotional bond between the audience and the film is *The Princess and the Cobbler's* greatest problem. It is easy to see why Calvert and the Completion Bond Company believed that building up the romance between the leads and the inclusion of the three songs by Robert Folk and Norman Gimbal were essential in building up the film's commercial appeal. The songs advance the plot and the relationship of the characters, and are used in the same way the Disney studio uses songs in its films.

So, if an acceptable version of this film existed, then why restructure it? In *The Los Angeles Times* article of August 30, 1995, Eberts is quoted as saying, "It was significantly enhanced and changed by Miramax after Miramax stepped in and acquired the domestic [distribution] rights. They made extremely good changes."

Eberts may have struck a brave pose for the press, but Miramax's treatment of the film didn't translate into respectable receipts at the box office. The film opened on only 510 screens, and grossed just over $300,000. In most areas, the film was out of first-run within two weeks.

In an effort to make Williams's work more accessible for family audiences, Miramax made a number of changes. Rather than try to sell the film as a modern milestone in animation and emphasize the film's strengths, the powers-that-be at the company tried to sell it as another kiddie show.

The company changed the title to *Arabian Knight*, which smacks of the worst of backroom brainstorming. It's not an accurate title (no one in the film is referred to as an "Arabian knight") and it makes a self-serving reference to Disney's *Aladdin*.

The company re-dubbed the film using "name" actors as an effort to build the box office appeal of the film. The completely acceptable performances by Bobbi Page as Princess Yum Yum and Steve Lively as Tack were replaced by performances by Jennifer Beals and Matthew Broderick. Additional lines were given to Tack, and, in a move that was decidedly bone-headed, the Thief was given a "voice." Actually, the Thief's "voice" is his thoughts, ("The Thief was a man of few words, but many thoughts," Broderick explained in the film), and these thoughts are voiced by Jonathan Winters. Designed to sound like ad-libs, Winters's lines come across flat and very unfunny. They detract from the visuals, instead of adding to them.

Miramax also made the decision to cut the Mad Holy Witch sequence out of an apparent commercial concern. The Mad Holy Witch is a wizened old woman with elongated and floppy breasts. One doesn't have to be Einstein to see the concern of possible ratings problems here. To complicate matters, at the end of the scene, she breathes in vapors, swoons a bit, lights a match and explodes! A drug and self-immolation reference may have also been responsible for killing the scene.

Miramax eliminated any box office draw that Williams's name might have by never mentioning in any ad that the film was from the animation director of *Who Framed Roger Rabbit*.

According to Williams's son, Alexander, who was working on the film, there was only about four months work left when the Completion Bond Company took over the project. The legacy of finger pointing and mystery unfortunately overshadow the accomplishments of the film, but at the heart of the controversy is a very thorny issue. In these kinds of stories, the good guys are always the artists who are victimized by the villainous money people, and the white and black hats are easy to see. But what about an artist, working in a very competitive commercial medium, who can't finish a project that has taken almost 30 years of his life? What responsibilities are assumed when an artist accepts outside funding in order to complete his project? What Miramax did to Richard Williams's work is inexcusable, but what about what Williams did to himself?

In a perfect world, an artist would be allowed to present his or her work unedited and untouched. Commercial animation is not a perfect world. Perhaps one day, someone will release *The Princess and the Cobbler* to laser disc and include as much of Williams's outtake animation as exists. After several years of low-key activity, Richard Williams once again is making himself known in animation circles. He is teaching animation in seminars in Los Angeles and London, and there are reports of his planning another feature.

Fred Calvert, who expressed nothing but admiration for Williams's skill as an animator, hopes Williams will be very active again.

"There is a quote from Chekhov, 'Talent forgives all,'" he said.

This article would not have been possible without the assistance of Luke Menichelli, Fred Calvert, Jerry Beck, James Gilbey, and the publicity office of Miramax Films. A special tip of the hat goes to Eric Lurio for alerting me to this story.

As of 2006, Richard Williams never worked on another animated production. Now living in Wales, Williams has written a highly acclaimed book on animation and has conducted classes on animation attended by professional animators who wish to learn from one of the acknowledged greats of the art. The Miramax cut of the film was released on DVD as *The Thief and the Cobbler* in 2006.

Chapter Four: The Rise of the Voice Actor

Animato #28 Spring 1994
The introduction for a section on voice artists

For too long a period in its history, animation has been a fairly anonymous medium. For the general public, the only names they knew were Walt Disney, Max Fleischer, Walter Lantz, and Leon Schlesinger. Certainly, some animators, writers, background artists, and directors received on-screen credits, but there was so little interest from the critical community for animation that even these recognized people seemed invisible.

The most unknown people, though, had to be the vocal performers. Aside from the late Mel Blanc, who negotiated screen credit in lieu of a raise, the only other actor to receive screen credit was the late Jim Backus for his work on the *Mister Magoo* series.

Quickly now, who did the voice of Gandy Goose or Sourpuss over at Terrytoons? Who supplied women's voices at Warners? Who played Bluto at Fleischers?

Imagine for a moment the feeling this anonymity must have caused in a performer such as the late Jack Mercer. For fifty years, he was the voice of Popeye the Sailor. *Fifty years.* And in that time, he received only one on-screen theatrical credit as Popeye (in the Robert Altman production of *Popeye*). Everyone knows your work, but next to no one knows your name. For years, there were people who claimed to have been Popeye's

In the animation gold rush of the 1990s the Comedy Central show *Dr. Katz* was an un-welcomed return to the static style of *Crusader Rabbit*. It was typical of shows that were dependent on voice talent – in this case, stand-up comics – rather than a marriage of voice and image.

voice, and each of these pretenders caused the real actor pain and embarrassment.

Why did this happen? Why did the producers think so little about voice actors?

The cartoon industry was, and still is, just that – an industry. In order to fulfill production schedules, the studio system had borrowed the mass production techniques of other industries. Winsor McCay didn't make his wonderful cartoons with an assembly line, but he wasn't trying to make a new cartoon every month. Bray, Fleischer, Lantz, Terry, Disney, Schlesinger, and Iwerks, to name a few, did indeed have such release schedules.

To make a schedule a reality, a producer had to be sure that *no one* was truly vital to a cartoon. A producer had to be prepared for a key animator, for instance, to leave and still be able to bring that short in on schedule.

Voice actors were no exception to that philosophy. Keeping people anonymous helped to keep them in line.

Was that right? No, it was wrong as it could be.

Did the directors and animators understand the importance of the voice actors? Certainly, but in the animation industry, the producers called the shots, and producers resisted giving many people who worked on a cartoon proper credit. That practice almost always included the voice actor.

The right voice could make a character. In fact, the right voice match has always seemed like some sort of wonderful kismet. Truthfully, now, how much of the success of a character such as Mr. Magoo came from the animation and how much from the wonderful vocal performances from the late Jim Backus? A good voice actor could make a difference between a barely tolerable character and a popular one. A one-note character such as Pepe Le Pew (once you seen one Pepe cartoon, who've seen them all), was made much more memorable thanks to Mel Blanc's efforts.

How many times in the last thirty years have talented voice actors carried a mediocre animated TV series? How many times have current producers cast "name" performers to do their *own* voice in a cartoon as an obvious way to dress-up woefully uninteresting animation? Take a look at how the recent Filmation production of *Happily Ever After* was advertised, and I think you'll see my point.

Thankfully, the status of the voice actor has increased in the last thirty years. Many voice actors today received a proper credit (especially in feature animation), although too many performers must endure an entry in a list thirty names long, which appears for five seconds on a television screen.

With the beginning of serious interest in animation in the 1970s, many major directors and animators finally began to receive the acclaim they deserved. But somehow, the spotlight never quite has focused on the voice actors. That is, until now. This special section of *ANIMATO* features interviews and profiles of a number of voice actors. It is by no means a complete look, but rather the beginning of ongoing coverage of this part of animation. The section also kicks off a new column by voice actor Hames Ware on the unsung heroes of vocal work from the Thirties and Forties.

By the way, despite what happens in the opening minutes of *Mrs. Doubtfire*, the voices are recorded first!

Many voice actors rose to such prominence in the 1990s that they achieved a true level of stardom. Rob Paulsen, for example, had a chat area on America Online in the early 1990s that had messages that extolled his work. Some messages even expressed how hot he was! I couldn't think of another time when a voice actor received that kind of response to his work.

Although the following piece on Jack Mercer had appeared before this introduction, covering voice actors was a priority with me. Besides the voice actors profiled here, we presented additional interviews with folks such as June Foray and Lucille Bliss as well as publishing columns by voice actor historians Hames Ware, Graham Webb and Keith Scott.

Animato #25 Spring 1993
Jack Mercer

Like most six-year-olds in America in 1960, I loved Popeye. I adored the cartoons I saw almost everyday, and, in fact, our television repairman dubbed me "Popeye" after one of his house calls.

As I grew older, my affection for those cartoons grew. My brother and I realized the best ones were those with the opening and closing hatch door. We watched everything, though, even the King Feature shorts, which somehow I knew just didn't hit the mark.

The constant through all of these shorts was Popeye's voice, which much later in my life was revealed to have a name, Jack Mercer.

Throughout his "life," Popeye the Sailor has been an underdog. The brilliant cartoonist E.C. Segar realized the rough sailor's appeal came from his lack of good looks and his scrawny body. Popeye never looked like a

The great Jack Mercer is seen here recording the voice of
Popeye for the series produced by Hanna-Barbera.

hero, and that made his heroics seem more significant than the rest of his
comic strip contemporaries.

When Max Fleischer bought the animation rights to the character in
1933, his studio wisely kept what Segar had established and built upon it.
The Fleischer Popeye was a gentle, self-effacing character who resorted to
violence only as a last resort. It's little wonder these wonderful cartoons
were such a hit with Depression era audiences. Popeye was the Everyman
who managed to win over great odds, and that also explains his enduring
charm sixty years later.

Singer and radio performer Sam Costello, from 1933 to 1934, first
performed Popeye's rough voice. A wage dispute apparently ended
Costello's tenure, and from 1934 to 1984, Jack Mercer was the voice of
Popeye the Sailor. With the exception of Mel Blanc and Mae Questel, no
one vocal performer had that long or distinguished a career.

Jack supplied a great number of secondary voices in Fleischer and

Famous cartoons, and actually received screen credit of his work in both Fleischer features. Ironically, he didn't receive a theatrical screen credit for his work as Popeye until 1980 and Robert Altman's *Popeye*.

In the early 1960s, Jack was the one-man voice cast for Joe Oriolo's *Felix the Cat* television cartoons. Jack never really cared for the shorts, and once described how difficult it was to go from Felix's falsetto to the gravelly tones of Rock Bottom and the Professor. Jack supplied the voice of Popeye for the King Features and Hanna-Barbera television productions as well as commercials, until his death in 1984.

I met Jack Mercer in 1977 when I conducted the following interview in his apartment in the Woodside section of Queens in New York City. He was at first reluctant to meet with me as there had been an increasingly steady flow of interview requests from animation fans. Once he realized I was working on a Max Fleischer biography with the blessing of the family, he set up an appointment. He and his wife Virginia were wonderfully hospitable, and Jack was very gracious in answering my questions, some of which he had heard hundreds of times before.

I had been told that Jack was one of the most modest people who worked in animation. Despite his accomplishments, he had never received the type of personal publicity his colleague Mae Questel gathered. The biggest difference between the two vocal performers was that Questel actively worked as an actress on television, the Broadway stage and in films. Jack, whose other main contribution to animation was his story work at Fleischer and Famous, didn't seek a career outside of animation in the way Mae had. The result was an unfortunate anonymity.

For years, there were a number of people who asserted to have performed the voice in the cartoons, and these untrue claims were painful to Jack. Even one of his co-stars in the cartoons made claims for years of having performed the voice. Years later I still can't get over the injustice of the situation. This very talented man had never been given the recognition his career deserved.

At the end of the interview, I asked Jack for an audio autograph, and he performed the *Popeye* theme song. It was a fulfillment of a childhood dream, and interestingly enough I couldn't watch him as he leaned toward the microphone of my recorder and sang. I just sat listening.

JACK MERCER: I was in show business, of course, my whole family was in show business, and they wanted me to do something else. I could draw a little bit, and my mother had an agent who booked her vaudeville act, and he was acquainted with someone at Paramount who suggested I go to the Fleischer Studios, and see if I could get some type of work drawing. When I first started, I was in the opaque department. I went through all the various departments, the inking department, the in-betweening department.

Did you like it?
I enjoyed it, yes. I hadn't done any professional drawing before that. It was just on my own.

How did the job as Popeye's voice come about?
I was imitating various characters in the inking department just out of my own amusement, and everybody seemed to get a laugh out of it. And a lot of the people suggested I try out for it [the Popeye voice]. I didn't know they were looking for anyone. So I eventually went home, and tried to improve the voice I was doing. So I finally got the voice after I practiced a while. I thought I could really do the voice, and got the quality I was after. I gave an audition over the phone to someone at Paramount. They heard it and from then on they said, "Why don't you come over and do some voices." Which I did. Sort of a breaking-in period, I guess. They told me I was going to do the Popeye voice. That's how it started. You know, fooling around while I was working at the other jobs.

Did Max Fleischer make that final decision?
Well, there's the thing. I don't know whether it was Max because I was more involved with Dave and Lou [Fleischer] at that time. Whether he was informed about it, I don't know, but he never came around to see. [Jack later commented that Max believed he was too skinny when he started

performing the voice and suggested he'd eat spaghetti and drink Guinness Stout!]

What type of a guy was Dave Fleischer to work with?

He was always kidding around. Very jolly. I had no conflict with him at all as far as I can remember. It was always sort of a happy family.

How about Max?

As far as I was concerned I was working for Dave and Lou Fleischer and the animators. Max was always in the front office. I very seldom saw him. He was always engaged in some innovation for the studio, the technical end of things, inventing machines like the turntable for dimensional effects, things like that. Every once in a while I'd run into him and we'd say "hello." So, as I say, I knew very little about him. He invited me once out to dinner in Miami when he got his new home. I guess that's the only social event I could think of outside of appearing at the parties. Sometimes he'd come in and look at a picture or sit in on a recording session or something like that. Very seldom.

He was like the "Godfather," though. If you had any troubles, you'd go to him and he'd straightened them out.

After the 1938 strike, was the studio still a happy family?

During the strike I was working in the story department, and that was sort of a section all by itself, you might say, and I didn't associate with the others. I didn't notice anything.

You see, with the story writers, we were just one big happy group. It was only the attitude of the opaquers and the inkers that might have been different. As far as I was concerned I didn't notice anything.

Other studio personnel were affected by the strike. Seymour Kneitel was injured by the strikers. Edith Vernick had to be escorted by the police through the picket line.

Well, I did have one incident. One day, of course, they asked everyone in there to pitch in and help anyway you could. If they needed someone to in-between I'd pitch in and help. The people out on the picket line used to take pictures of people going into the studio, and threaten you. One night I was going home on the subway, and some strange looking characters sat down on either side of me. There wasn't anyone else in the car at the time, so I felt perhaps they were trying to intimidate me in some way. It was very funny. These two fellows would come in and sit on either side of me. At the station before the one at which I usually got off, I got off the train real fast and left them sitting there! [*laughing*] The door closed, and the train went on. That's the way I got rid of them. Maybe it was just my imagination, I don't know. That and the fact they would harass you as you entered and left at work, and that they would take a photo of you going past their picket line.

What was the experience of Florida like?

They did increase [the size of the studio] a lot. A lot of people came in from the coast, and that did give us sort of a Disneyland atmosphere. All of those guys were crazy, and they brought a bit of Hollywood to Miami. I suppose that's why people thought it was all a party and I suppose there was, but I didn't get involved with it.

There was one fellow, Cal Howard; he did some crazy things. He had a car similar to mine, and he'd go around the neighborhoods screeching the tires. He sat up in the back of the car, and he had some arrangement by which he could reach the gas pedal. He'd sit in the back and steer the car. It was a convertible, and the cops were always after him.

I'd go out in my car, and they'd mistake me for him! I'd always have a siren blowing in back of me. I had a heck of time explaining it wasn't me. And he'd follow people around the studio: visitors, tourists. He'd make funny faces, all kinds of stuff and they would turn around because all the employees were laughing. He'd straighten right up, and act like he was one of them, and they couldn't figure it out.

Did it ever bother you that you didn't receive screen credit for your work as Popeye?

Yes, it certainly did. I think it would bother anyone because of this situation where so many people claiming to have done it. That's the biggest thing I felt was bad. But that was just their policy. Mae [Questel, the primary actress for Olive Oyl's and Betty Boop's voice] couldn't do anything about it. They said something about it took too much time in the credits. I don't know what their reason was – whether they felt if they wanted to make a change [in voice actors] they wouldn't want to change the titles.

Your vocal work was so important to the success of the Popeye cartoons.

Well, maybe, they didn't think so. I suppose they figured the character itself and King Features were more important than the voice work.

Everyone who watches the Popeye cartoons loves your adlibs.

Everyone questions the fact why they were discontinued. You see, when we were doing the sound along with the picture, you could see these ideas would come as the picture ran. It just seemed like a natural thing to ad lib as you were watching the action. But then when it was pre-recorded, it was a different situation. I would try to select little lines here and there that would serve as an ad-lib thought, and the ad-lib is supposed to be thinking to yourself. And then they insisted on having the mouth action along with these ad-libs, which sort of spoiled that situation, don't you see?

I always thought it was funnier if you didn't see the mouth moving, and they use that in some of the cartoons now as a side remark, and you just see the character standing. They used that now in the modern films. I don't know if they got that idea from the old Popeyes or not.

There's a difference in the thought of the line when it looks like it's just stuck in rather than actually having been written in.

Who performed Bluto's voice?

The first one I worked with was Gus Wickie, and he was a bass singer. And then we had several others coming and going, and I've forgotten them as they were coming and going! And we wound up with Jackson Beck doing Bluto more than anyone else did. I did some Blutos every once in a while, but it was too much. A conversation between Popeye and Bluto is pretty rough trying to switch back and forth.

Did you ever become hoarse? Your natural voice isn't as deep as Popeye's.

As a matter of fact, it's deeper now than it used to be. I used to talk up here more [in a near falsetto voice] you see, but now I've got it down here.

[Virginia Mercer: "He always hated his voice."]

You know, it would always embarrass me when we would be recording, and after doing a *Popeye* I would ask for instructions, or how do you want this line read, and when I would hear myself back, it would scare the hell out of me! Because the voice would come back like this: [exaggerated falsetto] I'd say "Jesus, is that me?!" [*laughter*] So I've been trying to get it down lower all the time. As I get older, it gets lower. Now when I have to do a high voice, I have to struggle.

Besides you, Mae Questel and whoever was Bluto, were there other people doing voices?

Once in a while, we'd have a larger cast, but most of the time there were just the main characters and the rest of us would pile in and do anything that came along. Someone would say, "You try this character, and you try this one."

And we each one would try out for it, and then they'd say, "You do this one. You take that one." And we get varied tonal qualities. So we didn't have too many people on a cartoon.

Could you describe a story session at Fleischer's?

What would happen would be if there were one story man or two story men, they would get together and try to get an idea for the character that was assigned to them. Everybody got the chance to do various characters. All just didn't have one character to work with, like Popeye. He [the writer] would try to get a synopsis, write that down, and send it to be accepted by the directors who were going to direct the picture. Lots of times they'd all get together, and decide if they wanted to do the story or not.

If they didn't like it, you'd try to get another angle, and as soon as they accepted one, then you'd go back, and "gag" the synopsis. Then you'd have to draw it up in storyboards. You'd have meetings with the director, and sometimes the animators would come in, and we'd all discuss the material; if it's funny or not, if it was too long, all sorts of problems.

Then, after it was accepted, as far as we were concerned it would leave the room, and we would try to get another angle on another character.

Also, we were asked to try to create characters. Now, with the Fleischers, they seemed to be interested in characters with some various capabilities – capabilities different than usual characters. For instance, a ghost that could walk through things rather than a character like, you know, like the Flintstones.

Did you have any favorite directors or animators?
No, we took them as they came! [*laughter*] Next! Whoever came in, we'd be interested in developing the story for them, and hoping we could sell the ideas to the directors.

Did you ever think of the violence as being bad in the Popeye cartoons?
It never struck anyone as being bad. It was supposed to be humorous. It always wound up in a funny situation even if Popeye was beating on somebody's head or something, it was funny. Bluto always wound up in a predicament that was humorous, humiliating, we thought.

I remember we heard one time that out on the coast they had pictures where the characters would be hit on the head with something, and they'd crack up like a plate, but they'd immediately come together again and be all right and run off. We tried to get some gags like that in our pictures like that, but the Fleischers said we'd better not pull any of that stuff because people are starting to complain.

Did you ever become bored with performing Popeye's voice?
Not really. Every cartoon was different. If you were doing a dramatic show on Broadway, and every night you were doing the same thing I imagine it would get boring after a while. But when you have different stories to do there is a constant creating there. We did have other characters to work with. It was a challenge. It was never boring.

I have a little pride in being Popeye's voice.

Spending an evening with Jack was a thrill that still brings tears to my eyes. It was one of those moments when you realized your childhood admiration was totally deserved. He was a great talent who never received the attention he so richly deserved.

Jack Mercer died in 1984. A new audience once – or if – the Fleischer Popeye cartoons are released on DVD, will appreciate his full genius as a voice actor.

Animato #28 Spring 1994
Jonathan Harris

That voice. Educated. Eccentric. Possibly just a little evil. Maybe a lot. Definitely elegant. If you grew up in the Fifties and Sixties, the distinctive voice (and features) of Jonathan Harris were a fixture on your television. Best known for that villain's villain, Dr. Smith on *Lost in Space*, Harris may no longer be seen on television, but he certainly can be *heard*.

Animato caught up with Harris at WishCon III in Springfield, MA, where he was a guest of honor. Coming to the *Animato* table for an interview, the dapper actor cracked jokes, assumed his Dr. Smith persona at a moment's notice, discussed needlepoint with my wife (he makes rugs), and made sure we took photographs at the correct angle.

"Never take someone's picture looking down at them," he admonished with a raised eyebrow. I felt like a chastened Will Robinson.

At an age when many actors simply seek retirement, Harris is still quite active. While he has "no interest or desire" to ever go before a camera again, Harris is very busy with commercial voice-overs and with characterizations for a number of animated series. He is currently heard on *Problem Child* on the USA cable network and on the upcoming *Aladdin* series for Disney.

Describing himself as "very lucky," Harris has appeared on 612 televi-

One of the most distinctive voices in show business, actor Jonathan Harris
made the transition from on-camera roles to voice acting in many cartoons.
Harris is seen here with me at convention in Springfield, MA.

sion shows over his career, which began with a Broadway debut in 1942.
He made many guest appearances besides being a co-star on *Lost in Space,
The Thin Man* and *Space Academy*.

Speaking to Harris about acting reveals the philosophy of not a "star,"
but of a working actor.

"Never be late to anything. Always be early," he instructed. "I'm always a half-hour early. I'm used to it."

Harris describes his training on the New York stage as "beautiful" with
a key word being "discipline."

Harris doesn't view acting merely with his voice as any less an assignment as any of his television or stage work. "You have to bring to play everything you've learned" to performing a voice. Unlike film acting, voice
work places a greater emphasis on projecting your emotions, said Harris.

Harris began his animation career by supplying voices for the series
Bugsville produced by Filmation in the early Seventies. "The best animated

series ever made," he proudly proclaimed. Harris played Lt. Grumblebee. He naturally supplied Dr. Smith's voice to the *Lost in Space* series.

Harris's accent has caused many fans to wonder if he's British or Canadian. Harris proudly revealed he's a New Yorker.

"I had a New York accent, and I was taught that to get rid of one accent, you superimpose another," he explained.

"I developed a persona which I sell for money . . . the Jonathan Harris sound," Harris said. Harris reminded me that the word "business" is prominent in the phrase "show business," and a performer has to understand his or her value in the market.

"It's easier if they put you in a place," Harris said, referring to typecasting. "Me, I'm an eccentric. A little strange. It's important to understand who you are and where they put you."

While Harris is certainly aware of the practical side of performing, he unabashedly declared his love of working.

"I do love talent," he said, and he gets to work with many talented people in his animation career. He admires fellow voice artists who "can do 12 different voices, and I can barely do me!"

A voice performer such as Harris is given a script, seated in a studio with an engineer, and often receives his instructions from a director miles away over a telephone line.

"You feel very free," he said of the recording sessions. "It's just an engineer and you. The direction comes over the phone. You can do it faster that way."

There's no room for adlibbing in animation, Harris noted. "You have to adhere to the lines on the page."

When not in a recording studio or at home with his wife, Harris keeps up a series of convention appearances regaling Baby Boomers and their kids with stories of working for Irwin Allen and others in the television industry. Harris also frequently appears with symphony orchestras around the country, narrating *Peter and the Wolf* and other classical pieces.

Harris is grateful, and perhaps a little puzzled, for the almost cult status his characterizations have given him. While he enjoys meeting fans, he admits there is one fan he is hesitant about meeting.

"Howard Stern wants me on his show. Gilbert Gottfried told me he wants me on, but I don't know . . ." Harris said with his voice trailing off.

If there were one person I'd bet could command the respect of the self-proclaimed "king of all media," it would be "Dr. Smith."

After this interview ran, I put Jonathan on our comp list. He would always write a letter acknowledging his receipt of the issue and he would always update me on his activities.

When he appeared on the east coast at the Chiller Theatre Convention, I would make it a point to try to see him. He was always gracious, always a gentlemen and always a lot of fun to talk with.

Besides his television work, Jonathan performed in two PIXAR productions *Toy Story 2* and *A Bug's Life*. His last voice work was in a short, *Hubert's Brain*, in 2001.

When I started *Animation Planet*, I received a letter from him encouraging the new venture and me. Jonathan passed in 2002.

I never had the heart to admit to him that as a kid I prayed for his death every week when I saw *Lost in Space*! In hindsight, I think he would have arched an eyebrow and told me that was what exactly what I was supposed to do.

Sid Raymond

Sid Raymond is delighted about the quote from President Clinton that ran in a recent issue of *Time* magazine. "I'm a lot like Baby Huey. I'm fat. I'm ugly. But if you push me down, I keep coming back. I just keep coming back."

For Raymond, the actor who originated the voice for Baby Huey in the Famous Studio series of cartoons, the quote comes at an appropriate time. Raymond will be recording the Baby Huey voice again for 10 new cartoons to be produced by a recently formed animation arm of Harvey

Comics, the publishers that bought the rights to the Famous Studio characters from Paramount Pictures in the late 1950s.

In Sid Raymond's case, this is not a case of coming out of retirement to perform once again. Speaking to Raymond one is immediately reminded of the old-adage: "once a performer, always a performer." The veteran television, stage and film actor may enjoy the temperate climate and sunny beaches of his home in Florida, but he longs for his native New York City and "being where there's action."

Raymond, who began in vaudeville, had a very active career in television, off-Broadway theatre, radio and the occasional film. He's worked with people such as Milton Berle, Ernie Kovacs, Edward G. Robinson, Garry Moore, Liza Minnelli, and Paul Newman. He was a fixture in television commercials, and his work has won two Cleos. But being in Florida hasn't kept him away from acting. He can be seen currently in a character bit in the new comedy *My Father, The Hero*, and has appeared with Richard Dreyfuss in *Let It Ride*, Rodney Dangerfield in *Easy Money*, and Dom DeLuise in *Hot Stuff*, among other films shot in Florida.

Raymond began his career playing resorts and nightclubs in the Catskill mountains of New York. Touring with a troupe of entertainers from the fabled radio show, *Major Bowes Amateur Hour*, Raymond's act included a number of impersonations.

"In doing my act, and doing a lot of impersonations, somebody called me from Famous Studios," recalled Raymond," and they showed me pictures of Baby Huey, this duck. And they asked 'What sort of a voice would you give his character?' I started to do a voice like that [a fast high-pitched voice], and then I did a voice like that [the familiar Baby Huey voice], and they selected that."

The Baby Huey shorts first appeared in 1951, and seldom strayed from one of several formulas. Baby Huey, a huge duckling clad in a bonnet and diaper, would either be rejected by his peers only to later save them from a horrible fate thanks to his un-baby-like strength, or find himself the object of a fox's appetite. Huey always overcame adversity through his goodness of character or his strength.

Raymond also provided the voice for Katnip the mouse in the Famous series, *Herman and Katnip*. Patterned after *Tom and Jerry*, Herman was played by character actor Arnold Stang. Raymond also provided incidental voices for other Famous cartoons, including Casper and Popeye shorts.

Recalling the recording sessions, Raymond said, "They were wonderful. They had directors like Izzy Sparber, Seymour Kneitel, Dave Tendlar, Myron Waldman. They were in the control room, and they could see me and I could see them . . . I did one line at a time, and I'd look at the director and he'd put his finger up meaning 'do one more,' and then he'd say over the loudspeaker, 'Sid, give it with more emphasis.' Then he put his hand up with a circle [meaning] 'okay.' Then I'd do the next line. If we had dialogue, the other guy, like Jackson Beck, would be at the other microphone, and he would pick it up."

Although Raymond has fond memories of his years at Famous, the lack of screen credit was frustrating. "They wouldn't give it to anyone except the director, the animators and Winston Sharples [the studio's composer]," said Raymond, who added the studio never would give a reason why voice people were excluded.

Raymond would occasionally ad lib lines or catch phrases that would find their way into a completed Baby Huey short. Huey exclaiming "That's logical!" or breaking into the song "I'm in the Mood for Love," were frequently the result of Raymond dropping them into a recording session.

"They always liked my timing," he said of his adlibs.

Raymond would receive $125 for a recording session as a major voice, and would receive an extra $25 a voice for the incidental characterizations.

"One-hundred-twenty-five dollars went a long way in those days," explained Raymond.

He also did voices for animated commercials. One spot had him providing the voice of a bottle of Lestoil household cleanser. The director had him do a voice with the inflections of Bert Lahr, the actor best known for his role as the cowardly lion in *The Wizard of Oz*. When a New York newspaper columnist wondered in print why Ben Lahr, a long established Broadway star, was reduced to doing voices for commercials, Lahr sued.

Raymond used this anecdote as the reason behind why he believes it's better for a voice artist to create his own voice rather than use an impersonation.

Raymond continues to audition for both on-camera roles and voice work. After he records the Baby Huey soundtracks in Vancouver, he'll return to his home in Florida where his next assignment will be a one-line character role in Sylvester Stallone's new movie, *The Specialist*.

"It's just one word, a curse word," he said. "But it's a good one . . . the things you can say today!"

After this interview Raymond recorded tracks for a new Baby Huey cartoon series that had much more of a *Ren & Stimpy* orientation than the slapstick formula of the original series.

He worked regularly, popping up in commercials and had a nice bit part in the 2003 comedy *Big Trouble*.

Sid died in late 2006.

Billy West

That intense psychotic growl and the brainlessly joyous sigh . . . they are probably the most imitated voices in America, thanks to the talents of Billy West.

Among the sound-a-likes and "name brand" celebrities who have dominated the field of voice artists in the last 30 years, West is part of a new breed of performer in animation. A brilliant mimic and solid stand-up comedian, West, like his colleagues on *The Simpsons* and *Rocko's Modern Life*, is setting new standards by bringing back the old ones.

Next time you're watching *Ren and Stimpy*, try turning off the sound for a while. Certainly the animation created first by Spumco, and now by Games, is competent enough (limited, but competent), but one quickly realizes just how much of the charm and success of the show rests firmly on the shoulders of the voice cast, and specifically on West.

With all of the controversy surrounding the show, the one point on which nearly everyone agrees is West's contribution. Although John Kricfalusi first performed Ren's voice, West picked up the duty when Kricfalusi became too busy with other aspects of the production. West not only provides the voice for both Ren and Stimpy, but does other incidental voices as well. He also is Doug on the Nickelodeon series of the same name, and keeps busy with providing voices for various commercials.

Like so many revered voice actors, West got his start as a voice actor on radio, first in his hometown of Boston, and then working with Howard Stern in New York. His first cartoon work was on the revival of *Beany and Cecil*, which led to his association with Kricfalusi and later to *Ren and Stimpy*.

A conversation with Billy West about his career quickly reveals the passion he has for voice work. Without hesitation, West can list off performers for whom he maintains great respect and affection; artists such as Daws Butler, Jackson Beck, Don Messick, and Jonathan Harris.

His feelings for his fellow artists undoubtedly help fuel his interest in doing something fresh and original, a task that is frequently difficult.

"To do anything different it takes a certain amount of courage on everybody's part," West explained. "It's kind of like a lot of people are afraid if you don't sound like everything that's been done previously that it won't be readily accepted. It's very hard to come up with something offbeat. The minute you do, though, and everybody is in agreement they're going to take a chance, people are just dying to hear something different. It doesn't have to be these cloying, annoying, high-pitch genderless cartoony little voices because it's a cartoon. You can do something that's rooted in some kind of reality; something that people can grab on to and relate to."

Originality is a large issue in an industry that has been known for shamelessly producing ten knock-offs for each innovative show. Too many times, especially in television animation, voice actors have been directed to imitate famous voices, rather than create something new.

"To me these guys were the geniuses, Daws Butler and Don Messick [the two primary voice artists of many Hanna-Barbera cartoons]. I think you had to twist their arm to do impressions. I don't think they liked doing impressions. And I understand why today. Because impressionists can put you out of business in two seconds. Once the hard work is done creating something, that's the hard thing, and then there's loads of people who can do it once it's established," said West.

(The point about the threat of impressionists is made clear with an anecdote West told about one of his heroes, Jackson Beck. Beck, whose career includes performing Bluto in the Famous Studio Popeyes and being one of the busiest commercial announcers in the country, was at an audition with one of West's friends. West's friend told Beck he had a friend, West, who did a great impersonation of him. Beck leaned over with interest and asked for West's name and address so he could kill him! He was kidding, of course.)

For West a celebrity's voice can be a springboard to developing a unique voice. Noting that Daws Butler brought his own vision to his famous Yogi Bear voice and resisted the urge to directly mimic Art Carney, West said his fascination with the Three Stooges led him to the voice of Stimpy.

"Everybody can do Moe and everybody can do Curley, but nobody gave a damn about Larry. To me he was the Keith Richards of the Stooges. Without him they wouldn't be anything. When I first started working in the preliminary stages of *Ren and Stimpy*, they loved that voice. They loved that stupid Larry persona. But we found out pretty quickly you couldn't have a cartoon character who sounded like a depressed old Jewish guy. This cartoon character had been able to go wild."

As West noted there is a lot of difference between Daws Butler's Yogi Bear voice and the voice of Art Carney; there is also a world of difference between Larry Fine and Stimpy. For anyone who has heard West's classic radio routine "Larry Fine at Woodstock," the contrast between his dead-on impersonation of Fine and the cartoon cat is readily apparent.

West views the trend of casting well-known actors in animated productions as just that . . . a trend, and a by-product of the compromise between the business and creative sides of the industry. He has to laugh, though, when he imagines that anyone would actually be compelled to see a film in order to hear Ed Asner or John Ritter.

For West, voice actors are artisans who create something new. Unlike a Lorenzo Music, whose characterization never changes from role to role (West did a perfect Music voice: "I'm Lorenzo Music, an astronaut. I'm Lorenzo Music as Garfield the Cat"), a true voice artist tries to bring something unique to an assignment.

"I base a lot of these voices on composites of people you couldn't even know about because I have a lot of experience. For years, I played in bands and I met hundreds of people a night. I used to meet club owners, and I used to meet couples cheating on each other and I just absorbed, and watched everything. I can just reach into this gallery of these people. If I were doing live performances, I would probably be doing some sort of performance art based on these people."

West gives great thought to the creation of a voice for even a secondary character. He revealed that the voice for Boomer on Doug is based on rock 'n' roll vet Flo of Flo and Eddie. West believes that a carefully designed voice with a hook in reality better serves a production than giving secondary characters "attention-getting" typically cartoony voices.

The technique of working with just a director and a sound engineer presents no problems with West. He would rather work on his own without attempting to interact with other members of a cast because he believes the performances come out "wooden." Since animators must have each line of dialogue isolated in order to properly time the mouth movements, actors can't overlap their lines, and since that element of performing is eliminated, West believes there's no point for voice actors to cluster together in a studio.

"You just have to be good. You just have to be believable. Just look at Mel Blanc. They mixed and matched all of his takes with himself. All you have to do is to have a good director who knows what they are doing."

Despite the precision which animation requires, there are instances in which a voice actor can ad lib, and one of West's was in the "Ren's Toothache" episode. While reading the storyboard in which the stench from Ren's rotted mouth prevented flies from enjoying their meal at Stimpy's litter box, West did a vibrating fly voice saying "taste, taste." He was actually only reading the instructions to the animators from the storyboard, but the director liked it, and incorporated the bit in the finished cartoon.

When he is not performing voices for television series, West is busy with commercials that he enjoys.

"One day you're a talking armpit and the next day you're a bottle of bleach," he laughed.

He does have another ambition, though, besides his voice work. A musician before he began on radio, West would love to compose film scores.

In the meantime, though, West is very happy as a voice actor. Thinking of the longevity of the career of one of his idols, Jackson Beck, West said, "It kinda makes you feel like 'hey, what a great business.' People don't decide for you when it's time to leave as long as you can still make your voice work, and you can still read."

Billy West has been a very busy guy since this interview. He performed the voice of Bugs Bunny in *Space Jam*, continued with a role of the Honey Nut Cheerio Bee in commercials, did the lead voice of Fry and a supporting voice in the long-running series *Futurama*. He was cast as Elmer Fudd in *Looney Tunes: Back in Action*. He performed Popeye in the television special *Popeye's Voyage: Quest for Pappy* as well.

Animato #33 Fall 1995
Rob Paulsen

Open the Toon Message Board of America Online, and very quickly one becomes aware of Paulsen fever. The many animation enthusiasts who leave comments and opinions are all avid fans of the man who currently supplies the voice for Yakko on *Animaniacs*, Throttle on *Biker Mice from Mars*, Pinky from *Pinky and the Brain*, Arthur on *The Tick*, Squishington from *Bump in the Night*, and *The Mask* from the CBS series of the same name.

Two of the most prominent voice actors in animation, Maurice LaMarche and
Rob Paulsen, formed a great team when they performed on *Pinky and the Brain*.

Rob Paulsen is one of the most versatile voice actors around, and certainly one of the most popular with animation producers and directors.
Yet, Rob Paulsen says the attention paid to him by animation fans "shocks
me in a positive way, but none the less it shocks me."

That's not a statement of false modesty. While Paulsen is happy for his
current status in the industry, he is also a huge fan of his colleagues. Give
Paulsen a head start of a few seconds and he can reel off the names of
fellow voice artists by whom he is awed ... Frank Welker, Jim Cummings,
Maurice LaMarche, Tress MacNeille, and Billy West just to name a few.

A thoughtful man with a passion for his work and an easy laugh,
Paulsen is extremely happy about his standing in animation and his popularity with fans, but he could have never predicted it.

Growing up in the Flint, MI area, though, acting and animation were
not part of his ambitions. Paulsen loved to sing.

"I've been singing longer than anything. I started out singing in high school, in choirs, rock 'n' roll bands. My parents were always willing to let me listen to Led Zeppelin and The Who as long as I listened to Prokofiev and Shostakovich."

Acting was a passion Paulsen developed by working in live theater.

"I got involved with some theater and traveled around the United States and Canada for about a year doing live theater," said Paulsen. "I moved permanently in 1978 to L.A. to pursue more TV stuff."

Paulsen established a busy career. He appeared in over 40 on-camera commercials over the first eight or nine years in Los Angeles, and had guest roles on a number of television series including *Hill Street Blues* and *MacGyver*. He also appeared in two pilots and six feature films.

Although Paulsen had appeared in the *G.I. Joe* animated series in 1983 as the characters Snowjob and Tripwire, he really considers his career in animation beginning with a successful audition in 1984. At a general audition for new actors at Hanna-Barbera, director Gordon Hunt selected him for several productions, the first being the direct-to-video series, *The Greatest Stories of the Bible*.

Paulsen followed that assignment with the role of Hadji in the second *Jonny Quest* series at H-B in 1985.

Other roles piled on top of another, and Paulsen found that he was appearing more behind a microphone and less in front of a camera.

"I started phasing the on-camera stuff out not because of any particular reason other than I started getting more and more voice work," recalled Paulsen, who credits his wife with diplomatically reminding him that if he was getting voice work, he should concentrate on it.

Since he hasn't appeared in an on-camera role for more than six years, Paulsen is both flattered and slightly puzzled about all of the fan interest in his feature film work.

"Virtually all of the films are pretty crappy," he said with a laugh.

Stewardess School can currently be seen as part of cable's Comedy Central movie package, and Paulsen plays what he termed "a very broad character about whom there is no question of his sexual identity" in the 1987 comedy.

"It was a really great job. I worked for 12 weeks at Columbia [Pictures] and all my checks cleared. You couldn't really ask for more," he chuckled.

The sexual and movie politics made his role in Brian De Palma's sexual thriller *Body Double* (1984) a far less comfortable shoot for Paulsen.

"*Body Double* was a little disconcerting for me because it was real clear for some reason that Brian De Palma had this preoccupation on new ways to dispose of women and there were some pretty odd ones in this movie. It was beautifully shot, but I said to myself I'm not sure I want to do this anymore."

Paulsen's son was quite young at the time he appeared in *Body Double*, and while he doesn't consider himself a prude, he thought about the types of films in which he wanted his son to see him. The mean-spiritedness of the De Palma film was not something with which he wanted to be associated.

Voice actors differ on the way they create a characterization, and Paulsen says, "I guess it's the function of being an actor, and it's a kind of an organic process that has happened to me ever since I can remember."

The process is "a real collaborative effort," said Paulsen. Sometimes a director will have an idea of what a character should sound like, while others might say, "We'll know when we hear it."

Improvisation is extremely important. "What really helps me a lot is to improvise in the character I'm trying to come up with."

In creating Squishington for *Bump in the Night*, for instance, Paulsen worked with the directors of the show to come up with the voice. Seeing a picture of the character gave Paulsen a clue about the voice. He remembered that Squishington's roundness led him to a Droopy-style voice, and then he added a Shirley Temple-esque flavor to it when he was told that Squishington is a little shy.

Then Paulsen begins talking "in-character."

"The character starts saying things from the character's brain or his soul and the lines [of dialogue] start making sense," he explained.

For Paulsen, the best characters are those who operate with a complete personality and an internal logic.

"When I see well-developed characters, whether they're live-action or animated, I know they come from somewhere," said Paulsen. "I try to create them with a life to the extent they could talk to anyone about anything from their perspective."

Paulsen improvises during recording sessions and frequently contrib-
utes lines and ideas that are used by directors. But the goal of the improvisation is not necessarily to add something to the finished cartoon. It's just
the method that Paulsen uses to maintain the character he's created.

Paulsen notes that the directors at Warner Brothers and at *Bump in
the Night* especially want him to "bring something to the party." His im-
provisations are not a critique on the scripts he's given as Paulsen has the
highest respect for the writers of his series.

Unlike voice actors of 30 years ago, Paulsen has not been asked to do
a cartoon voice that is an outright impersonation of a famous actor. He
did note that in the "long and arduous audition process" for Yakko he was
asked to bring the "sensibility of Groucho Marx" into the characterization,
but not to do the distinctive Groucho voice.

In creating the voice for Pinky, the rodent's huge teeth were a starting
point. Paulsen played around with a voice that reflected a sizable over-bite
and then recalled some favorite voices from his childhood. Paulsen was a
fan of British humor while growing up. He enjoyed not just Monty Python,
but also the *Carry On* film series, and performers such as Billy Connelly,
among others. Paulsen has practiced various British accents for years, and
thought that Pinky could be a British mouse.

One can easily see why Paulsen enjoys his work with the Warner Brothers producers when he relates the story of just how far the producers of
Animaniacs are willing to go for an inside joke.

Most of the viewers of *Animaniacs* were probably perplexed about the
Pinky and the Brain episode in which the Brain is asked to record a number
of commercial voice-overs. After all, we're used to see the Brain trying to
make his next evil plot to take over the world a reality. So why is he recording narrations about frozen fish with crispy crumb coating?

The explanation shows the level of respect the producers of *Animaniacs* have for their voice talent, related Paulsen.

Floating around audio collector circles is a priceless group of outtakes
from a recording session sometime from the early 1980s in which the late
great Orson Welles is attempting to read narrations for a series of British
frozen food commercials. Welles, who could be a tyrant, objected fre-

quently, profanely and hilariously, to the voice-overs as they were written and to the direction he was receiving. At the end of the tape, Welles leaves in a dramatic huff.

Rob Paulsen revealed to *Animato* readers that his *Pinky and the Brain* co-star Maurice LaMarche is a huge Welles fan who had memorized the outtake tape. Whenever a recording level was needed, LaMarche would perform parts of the outtake tape much to the delight of the engineers and directors.

The producers decided to use the outtake tape as the basis for a *Pinky and the Brain* episode, and commissioned a script which was planned to be a surprise for LaMarche.

"We came into work and we were all sitting there with smiles on our face," recalled Paulsen. "And Maurice walked in and said 'Hi guys. What's up?' He sat down and started glimpsing the script and I remember it was just precious. It was a like a little kid at Christmas time going, 'Oh my God! Are you kidding me? Is this a joke?'... It was thrilling just watching him be thrilled."

Paulsen admires his fellow voice actors and enjoys the spontaneity that comes from a group recording session. While occasionally he's required to perform lines by himself, he believes the interaction between the actors improves their performances.

Unlike many voice actors of years past who labored in relative (and sometimes total) anonymity, Paulsen and his *Animaniacs* co-stars make frequent appearances at Warner Brothers Studio Stores across the country. They are part of a new generation of voice actors who are being recognized for their contributions to animation and being allowed to interact with the fans who love their work.

Rob continues to be one of the busiest voice actors in the business and has contributed to *Powerpuff Girls*, *Star Wars: Jedi Starfighter*, the *Lilo and Stitch* television series, *Danny Phantom*, *Jimmy Neutron: Boy Genius* and *Teacher's Pet*, among many others.

Animato #33 Fall 1995
Mae Questel

The recent passing of Mae Questel at the age of 89 was another signal that a wonderful era in animation is fading into the past.

No one person has been associated as much with Betty Boop as the character's primary voice artist, Mae Questel. Although several performers voiced the character before Questel, hers is the rendition that stuck with the Fleischer Studios and with the public.

Questel attempted to begin her professional show business career at the age of nine when she auditioned for the Broadway show *Daddy*. Although the producers liked her, her grandparents didn't believe the theater was a proper career for a young woman, and Questel's show business aspirations were put on hold for a few years.

In 1930, her high school sorority sisters entered her name into a Helen Kane impersonation contest. Questel won the contest that meant four days booking into one of the leading vaudeville houses in New York, the RKO Fordham, and $150 in prize money. Helen Kane even autographed a photo, "To Another Helen Kane." Neither performer could imagine how ironic this inscription would become in just a few years.

Her four days at the Fordham resulted in bookings in the prestigious Palace Theater and then subsequent bookings from Boston to Baltimore. At the relatively tender age of 18, Questel began her show business career with an act consisting of impersonations of well-known performers such as Mae West, Marlene Dietrich, Eddie Cantor and Jimmy Durante.

Max Fleischer hired her in 1931 to perform the Betty Boop voice, an assignment that had also been given to four other actresses. Where the other mimics failed, Questel succeeded and she had the job through the end of the series in 1938. Questel told me that she didn't want to move to Florida with the rest of the Fleischer studio, and by that time the Betty Boop series had naturally run its course.

In this photo, taken during the late 1940s at the Famous Studios,
Mae Questel is flanked by Jack Mercer (left) and Jackson Beck.

A short brunette with large eyes, Questel bore an amazing resemblance to La Boopster.

Questel's mimicry extended to her characterization of Olive Oyl in the Popeye cartoons. Although at first the Olive voice was a deeper voice, Questel's version was based on popular screen comedienne ZaSu Pitts.

Unlike her frequent partner behind the microphone, Jack Mercer, Questel worked hard to have an acting career in front of the camera. She appeared in several Paramount musical two-reelers with Rudy Vallee in the early 1930s and in the film *Wayward* supporting Richard Arlen and Nancy Carroll (1932). She retired from show business in the late 1930s for three years after the birth of her son.

She returned to voice acting with numerous appearances on radio programs during the 1940s and essaying Olive Oyl and other cartoon voices when Paramount moved the Famous Studios operation back to New York in 1942. She worked on the Casper cartoons and was the voice of Little Audrey. According to Jackson Beck, who played Bluto at Famous, Questel even played Popeye in several shorts made during World War II when Jack Mercer was unavailable.

She provided the voice for the television character Winky Dink on the show *Winky Dink and You*, and did scores of voice-overs for commercials. And at an age when performers worry about making the transition to older parts, Questel had no problem with character roles. In 1960, she was praised for her role in the Broadway hit *Majority of One*, and encored her performance for the movie version starring Rosalind Russell. Other Broadway roles came in *Enter Laughing* with Alan Arkin, *Bajour* with Chita Rivera and *Come Blow Your Horn*. She had prominent parts in Jerry Lewis's *It's Only Money*, *Funny Girl* and *Move*. Her television appearances included guest shots on series such as *Mrs. G Goes to College*, *The Naked City* and *77 Sunset Strip*.

Questel even starred on her own comedy record in the early 1970s. *Mrs. Portnoy's Retort* was a satiric response to Philip Roth's bestselling book, *Portnoy's Complaint*. Roth's book was known for its candid depiction of obsessive masturbation, and the album took full advantage of this theme for a series of cheap laughs with Questel playing the role of the fictional Portnoy's mother.

In the mid-1970s Questel was picked for the role of "Aunt Bluebell" in a series of commercials for Scott Towels, and was a fixture on television for years.

I've spoken to Questel several times since 1977, when I began my research at the Fleischer Studio, and always found her to be bubbly, outspoken, and self-confident. Her character of Aunt Bluebell, who would butt into other people's problems with her unsolicited but friendly advice about paper towels, never seemed to me to be too far from reality.

At a meeting of the Sons of the Desert (the international Laurel and Hardy fan club) back in the early 80s, I met Questel and she proved to be an old-fashioned showbiz trooper. She was ready to do Betty's voice upon request and was delighted that one member of the organization had brought along her *Musical Justice* live-action short with Rudy Vallee.

Sometimes too candid for her own good, she wasn't shy about revealing her unhappiness that she wasn't selected for Hanna-Barbera's revival of Popeye in the '70s, and was quoted by her son in a 1977 article that she was always hoping to get a telephone call from someone making more Betty Boops. She finally did get a chance to do Betty again in *Who Framed Roger Rabbit*.

Questel's last performance of note was in Woody Allen's segment, "Oedepus Wrecks," of the 1989 anthology film *New York Stories*. Although the film as a whole received mixed notices, Questel's performance was singled out for praise.

In poor health for a number of years, Questel lived to see and benefit from the rediscovery of Betty Boop.

Mae Questel died in 1998.

Animato #31 Winter 1995
Don Messick

When the Seventies situation comedy *The Duck Factory* cast the actor to play the fictitious animation studio's voice talent, for once Hollywood got it right. Don Messick, the man who, along with the late great Daws Butler,

Don Messick was one of the greatest assets of Hanna-Barbera.

created many of the voices heard by two generations of television viewers, played the role.

Messick is the man responsible for the voices of the following characters: Boo Boo and Ranger Smith on *Yogi Bear*; Pixie of Pixie and Dixie; Dr. Benton Quest and Bandit on *Jonny Quest*; Scooby and Scrappy on *Scooby-Doo*; and Papa Smurf on *The Smurfs*. Who was the narrator on all those old Hanna-Barbera cartoons like *Huckleberry Hound*? That's Don Messick as well. But, that's just scratching the surface. You can also add to the list Hampton on *Tiny Toon Adventures*, Astro on *The Jetsons*, and Droopy on *Droopy and Dripple*. So far, Messick has performed on over 40 animated television series.

The soft-spoken voice actor (whose regular speaking voice sounds very much like his Dr. Quest characterization), describes himself as "reticent and an introvert," but he is obviously proud of his long career in animation. He spoke to *ANIMATO* from his home in southern California.

Messick started his show business career at the tender age of 13 in his native Maryland as a ventriloquist. Performing with his dummy "Woody DeForest" at area events such as Lion's Club meetings led to his own weekly radio show in Salisbury, Maryland by the age of 15. Acting as both the writer and the performer on that show, Messick discovered his voice's flexibility. Rather than performing impersonations or impressions, he began developing his ability to create and perform various different characterizations.

"I loved radio. That really was my first love," Messick recalled fondly.

After high school, Messick moved to Baltimore, and attended an acting school for two years, and performed in little theater productions.

"Studying acting I realized how bad I must have been on the radio," Messick said with a laugh. He worked on eliminating his eastern Maryland shore accent.

His acting training was interrupted by a 20-month stint in the Army. Assigned to Special Forces, Messick found himself traveling around the country entertaining troops. The Army brought him to the west coast, and after he was discharged, he went to Los Angeles to continue his fledgling show business career. Messick appeared in a few plays, and eventually attended a radio workshop for ex-GIs, which included performing in a weekly radio play.

His connection with the radio workshop led to the role of Raggedy Andy in a radio version of the popular children's stories. That show ran 39 weeks, and was derailed by a musicians' strike. Another show business gig brought Messick back to the east coast.

In New York City, Messick survived an experience that many young actors suffer; extreme poverty. Although he appeared in several off-Broadway productions, Messick recalled that in order to make ends meet, he sold his blood at $5 a pint.

His career took an upswing when he received a message from animation legend Bob Clampett. Clampett had left Warner Brothers to form his own production company, and had a hit with a puppet show entitled *Time for Beany*. Clampett had developed a new puppet show, *Buffalo Billy*, and wanted Messick in the cast.

Clampett put Messick under contract, and brought him back to California. After rehearsing the show for several months in Clampett's garage (in which he had a puppet stage set up), Clampett sold the show to Fanny Farmer Candy, and Messick returned to New York for the show's 13-week run.

Another puppet series then brought him back to Los Angeles. Messick noted that local stations eventually believed originating a live puppet show was too expensive, and instead developed children's shows featuring old theatrical shorts hosted by "cartoon jockies."

With the puppet shows on the wane, as was dramatic radio, Messick made the rounds to animation studios looking for voice work. He was unaware that like dramatic radio, theatrical cartoons were also endangered.

MGM eliminated their animation unit in 1957, and long-time partners and Oscar-winners William Hanna and Joseph Barbera found themselves unceremoniously fired. After securing a deal with Screen Gems, the television arm of Columbia Pictures, Hanna and Barbera produced their first made-for-television cartoon series *Ruff 'n Reddy*. Hanna and Barbera remembered Messick from an interview with him, and hired him and Daws Butler for the show.

Although there had been earlier animated series made for television,

Ruff n' Reddy was a hit, and in no small way the vocal team of Daws Butler and Don Messick was responsible.

For Messick the association with the studio is one that continues to this day. Hanna-Barbera was "like a second home. Some of the other actors would say to me, 'Don, you have a room here?' It really was, and has been [a second home] although it is a little different under the new ownership."

As the studio prospered, Messick was kept busy appearing in series after series.

At Hanna-Barbera, directors liked assembling the complete cast of vocal performers, if possible, rather than record the actors individually. Messick likes this ensemble performance approach.

"I found it was better to work that way because of my experience as an actor in radio and on the stage. I like to feel the relationship of the other people I'm working with; so that we can play with each other. As Daws Butler once put it, working with me was like 'chamber music.' We performed and each [of us] kind of anticipating the reaction the other would have."

Both Messick and Butler sneaked in some adlibs. "They don't discourage that sort of thing unless it gets out of hand. All of us have at one time or another ad-libbed. Daws would say, 'Well, Snaggle Puss wouldn't say it that way,' or I would say [a line] would not be a natural way for Boo Boo to speak."

Messick views his job, not just as supplying a voice for a cartoon character but also as acting. "It's like acting, theatrical acting." He noted that he and others would get involved with a character as a performer. For example, he recalled how Casey Kasem would often change Shaggy's lines while recording *Scooby-Doo*.

Messick matter-of-factly stated that he does not do impersonations, and said he was never asked to base a characterization on an established voice, something the late Daws Butler did a number of times. While Messick readily admits that Hanna-Barbera patterned Yogi Bear after Art Carney's character on *The Honeymooners*, and patterned Snaggle Puss's voice after stage legend Bert Lahr, he says that Butler went far beyond a mere impersonation, and these voices became something unique.

Messick enters into the process of creating a voice the same way he would work on performing a role on the stage, or before the cameras. For him, it's all acting. He wants to do more than come up with a funny or appropriate voice. He wants to create a character for the drawing before him.

The opportunity to do an ongoing role in a series means the chance to refine the characterization.

"That's what happens when you get into a series where you have the opportunity show after show to let the character evolve," explains Messick, who added that he wasn't pleased with his early performances as Boo Boo because "it sounded like he had a cold in the nose." Over the course of the series, he refined Boo Boo's voice to reflect his vision of the cartoon bear's personality, "a naive, simple, but lovable little guy."

In the beginning of the Hanna-Barbera studio, Messick notes that Joe Barbera directed everything, and he was a "tough taskmaster."

"The actors, I believe, always came away feeling, 'I didn't do it right. I tried, but . . . ' You got the feeling that Joe thought, 'Well, that's as close as they're going to get to it, so . . . ' He was always acting it out himself, and unless he heard it from the actor exactly as he heard it in his mind then it's not up to standard."

Regardless of what happened in the recording studio, Barbera must have appreciated Messick's talents (in his recent autobiography, Barbera refers to Messick as a "great" voice actor), as Messick still is associated with the studio nearly forty years later.

Who's the character closest to Messick's heart? Without missing a beat he responds "Scooby-Doo." He says with pride that Scooby-Doo was in production for 22 years, a record for television animation.

"I got into the character. I enjoyed it. People come up to me and tell me they grew up with Scooby," Messick says warmly.

That's the reward of creating memorable vocal characterizations.

I received a nice note from Don after this article ran saying it was the best thing that was ever printed about him. Whether or not that is true, the sentiment shows something of this extremely talented and gracious performer.

Messick's voice pops up in the most surprising places. I was watching the puppet film Bob Clampett made for a radio industry charity on the *Beany and Cecil* DVD the other day and who was the narrator of the piece but Don Messick!

Messick passed away in 1997.

Animato #34 Spring 1996
Jess Harnell

Singing in bands doesn't sound like a way to prep for a career as a voice actor, but Jess Harnell has made the transition from rocker to actor very successfully. Harnell is best known as the voice of Wakko on the hit show *Animaniacs*.

The good looks and rock star haircut would certainly help Harnell on a stage in front of fans, but aren't prerequisites for a voice actor. Talking to Harnell, though, you quickly see why he's such a sought-after performer. He's an impressive mimic, a quick wit, and has lots of common sense.

As Harnell grew up, he found himself singing in a lot of rock bands "because I had the right haircut." That led to employment as a session singer and Harnell built up a career singing jingles for commercials and performing a lot of background music for television and movies.

Because of a talent for mimicry, Harnell was in demand as a "sound-alike." Harnell explained that in order to save money, a producer would hire a sound-alike to perform a hit song in the style of a popular singer, rather than use that singer. Harnell performed hundreds of sound-alike songs and credits the experience as honing his skills as a mimic.

Music was the gateway for his new career. Harnell had been working with music producer Dan Savant who was putting together a soundtrack to accompany the Splash Mountain ride at Disneyland. Savant needed a singer who could also do the voice of several Disney characters from *Song of the South*, and Harnell filled the bill. He did eight voices on the ride's soundtrack, including those of Brer Rabbit and Brer Bear.

Jess Harnell's career in voice acting came from his career as a singer.

A year later, he recorded a similar soundtrack when the ride opened at Walt Disney World. Harnell impressed the Disney staff so much that he was asked to do the Roger Rabbit voice when Charles Fleischer was unavailable. He performed the voice for several years.

Harnell quickly and gratefully acknowledged the help of Rick Dempsey, the head of Disney's Character Voice Department. Harnell was without an agent, and Dempsey wrote a letter on Harnell's behalf to a number of agents. Harnell was signed with showbiz giant ICM and, within a year, he landed his first series, *Animaniacs*.

Wakko, for the uninitiated, is the Warner sibling who wears a hat, eats a lot, and has an unmistakable Beatle-esque sound.

"People ask me if they were looking for a Beatles kind of thing but that didn't happen at all," explained Harnell. His first audition went well enough that the voice casting director Andrea Romano called him back. Harnell asked Romano which mic to use in a John Lennon impersonation. Romano was intrigued, and asked him if he could do other Beatles. When he confirmed he could do all four, she asked for Ringo. Romano liked the voice, and showed him a picture of Wakko. Since Wakko wasn't adult, Harnell made him a "baby Beatle."

What he didn't realize is that the *Animaniacs* creative crew was having some difficulty forming Wakko's character, and his voice helped them further develop Wakko.

Aside from Wakko, Harnell essayed the role of Secret Squirrel in the recent revival of the Sixties show, had roles on *Biker Mice From Mars* and *The Twisted Tales of Felix the Cat* On the recent *Pink Panther* show he was the Panther's nemesis Manly Man. The directors of that show thought his character should have a different voice each time he appeared so Harnell had to come up with a variety of voices. He called that assignment "voice-over aerobics."

He has also had guest spots on the new *Casper* show, *Tiny Tunes, Bonkers,* and *Goof Troop.* He also plays the Sewer Urchin on *The Tick.*

As with every voice actor, Harnell has his own technique for creating a characterization.

"That's the great mystery of voice acting; how do these people arrive with the voices for these characters," he said. "The more input that you get as an actor the better off you are. A character description is helpful, but a photo is even more helpful. A paragraph of dialogue is good, a page of dialogue is even better."

Harnell used the Sewer Urchin as an example. When he read a description of the character, he noticed the Urchin was "nervous and fidgety." He zeroed in on the fidgety part, and was reminded of Dustin Hoffman's role in *Rain Man.* He took a little of Hoffman's obsessiveness, and turned it into the Sewer Urchin.

Singing in character is a real challenge for a voice actor, Harnell explained. Something that would be easy to sing in one's own voice can be difficult when you're in a character voice and already pushing your larynx up and down your throat. Harnell didn't know when he got the role of Wakko that singing in character would be such an important part of *Animaniacs.* Luckily for the producers, Tress MacNeille, Rob Paulsen and

Harnell all come from musical backgrounds. When we spoke, Harnell had just finished recording a third *Animaniacs* CD.

"How would that character sing 'Happy Birthday' and how would that character cry and laugh and how would that character sound when he was angry" are all tests for the voice actor, said Harnell. "As long as you can adapt it into a lot of things that's when you know you've got a character that's a person."

Another test is doubling up on voices. On many *Animaniacs* episodes the three stars do multiple voices. Harnell noted that Rob Paulsen meets himself coming and going, so to speak, when Yakko has a conversation with Dr. Scratch'n'Sniff.

Harnell estimates that 95% of the recording work he does is with other voice actors. While a "wild" recording session (in which an actor reads his or her lines without other members of the cast) can be quick, Harnell said that a performer doesn't get the interplay with fellow cast members which can result in ideas that can find their way into a finished cartoon.

Harnell is very gratified with the response the *Animaniacs* crew has received from fans, and is amazed by the cyber fan activity on such computer services as America Online, where there is a Jess Harnell folder in the cartoon area. Unlike other successful television performers Harnell can still enjoy a somewhat anonymous life.

When Warner Brothers schedules tours for the vocal performers to the various Warner Brothers stores, though, Harnell gets a real taste of celebrity. Fans crowd Harnell and his co-stars for hours, and he remembered one appearance in which 1,500 admirers turned out.

Ask him if he is content with the current state of his career and he deadpans, "What I really want to do is direct."

"No, I'm just kidding," he continues with a laugh. "I'm very satisfied. I work with people who I would hang out with if I weren't working with them. My job, in a small way, I'd like to believe, make people happy and there's nothing more than you can say about a job than that."

Harnell recently finished a CD that he'll give to friends, family and people in the entertainment industry that showcases his singing. If something happens from that he'll be happy, but if nothing happens, he's pleased to continue voice acting.

"I'm in a very nice position in my career, I love being a voice actor," he said with pride,

Harnell has strong feelings about performers who become famous by creating a ch aracter and "then spend the rest of their life bitching about how they can do more." His response to them is a Wakko-like "Shut up!"

For him, the mere thought that he's met ten people who loved Wakko so much to endure having a Wakko tattoo is a testimony to the strength of the character and the validity of what he is doing.

He is a realist, though, about certain conditions of voice acting. Harnell accepts the fact that voices are property of the producers and believes if he was offered a percentage of ownership in Wakko, a similar offer should be made to all the artist and writers whom he views equally responsible in bringing Wakko to life.

A skilled mimic himself, he also understands that a producer could re-place the original performer of a voice with someone who also can do that voice. Recreating voices has always been a "weird" experience for Harnell. "I couldn't bring a whole lot of me to it," he said.

Despite the voice actor's precarious position, Harnell feels very com-fortable at Warner Brothers. "Warner Brothers is very kind to us. They let us do the voices on TV shows and on radio. Some shows won't let you do that,"

Harnell has three rules that he believes can help assure success in show business. After a person gets a break, they need to . . .

1. Hustle. Stay on top of the business. Be aggressive in a nice way.

2. Be a nice person to be around.

3. Be talented.

Obviously, Harnell has followed his own advice.

Jess Harnell, like his *Animaniacs* co-star Rob Paulsen, has had a busy career since this interview with vocal performances in such shows as *The Grim*

Adventures of Billy & Mandy, Codename: Kids Next Door, Mucha Lucha, Duck Dodgers and *Drawn Together.*

Animato #34 Spring 1996
Jackson Beck

Close your eyes. Isn't that deep voice of the guy performing the announcing chores on that Little Caesar Pizza ad familiar? Sure, you've heard it hundreds, no, thousands of times on television and radio, but isn't there something slightly . . . Bluto-ish about it?

Well, if Jackson Beck the announcer sounds a little like the Bluto/Brutus of the Famous Studio Popeye cartoons, that's because Jackson Beck the actor portrayed Popeye's nemesis. Beck also played the Fox in the Baby Huey series, King Leonardo in the early Sixties series *The King and Odie,* and was the announcer in Filmation's *Superman* series of the early Seventies.

Today, the veteran actor and announcer is comfortably busy in his home base of New York City.

"Everything I do is fun because I like what I do," he said during an interview conducted last August.

Beck has fond memories of his time behind the mic at Famous.

"It was very pleasant working for them [Famous Studios]. I asked for more money once or twice but I never got it. But what the hell? I would have only pissed it away on wild women," said Beck with a hearty laugh.

Beck was one of a core of performers who supplied the voices for the Famous shorts. Joining Beck were Jack Mercer (Popeye), Mae Questel (Olive Oyl, Little Audrey and others), Sid Raymond (Baby Huey) and Arnold Stang.

When Beck joined the cast at Famous he was already a veteran of radio and the stage. Bit by the acting bug at an early age, Beck joined a repertory stage company for a tour of several cities. The trip began with a bad omen: the bus broke down in nearby Newark, New Jersey. By the time the troupe reached Philadelphia there were no bookings and no money.

The fledgling actor was stuck in a cheap hotel with other cast members and was eventually rescued by his family who sent him money.

Upon returning to New York, Beck thought over his decision to be an actor, and put his energies toward a new acting opportunity, radio.

Listening to radio today gives a person little idea of what the medium was like 50 and 60 years ago. Radio, for lack of a better definition, was television without pictures. Programs of every type, from dramas to comedy to news, were heard over national networks or independent stations.

Beck decided to break into radio, and came up with a system. Taking the addresses of stations, producers and advertising agencies that often created shows, Beck worked out a walking route in Manhattan. He would routinely visit the offices of these decision-makers once a week, making sure he left an updated card for their files. When he could, he'd make sure that the card was slightly over-sized so his card would stick out of the file.

"They got used to me," said Beck.

Beck believes in the importance of self-promotion and trying to be different. He recalled how he wanted to send a Christmas greeting to his list of potential employers, but didn't want to send a card that might never be noticed. So he went to a novelty store and bought 200 children's birthday horns, the kind that has a paper tube that unfurls when the horn is blown. Beck had slips of paper printed with his name and a Christmas message and, with the help of his parents, glued the slips to the end of the tubes. The unusual Christmas "card" got noticed!

Beck and other struggling actors would go to smaller station in the city (there were over 20 stations at the time) and stage radio shows for free in order to build up credits and gain experience.

His real break, though, came when he was hired by the promotional office of Columbia Pictures. Columbia would produce one-hour adaptations of their current releases and send the program free to radio stations. Naturally, if the stations played the show, Columbia would get a free commercial.

Beck could mimic a number of Hollywood leading men, and received roles on these programs. These were his first paying jobs.

One might wonder why, in the middle of the Depression, Beck persevered in his quest to be an actor.

"You are born an actor. You never quit," said Beck with great feeling. "And if you do, you're the saddest person in the world because once you quit you can't get back. Never again. It's like you ride the rocket and you never get off."

Beck believes that acting can't really be learned. "You can't learn inspiration. You can't learn creativity."

He also has great pride in his craft.

"Even the crap I do from time to time, and I'm not referring to my commercials, even the crap you have to put something of yourself into it."

As Beck received more and more employment in radio, he was considered a character actor who specialized in a variety of voices and dialects. He noticed, though, that the people who had a permanent place in the stations were the announcers, so Beck began to seek announcing assignments as well as acting gigs.

An agent friend tipped Beck to an opportunity at the Famous Studios in 1944. The studio needed a voice actor for Bluto/Brutus, and Beck auditioned. At the end of the session, the director told him to report back the following Monday for his first recording job.

He has nothing but praise for his co-stars. "Mercer was the most versatile voice man that I knew," said Beck, who puts Mercer in the same league as Mel Blanc. He explained that while Mercer didn't have the dramatic range of Blanc, he could create sound effects that Blanc couldn't.

"If you were short of a sound effect, he'd do it with his voice," said Beck, who characterized Mercer as "self-effacing and brilliant."

Sid Raymond was "pure vaudeville," and Mae Questel was a "great artist and wonderful lady." Beck confirmed that Questel had performed the Popeye voice in several wartime shorts.

Beck remembered that "everyone would ad lib."

"None of them are memorable because when you're doing Bluto none of them are memorable remarks," Beck said laughter.

"Most of the fight scenes were ad lib. We had to say certain things like 'Why you!' [and] anything else that was suitable. If you felt it, you said it. You always had a little latitude. Nobody held a watch."

The Famous voice actors weren't under a formal contract. They were paid by the recording session. Only Mercer, who was part of the writing staff at Famous, had a more concrete tie to the studio. This allowed Beck to appear on radio and record children's records. When Famous Studios stopped production on the Popeye shorts in 1957, Beck continued mixing acting and announcing assignments.

The late Fifties signaled an end to much of the entertainment industry in New York. Animation studios closed or shifted to the west coast. Live television production was replaced with filmed or videotaped programs from Hollywood. Dramatic radio was overcome by television. While Beck took jobs on the west coast, he remained firmly based in Gotham.

"I was born here. It's in my blood."

Beck is a man of principle and is at a point in his career where he can afford to turn down work if the people, price or working conditions don't match his standards. He recalled turning down a voice-over job at *Saturday Night Live* a few years ago because of the material's ethnic humor which Beck considered insulting.

"You can't be a whore in this business," he said.

Although he has appeared on camera in the past, Beck doesn't seek those sorts of roles now. "It takes so long, it really isn't worth the effort," he explained.

He made an exception, though, for an old friend, director Sidney Lumet. Lumet made a political drama with Gene Hackman and Richard Gere in 1986 entitled *Power*. Gere and Hackman play political consultants, and, at one point in the plot, they need an announcer for a crucial set of commercials. Gere barks, "Get me The Voice!"

Perhaps it was typecasting, but "The Voice" was, of course, Jackson Beck. If I was running for office, I'm sure I'd want that authoritative voice in my corner!

Jackson continued working up until his death in 2004.

Animato #35 Summer 1996
Maurice LaMarche

The moment I became an *Animaniacs* fan is when I saw the *Pinky and the Brain* cartoon in which the world's smartest lab mouse is trying to record a series of narrations for a series of TV commercials. I realized immediately that this was almost a word-for-word adaptation of a tape of actual outtakes from an unsuccessful recording session with the late great Orson Welles. While the cartoon as a whole was brilliant, I couldn't get over the great vocal characterizations, especially the Wellesian tones of The Brain. Who was that voice actor?

Little did I realize then I had been hearing that actor's work all over the television dial. He was Egon Spengler on *The Real Ghostbusters*, Mr. Wilson on *Dennis the Menace*, Dishonest John on *The New Adventures of Beany and Cecil*, Popeye on *Popeye & Son*, dozens of different voices on *The Critic*, and had roles on shows such as *Duckman, Freakazoid, Tiny Toon Adventures, The Tick*, and *The New Pink Panther*.

Maurice LaMarche has built up a reputation as a voice actor's voice actor. Talk to almost any current vocal performer and his name will surely be mentioned. His success can also be seen in the legions of fans that turn up at signings and talk about his work on the Internet.

An hour before an autograph session began at the Boston Warner Brothers Studio Store earlier this year, fans were eagerly lining up to see the two stars of *Pinky and the Brain*, LaMarche and Rob Paulsen.

Asked about how he reacts to such enthusiasm for his work, LaMarche replied, "I'm floored by it. Unbelievable numbers to come see us and tell us 'you guys are doing a great job' and that means so much to me." Quick with a joke or impersonation, LaMarche is part of a new generation of voice actors who justifiably take great pride in their work. LaMarche is also a fan of his colleagues' work.

"Rob Paulsen is probably the most giving actor I've ever worked with and you couldn't meet a nicer guy," said LaMarche, adding, "Billy West [*Ren and Stimpy, Doug*, etc.] is one of the most monstrously talented persons I've ever met and I'm happy to call him my friend."

A former stand-up comic, it's easy to see his on-stage roots at an autograph session. LaMarche and Paulsen just don't sit at a table and sling out signatures. They talk to the fans, pose for pictures, and perform for them. Ask for one of their voices and, voila, there's the character right in front of you.

They even make taking a break performance art. A time out for the two actors elicits a Pinky exclamation from Paulsen of "Potty Time!" and an affirmative "Yeeess!" from LaMarche. Both actors clearly relish the opportunity of meeting the fans.

"In voice acting you're paid very well, but you toil in relative anonymity," said LaMarche. He characterized his career in animation as "a case of failing upward, by accident."

Working the comedy club circuit in the late Seventies, LaMarche found himself in Toronto working at a club called Yuk Yuks. Representatives from the Canadian animation studio Nelvana were in the audience to see if they could find some potential vocal performers. They were impressed enough with LaMarche's mimicry to offer him two roles in their new television special *Easter Fever*.

LaMarche supplied impressions of Steve Martin and Don Rickles for characters participating in a roast for the Easter Bunny in the 1978 production. While he liked the work, success in stand-up comedy was still his goal.

"My dreams for myself were very lofty," remembered LaMarche. "I saw myself in a big TV series making 60 bazillion dollars an episode, the fancy cars, the 15 houses and all that stuff. And I've come to discover through friends of mine who've gone on to that, that that's not what makes you happy. It's just fine with me that I don't have that for myself."

Unlike his friend Jon Lovitz, who is constantly recognized, LaMarche enjoys the acclaim he's received for *Pinky and the Brain* (the only real hit of the fledgling WB Network) without the accompanying hassles of television stardom.

He deeply appreciates the respect he and Paulsen received from the producers of *Pinky and the Brain,* who insisted the two stars be given a separate card in the end credits.

Despite his success, there are no star trappings with LaMarche. He is quick to acknowledge a number of people who have been instrumental in his ca-

Pinky and the Brain set new standards in voice work and writing for television animation.

reer. He's deeply thankful to his agent at William Morris who took a chance on him by signing someone who hadn't already made a name for himself in the industry, and he is truly appreciative of the support veteran vocal performer Frank Welker gave him by talking him up to producers and directors.

Even with the help he was getting, LaMarche found breaking into the field was not easy. "I found out it's very hard work and it was a year before my first job. Auditioning, auditioning, auditioning and not getting it, not getting it," said LaMarche.

A role in *Inspector Gadget* as Chief Quimby was a big break and it was followed by Egon Spengler on *The Real Ghostbusters*. LaMarche was still pursuing his comedy career and split his day between the two.

Family tragedies cut short his comedy career, though. In 1987 La-Marche lost his father to a murder, and then his sister was killed in an automobile accident in 1989, LaMarche lost his drive to perform before an audience, and concentrated on his vocal performing.

When asked if he misses stand-up comedy, he thoughtfully replied, "Every now and again I get a little twinge for it. We [Rob Paulsen] checked into the hotel last night [for a signing appearance] and in the lobby was a comedy cabaret. Rob said to me, 'Hey, Moe, why don't you get up there and make your big comeback in Cherry Hill, NJ.' And I thought, 'Big joke.' But, sure enough, after dinner, we went by and I was looking through the window like a little kid at a candy store.

"I may go back to it one day, I have to take the Reagan jokes out of my act, and maybe punch up the *Fantasy Island* piece like maybe throwing it right out the window!" he continued with a laugh.

"If that happens great, but I get a lot of creative juices flowing right in the arena of the studio. How much more can you ask for when you do 27 different voices on one episode of *The Critic?*"

Those 27 voices on a *The Critic* episode is LaMarche's record for number of different voices in one show. "One of the most rewarding moments of my career was my two years on *The Critic,*" he said with pride.

The vocal cast of *The Critic* would read each script aloud with the show's producer James L. Brooks, a man who has helped create some of television's most memorable comedies. For LaMarche, sitting at a large table with the rest of the cast and making Brooks laugh stands out as a significant moment in his career.

Despite good reviews, and respectable ratings when the show moved to FOX, LaMarche said *The Critic* fell prey to the priorities of a new management team and was cancelled.

LaMarche relished working with Brooks, who is a legend in television, and subsequently had the chance to the work with another legend, Ralph Bakshi, on the trouble-plagued feature, *Cool World.*

"I heard all these horror stories about Ralph Bakshi, but apart from his trait of standing right next to you at the microphone smoking cigarettes in your face, that's the only negative he had about him," said LaMarche.

"I thought he was tremendous. He encouraged a lot of improvisation in the characters. For some reason he really took to me," continued LaMarche. "Ralph would show me a drawing and I just went nuts. I found my inner Billy West."

One of the great compliments he received during the recording of *Cool World* occurred, LaMarche recalled, when "Bakshi told his engineer, 'Keep that f****** thing rolling. Everything that comes out of this f****** guy's mouth is brilliant! He's a f****** genius! Keep rolling! G** ****** don't even stop the f****** machine!'" (This anecdote was told in a letter-perfect Bakshi impersonation.)

"That's not to say I am a 'f***** genius,' but rather at that point in time Ralph Bakshi thought I was! I loved working with him, and I'd kill to work with him again."

LaMarche would like to do more work in animated features and frequently auditions for roles.

"I did get a shot with *Pocahontas* and *Hunchback [of Notre Dame]*, but it wasn't my time yet at Disney." LaMarche does admit to having a "little twinge of resentment" toward the Disney policy of hiring movie stars to perform voices, but he has no ill feelings toward the actors themselves. He said he can't blame superstars such as Mel Gibson for being interested in voice work as "it's a real kick to see your voice coming out of a character."

Voice acting is acting, LaMarche pointed out, regardless if the actor is a Mel Gibson or a Maurice LaMarche. There is far more to the craft than just making goofy voices. For LaMarche, The Brain is simply not a voice, but a real characterization with considerable depth.

LaMarche noted, "*Pinky and the Brain* works because Rob Paulsen and Maurice LaMarche play two best friends who love each other dearly in spite of the antagonistic relationship."

LaMarche's technique for creating a characterization is to look at a drawing and "ask 'What does he want?' I then find that part of me. If it's greed [for example], then out comes a greedy voice. With the Brain it was a pure case of looking at a character and saying, 'Oh! He's Orson Welles.'"

Equally challenging as creating a new voice is continuing an established voice. LaMarche played Popeye on *Popeye and Son* and has also performed as Yosemite Sam.

"The greatest challenge is not to bring too much of yourself to it," he explained. "I was very careful to stay close to Mr. Mercer ['s characterization] as possible, and I call him 'Mr. Mercer' because of my respect for him." LaMarche considered playing Popeye a "great honor."

Next up for LaMarche is a new series he recently started recording, *Capt. Simian and the Space Monkeys* from Epoch Ink. An intergalactic spoof about a spacecraft commanded by an evolved ape, LaMarche plays Dr. Splitz, an orangutan with two personalities. Considering this is the actor who did 27 different voices in one show, two voices won't be too much of a stretch!

LaMarche continues to be one of the most popular voice actors in the business. Recent credits include *Catscratch*, *Barnyard*, *Balto III: Wings of Change*, *Futurama*, and *Harvey Birdman*, *Attorney at Law*.

The Chicopee (MA) Herald June 5, 2000
June Foray

Few people know that Rocky the Flying Squirrel is a native of Springfield.

For that matter, most people are unaware that Tweety's protector Granny also hails from the City of Homes. In fact, Natasha Fatale, Witch Hazel, Jokey Smurf, and Nell Fenwick also have ties to the city.

That's because all of these cartoon characters have been given their voice by June Foray, long considered one of the premiere voice actors in the animation industry. Now, Foray has another role that of Grandmother Fa, in the new Walt Disney Pictures animated feature *Mulan*, opening June 19.

"My agent called and said they wanted me," Foray said in an interview from her home in California. "They liked the texture of my voice and they needed a particular voice, one that could be strident and yet soft and gentle."

Mulan re-tells an ancient Chinese myth concerning a young woman who saves her father's life and her family's honor by disguising herself as a man and serving in the emperor's army. Foray plays the title character's grandmother who is viewed as outspoken and unconventional and serves as the young woman's role model.

While some actors couldn't imagine spending their careers in relative anonymity, Foray explains that acting with just one's voice is a high form of the art.

"The voice actor is the nexus between the animator and the audience," she explained. "It's extra important to create an emotional connection."

Foray recorded the role of Grandmother Fa in six recording sessions over a three-month period. While the casts of most animated television shows record their dialogue as an ensemble, Foray noted, "in a feature you don't work with anyone else. You always work alone. It's more difficult in a way, unless you're an experienced actor, because people like the give and the take of an ensemble."

Unlike her colleagues who act before a camera, Foray must rely solely on her voice to create the character created by an artist. "You don't have the benefit of using your eyes and body motion," she said.

Foray was born in Springfield, MA, and lived at 75 Orange Street. She said she knew she wanted to be an actress when she was six years old and her parents helped her by sending her to acting lessons. By the age of 12, she had made her professional debut acting on the former WBZA radio station and was asked to join the station's acting company at 15.

Her family moved to the Los Angeles area in the late 1940s when she was 17, and Foray had her own show, *Lady Make-Believe*, two years later. She also worked on a number of network radio shows originating from Los Angeles such as *Lux Radio Theatre*, *The Danny Thomas Show*, and *The Jimmy Durante Show*.

Although she has never been back to Springfield, she has fond memories of the city and recalled with pleasure walking to Forest Park and ice-skating on Porter Lake.

In 1950, she received the role that changed her life. She was chosen to make the feline noises for Lucifer the cat in Walt Disney's animated feature *Cinderella*. That film and her work on children's records with the late Mel Blanc, the man who created the voice of Bugs Bunny, Daffy Duck, and almost all the rest of the Warner Brothers cartoon stars, led to work at Warner Brothers on Tweety and Bugs Bunny shorts.

Foray really hit her stride when she was cast in a number of roles in the *Rocky & Bullwinkle & Friends* in 1959. The long-running animated television series was a hit in its original run and is currently seen on The Cartoon Network. Foray not only played Rocky, but also a nemesis of Rocky's, the evil spy Natasha Fatale. Nell Fenwick in the *Dudley Do-Right* shorts, assorted heroines, children, and fairy godmothers were also among her roles on the show.

Foray has become a well-known advocate of animation and has appeared at festivals promoting the medium throughout the world. She is now serving her sixth term on the Board of Governors of the Academy of Motion Pictures Arts and Sciences and continues in her role as chairman of the Short Films branch.

Despite her position in the industry, and her credits that include hundreds of appearances in animated cartoons, radio programs, and recordings, Foray isn't about to rest on her laurels. She maintains a busy schedule with voice work for television shows, and in recording audio tapes for children. She just completed narrating several *Mulan* read and sing-along tapes, and has a deal with Turner Publishing to record her *Lady Make-Believe* stories.

She continues to take great joy in her art and said, "There's a little bit of me in all the characters that I've done."

Foray has the distinction of performing the same cartoon voice for 62 years. She has been "Granny" in the Tweety cartoons since 1943. Her characterization was part of Joe Dante's *Looney Tunes: Back in Action* feature.

She reprised her role of Grandmother Fa in the direct-to-video production of *Mulan II*.

Comic Book: The Movie

The popularity of voice actors culminated in an interesting film that was released in 2004. If you are a fan of voice actors, then you need to watch *Comic Book: The Movie*

I'm not sure how people who are neither animation nor comic book fans would take *Comic Book: The Movie*. Although it is done in the impro-visational mock-u-mentory style of *Spinal Tap* and *A Mighty Wind*, the sub-ject matter might not have as broad an appeal as rock or folk music.

Produced and directed by Mark Hamill, a veteran voice actor himself, the film is about a fervent comic book fan who learns that his favorite character is about to be adapted by a Hollywood studio. To win favor with the fans, Hamill's character is given the assignment to shoot a short docu-mentary about the character and his creator. He discovers the grandson of the long-deceased artist and brings him along to the San Diego Comic Convention where the documentary is to be shot.

Billy West plays the grandson and Hamill's camera operator is Jess Har-nell. Voice actors play almost all of the speaking parts. The cast includes Tom Kenny (*SpongeBob SquarePants*), Roger Rose (*Rugrats in Paris*) and Darian Norris (*Fairly OddParents*).

Like other films in this genre, much of the film is adlibbed and while the voice actors are all up to the task, the framework of the film sometimes undercuts their efforts. With much of the action taking place at an actual convention, the film sometimes has that *Trekkies* feeling of making fun of the fans. Hamill, though, is a fan boy himself, so no one gets roughed up too much.

The casting of the voice actors was undoubtedly intended to show their range as performers, but because the cast is nearly all voice actors there is a novelty feel to the production that doesn't help it. Sometimes the film comes across as more of a stunt.

The extras are a lot of fun as they show the cast appearing at a panel at the convention (as themselves) discussing the industry and their kind of performing.

Despite its shortcomings, *Comic Book: The Movie* is a must-have for voice actor fans.

Chapter Five: Toon Reviews

The following are reviews I wrote of VHS releases in the two magazines. The irony of the new DVD age is that much of this material is not available in the new format. Despite the advances in the 1990s, it's much more difficult to be an animation fan today, especially if you're interested in classic animation.

As I write this in December of 2006, the *Betty Boop* cartoons have yet to be released on DVD. After years of waiting, Walter Lantz's cartoons will be released on DVD in the summer of 2007. The most readily available classic animation is the shorts that have fallen into the public domain, but print and reproduction quality is always an issue.

Time-Warner has announced the Fleischer Popeyes will be brought out sometime in 2007.

The MTV animation shows such as *Liquid Television, Daria, The Head* and others are not on DVD either. Only recently has *Beavis and Butt-Head* been brought to the new format.

Most of these reviews are about home video releases, although there are also some that cover television productions – some of which have never seen a secondary release.

If any of these productions sound interesting to you scour the Internet or flea markets. That's the only place you're going to find many of them.

American Pop
Columbia/TriStar Home Video

In a 1981 interview, Ralph Bakshi bemoaned the fact that the title for his new film was all wrong. *American Pop* had people thinking the film was an animated history of American popular music. Although music plays a very significant role in the film, it really is an epic story of four generations of an immigrant family in America. The "pop" meant "father" more than "music."

I have to admit I never saw the film when it was first released as I had been so unimpressed with *Lord of the Rings* that I just couldn't face another Rotoscope feature. I was particularly incensed that Columbia was promoting the film with the line "the state of the art in living animation."

The fact of the matter is Rotoscoping was certainly not state-of-the-art in 1981. It was a process developed by Max Fleischer in 1915 in which the animator would create a cel by tracing over a frame of live-action footage. Fleischer found it was more expensive to use the Rotoscope as it added an additional level of production cost. There were competent cartoonists he could hire who didn't need it. In 1981, though, the economics were reversed. It was now cheaper to shoot live-action footage and hire younger, inexperienced help to use the Rotoscope to produce animation.

Looking at this film today, one can see that in story and execution, *American Pop* is as "live-action" as any animated film could ever be. Clearly, it was produced in animation because the epic story, spanning most of the century, would have been an expensive period live-action piece. The sets and props called for by the script would have been a daunting production challenge. In animation, though, building those New York streets and finding those vintage automobiles is just a matter of ink and paint.

One of the problems with the Rotoscoped action is that the movement of the characters is smooth and life-like, the facial expressions are not. They lack the exaggeration needed to portray emotions.

The story revolves around one family, Russian Jews, who escaped persecution by immigrating to America. Their life here is no real blessing. The mother is burnt alive in a sweatshop fire leaving little Zalmie to fend for himself. He is taken in by a song plugger and the two form a team to attempt to break into vaudeville.

Their lack of success propels them into working for a local crime boss. Zalmie marries and has a son, Benny, who is also fascinated by music. Zalmie's wife is killed in a botched mob hit, and Benny goes to war and is killed by the Nazis. Benny's son, Tony, eventually runs away from home, and winds up in Haight-Ashbury writing songs for a successful rock-folk group. He becomes a junkie and, at his lowest ebb, a child named Little Pete shows up at his door. Tony comes to understand that this kid is his son from a one-night stand with a waitress in Kansas.

The two go to New York where Tony tries to write more songs, becomes a dealer, and eventually abandons Pete who grows up to become a drug dealer to rock bands. While at a sale, Pete forces a rock band and their producers to listen to one of his songs, and the film ends with Pete finally achieving what his father, grandfather and great-grandfather had all aspired to . . . success in America through music.

Bakshi did not write this movie (the script was by Ronni Kern), but it certainly has much of his style. Much of the dialogue overlaps and sounds improvised, and Bakshi clearly is sympathetic with these street characters. The backgrounds are effective, and the music score, which uses dozens of pop tunes (most performed by the artists who made them a hit) from the turn of the century to the Eighties, is very impressive. The music provides a nostalgic point of reference for the story and also is an ironic underpinning for the grim events on-screen.

The difficulty with the film is that there isn't a single character that is actually sympathetic. Zalmie is perhaps the character we understand the most. Benny is on the screen for a limited amount of time and really doesn't develop a character.

Tony comes across as a pathetic little jerk. The scene in which he abandons his son is extremely distasteful. Obviously, Bakshi himself realized just how grim that part of the story comes across. We see Pete, age 12 or so, sitting on a park bench, and the scene dissolves to Pete in his early twenties sitting on the same park bench. What happened in the meantime is so potentially painful, it's ignored.

The conclusion of the film is also flawed. Pete is a very angry young man whose musical voice is undoubtedly punk. His song, though, is Bob

Seger's *Night Moves* (performed by Seger). Not only is this song inappropriate for the character, the two voices are not much of a match. The character's musical triumph doesn't ring true.

American Pop is a depressing piece of work that doesn't have the kind of street humor of Bakshi's earlier pictures. Of his trilogy of Rotoscoped features (*Lord of the Rings, American Pop, Fire and Ice*) *American Pop* may be the most ambitious in trying to use animation as a vehicle for a dramatic, non-fantasy story, but is also the most self-conscious.

Animalland
Just for Kids Home Video
80 minutes

This collection will do much in shedding light on a fascinating footnote in animation history. At the end of the Second World War, the British film studio J. Arthur Rank Organization recruited David Hand to head up an animation unit to make theatrical cartoons for the British market. Hand had been a key person at the Disney studio specializing in production organization. He put together a team of directors and animators, and produced almost 20 shorts until the economics of the film industry in the 1950s made theatrical cartoons a thing of the past.

Although some of these cartoons have been released in the previous collections, this tape boasts excellent prints and an effective video transfer. The animation is certainly up to the quality of Warners and Famous during that time, but the shorts remain historical curiosities. The stories and gags simply aren't very appealing today, especially to an American audience.

The nominal star of the series was Ginger Nutt, a squirrel, and these shorts had a lackluster "funny animal" format. The animation unit certainly had talent in getting images on the screen that moved well, but the stories were neither funny nor appealing.

Still, these shorts are gentle and young children might find them fun.

Arise - 1991; 80 minutes directed by Rev. Ivan Stang; PolyGram Home Video $19.95.

PreDobbs STANGFILMS directed primarily by the Rev. Ivan Stang; $20.00. Both films are available from The SubGenius Foundation, Inc., PO Box 140306, Dallas, Texas, 75214

Do secret forces control us? Are alien space monsters bringing a startling new world? Do people think you're strange? Then, you may be on the right track! That's a quote from the Sacred Pamphlet of the Church of the SubGenius, a Dallas-based religious group that has been spreading the word of one J.R. Bob Dobbs (possibly a relation to this writer, who knows?) since 1979. The Church has an intricate dogma that ties together the end of the world with Yetis, UFOs, the Fighting Jesus, Jehovah I, the Space God, a Conspiracy of Normals and the Bleeding Head of Arnold Palmer. Intrigued? Well, *Arise* will probably answer many of your questions about the Church and its elusive founder, Bob.

Not really pure animation, *Arise* is a hypnotic collage film using clips from various public domain sources, animation, sequences from various Church revivals, and video effects. The film probably runs too long for one sitting as the images and narration are rather densely packed. I'd recommend viewing it over several evenings. Actually, after a hard day broadcasting the corporate line at my day job, it's truly refreshing to relax to sheer chaos.

PreDobbs STANGFILMS is probably a tad more accessible to audiences who aren't inclined to change their religion. A collection of animated films, which highlight the talent of SubGenius Church guru Rev. Ivan Stang, this tape has the hilariously gross *Reproduction Cycle* and the outstanding Art Break video on the Church financed by MTV.

Bebe's Kids

There certainly have been animated productions based on stand-up comedy routines before (Lenny Bruce's *Thank You Mask Man* springs to mind), but I can't remember when a feature-length film was based on such subject material. *Bebe's Kids* breaks ground in that field as well as being a pioneer in animated ethnic humor.

Based on the late comedian Robin Harris' routine, *Bebe's Kids* tells the story a date from Hell. Like Harris' routines, this film isn't afraid to exploit scatological humor and use references that a lot of white America may not get.

For example, I was the only person in the audience who laughed when Harris described a *Dolomite* movie! When a group of men are admiring an attractive woman one remarks, "Reminds me of *Players* magazine, June 1973." Another rejoins, "Yeah, Pam Grier!"

The rating of PG-13 certainly is appropriate.

The central character is a caricature of Harris, and he recounts his experiences over drinks in a neighborhood bar. After meeting a beautiful woman at a funeral, he sets up a date with her and her son to go to an amusement park called "Fun World." His dreams of an idyllic time are shattered when he picks up his date and finds there are three more children slated to go with them. Bebe is a friend of his date, Jameka, and has dropped her kids off to go along. Naturally, Robin is not pleased, especially when he realizes these kids are foul-mouthed and ill-mannered.

The best moments of the film are when Harris is trying to balance dealing with the kids with getting to know Jameka better. The problems of this film are several-fold.

Throughout the film, the audience's sympathies are with Robin and Jameka, but in a very self-conscious scene the actions of Bebe's kids are justified by the kids themselves as an expression of freedom. This is supposed to make us like the kids better and sets us up for the conclusion of the film.

Instead, it undercuts the comedy that both precedes and follows the scene. Up until this point, the film was a loose street-wise look at modern dating, but after it (a very silly rap song during a "trial" of the kids), the tone shifts to one of social relevancy. It really doesn't work.

Another big problem is the animation itself. Produced in six different locations, the production is at the level of a Saturday morning cartoon. Some of the character animation is fairly effective, but once again it's the case of the voice out-acting the animation. Faizon Love, however, does a fine job impersonating Harris.

Despite its flaws, it's refreshing to see someone attempt to do something different.

The feature was accompanied by the short *The Itsy Bitsy Spider* written by former *Saturday Night Live* writer Michael O'Donoghue that displays a PG-rated version of his caustic wit. Even though the direction by Matthew O'Callaghan has more flair than the feature possesses, the short is fairly mediocre. Again, though, it's great to see a company other than Disney making a commitment to short subjects.

Beavis and Butt-Head Do Christmas
Sony Home Video

I have to make two admissions. First, I've grown to like Mike Judge's infantile characters, and second I never thought I'd hear the word "bunghole" in what was passing as a Christmas special. Two Yuletide episodes with appropriate bumper segments are presented in this collection.

It's a Wonderful Life and *A Christmas Carol* are both given the B&B treatment with fairly predictable results. In the first segment Beavis is visited by the three ghosts of Christmas, but still doesn't get the point, while Butt-Head sees how the world would be if he had never been born. This latter segment has some very black humor, including a plot point in which heavenly powers confer with one another and conclude that B&B must die!

The bumper segments feature what appears to be real-life Christmas letters to the little wieners. As usual, I don't know if I should laugh or be very frightened.

The Best of Liquid Television 2
Sony Music Entertainment/MTV

Liquid Television was a great experiment with fantastic successes and dismal failures. On this second tape there's quite an offering of both, and one thing you can't say is the program didn't offer a variety of animation and subject matter. The truly creepy *Billy and Bobby* are represented with two shorts, and the surrealistic *The Adventures of Thomas and Nardo* is also here. Unfortunately, the collection includes such wastes of time as *Art School Girls of Doom* and the evil puppet production *Winter Steele*. I think the enjoyable material outweighs the boring in this collection, though.

Boop Oop A Doop
74 Minutes $29.95; Ivy Classics Video

While this cartoon compilation is certainly not a documentary in the same sense as Leonard Maltin's wonderful look at the Fleischer Studios, it nevertheless is an entertaining look at the Fleischers' cartoon heroine.

Narrated in a straightforward fashion by Steve Allen, the tape opens with Allen standing in front of 1600 Broadway in New York, the building which was the Fleischers' home during most of the Thirties. It then traces the development of Betty from both a supporting character to a star and from a dog to a human being. The production also points out how the Fleischers used contemporary jazz and pop stars such as Louis Armstrong and Cab Calloway to great advantage in many of their shorts.

Many of the classic early Boop cartoons are shown in their entirety, and the print quality is quite good. The tape characterizes some of the cartoons as being tinted, but as far as I can tell the only shade used is sepia.

The narration touches on who the Fleischers were, the debut of Popeye the Sailor in a Betty Boop cartoon and other aspects of the Boopster's career, but goes into more depth on Betty's sexuality. At one point, there are two single frames in which the film asserts Betty's genitalia were portrayed. I have to admit being a little doubtful of this myself, as what is being discussed is a single and short pen stroke. Frankly, the segment seemed to be attempting to cash in on the *Who Framed Roger Rabbit* controversy, but thankfully, the production does not dwell on this revelation.

The Cartoons that Time Forgot
Kino on Video

The cartoons of both the Iwerks and Van Beuren Studios are certainly well known to animation buffs who've built up any considerable size of public domain material. There are a number of different collections and much of this material is available in varying degrees of quality, but even the best of the other tapes pale next to the print quality and presentation of this new series from Kino on Video.

Animator and animation historian Greg Ford has done a great job assembling the series, but also has provided knowledgeable liner notes that create the proper context in which to watch the shorts.

The seven-volume set includes *All Singing! All Dancing!* (75 minutes), *Down and Out with Flip the Frog* (76 minutes), *Things That Go Bump in the Night* (75 minutes), *Willie Whopper's Fantastic Adventures* (75 minutes), *Free-Form Fairy Tales* (77 minutes), *The Odd and the Outrageous* (80 minutes), and *Rainbow Parades* (73 minutes). They retail for $29.95 each.

If nothing else, this series should firmly rewrite the popular assessment of Ub Iwerks. Iwerks was the man most responsible for the success of Mickey Mouse in *Steamboat Willie*, and the succeeding early Disney shorts. Like Max Fleischer, Iwerks was an inventor who sought to advance the technology of animation. The not-so-silent partner and distributor of these early Disney shorts, a shady character named Pat Powers, was certain that Iwerks was the man in the Disney operation with all the talent, and convinced Iwerks to leave Disney to set up his own studio.

Iwerks assembled animators such as Grim Natwick and Shamus Culhane from the Fleischer Studio, and brought Carl Stalling over from Disney to compose the scores. Powers worked out a distribution deal for many of the cartoons through MGM, and, on paper, everything should have worked out fine. The Hollywood legend is these cartoons were all miserable failures, and that a chastened Iwerks limped back to Disney, where he developed his multi-plane camera for 3-D effects and lived out the rest of his life in anonymity. The truth is obvious, though, when watching these tapes. Iwerks' shorts were uneven in quality, but many of them had the racy Pre-Production Code feel of the early Fleischers. A further distinction was that Iwerks extensively used the two-color Cinecolor system for many of his films, a relative rarity in animation during that period.

Iwerks may not have had the story or the business sense Disney had, but the cartoons he produced were not as bad as two generations of Disney loyalists would like people to believe.

In an interview with *ANIMATO*, Greg Ford, explained. "I tried to program them [the series] for contemporary audiences."

While some might find the *Comicolor* fairy tales "slow," Ford said he feels confident modern viewers will like the Flip the Frog cartoons for "their Pre-Code sense."

Ford, who is currently finishing a documentary on the career of Friz Freleng, recounted the difficulty in obtaining the prints for this collection. The process of producing the series took a year and a half. Although he tried to always make transfers from 35mm prints he said, "At times we were forced to go to 16mm prints. There was a lot of nitrate deterioration." The prints came from a variety of sources, with most of the Van Bueren cartoons coming from private collectors. With some titles, Ford was forced to use more than one source print in order to present the cartoon as it had been originally intended. Besides the inevitable nitrate problems, Ford said the negative of *Balloon Land* had been edited at one point. All references to the Pin Cushion Man, the villain in the short, had been deleted!

"It was unbelievably difficult to restore it to the original version," Ford said.

"I think the early Iwerks cartoons are a critical link between Disney, Warners and Fleischer," he explained. The departure of Harmon and Ising from Disney to Warner Brothers, the creation of the Iwerks Studio, and the raiding of the Fleischer Studios for talent such as Shamus Culhane and Grim Natwick are all moves which created a unique cross pollination in the 1930s animation industry.

The rule by which animation studios were judged during that time was the success it had in creating memorable star characters. Iwerks' principal star was Flip the Frog, a thinly disguised attempt to create a Mickey Mouse clone – an agreeable straight character. Perhaps it was the influence of the former Fleischer staffers, but Flip transformed from a recognizable amphibian living in the woods into what looked like little guy with a big nose trying to survive in Depression America.

Down and Out with Flip the Frog is a great collection of these frequently entertaining gritty cartoons. They're topical and risqué, but they don't firmly establish just who or what is Flip. For our tastes today, that might not be important, but it did little to help Iwerks sixty years ago.

Iwerks' other attempt to establish a character is Willie Whopper, a boy who tells fantastic lies. *Willie Whopper's Fantastic Fables* is one of the most entertaining collections in this series Shamus Culhane described Willie as "a boy Baron Munchausen," and the description is accurate. This tape features one short that was never released to theaters, *The Air Race*, which has an unforgettable gag of St. Peter flipping off a buzzing airplane!

Things That Go Bump in the Night is a wonderful collection of spooky cartoons that is headed by a very Fleischer-esque Flip the Frog short, *The Cuckoo Murder Case*. The other real highlight is a complete print of the cult favorite *Balloon Land*, a truly grotesque color extravaganza with the evil Pin Cushion Man mass murdering the easily punctured inhabitants of Balloon Land. It is among the first use of Iwerks's multi-plane camera.

With this series, Iwerks' reputation will be restored, but the last two tapes in the series may confirm the status of the Van Beuren Studios. Headquartered in New York, the Van Beuren Studios had undergone profound changes at the beginning of the sound era. Paul Terry had left to form his own outfit, and in his place, the studio struggled to find a style and some starring characters.

At various times during their history, the cartoons resembled not only those made at the neighboring Fleischer Studios, but later the more polished Disney productions. *The Odd and the Outrageous* features examples of the early Van Beuren releases. *Piano Tooners* stars "Tom and Jerry," a tall and short duo of vaguely human characters who exhibit not a whit of personality. *Opening Night* features another unsuccessful Van Beuren attempt at a star character, "Cubby the Bear."

Taking a cue from the Fleischers, the Van Beuren Studio contracted with King Features to license one of the syndicate's comic strip characters. Inexplicably, for sound cartoons, they chose the almost dialogue-less *Little King* strip by Otto Soglow! *The Little King* short in this collection, *Christmas Day*, attempts to establish the King as both wistful and willful, not a very appealing characterization.

Two "cult" cartoons are featured on this tape: Ted Esbaugh's *The Sunshine Makers*, featuring the fight between the "Joys" and the "Glooms," and *Candy Town* with the bottle of castor oil chasing the cat couple who had just eaten way too much candy.

The later Van Beuren efforts are well represented by the final collection in the series, *The Van Beuren Rainbow Parades*. Burt Gillette, the director of Disney's *The Three Little Pigs*, was hired to change the look of the company's cartoons. Gillette's color cartoons, entitled "The Rainbow Parade," are an attempt to forge a new identity for the company, but ape the look of the popular Disney color shorts. This is perhaps the weakest tape of the series because the cartoons are largely disappointing.

The studio purchased the rights to produce cartoons based on Fontaine Fox's popular comic strip *The Toonerville Trolley*. Considering the highly individual style of Fox's writing and drawing (he was a stylist of the caliber of George Herriman, Cliff Sterritt and E.C. Segar), one is amazed at the fine job the studio did in translating the strip to celluloid. Two of the series are included.

Felix the Cat was already familiar with audiences who, along with Ko-Ko the Clown, were the two most popular cartoon stars of the silent era. The Van Beuren Studio revived the character in three color cartoons, two of which are in this collection. While *Bold King Cole* and *The Goose That Laid the Golden Eggs* are not poorly done, they just don't capture the character that had been established by Felix's creator and animator, Otto Messmer.

The efforts to establish their own cartoon star is summed up in the presentation on this tape of the Molly Moo Cow cartoons. Molly was a benign cow always helping out fellow animals in trouble, and perhaps is one of the least likely candidates for cartoon stardom one could imagine. Because these shorts were made after the enforcement of the Production Code, Molly could not be drawn with an udder! The horror!

This series is both a historically essential and greatly entertaining addition to any serious animation collection.

The Castle of Cagliostro 1980 (1992 video release)
Streamline Pictures 100 minutes

If your exposure to Japanese animation has consisted of either the high polish of Akira or the numbing repetition of any number of space operas, this 1980 Japanese animated feature will be a pleasant discovery. For once while watching an English translation of Japanese animation I didn't get the sense I was missing something!

The Castle of Cagliostro is the story of a master thief named Wolf who becomes involved with restoring the rightful heir to the throne of a tiny European nation named Cagliostro. Unlike most American animated features, which have plots that can be easily described in a few sentences, The Castle of Cagliostro doesn't. I certainly have never seen another animated feature before that artfully mixed a gentle parody of Sixties caper movies with a plot concerning a royal family who has been controlling the world's economy for generations by printing counterfeit cash!

Adventurous and funny, The Castle of Cagliostro is a film that kids will like, but won't bore an adult.

Cartoon Gate
Kino on Video

This compilation produced by animation director Greg Ford is a mixed bag of partisan animated political commercials and propaganda, one theatrical cartoon, and an overly long political satire. The result is a tape with some material well worth having in any animation collection, but also with plenty of opportunities to hit the fast forward button. The producer was obviously hobbled by having to use mostly material in the public domain.

Hell Bent for Election is undoubtedly the highlight of the collection. This 1944 color short was produced by a group of labor unions to encourage working people to elect Franklin D. Roosevelt to an unprecedented fourth term. The election battle is characterized as a race between a sleek streamlined train with FDR's famous profile and an old-fashioned locomotive belching smoke and oil with the year 1929 on its side.

The public is represented by a rail yard worker who is given instructions by his Uncle Sam to make sure the Win the War Special makes it into the station first.

Produced by UPA founder Steve Bosustow and directed by Chuck Jones, the short's design are highly similar to the flat designs that UPA would make famous in just another few years.

The amazing aspect of the cartoon is the level of vehemence the propaganda takes. In one scene, a character who is clearly a Republican Congressman is transformed into Hitler! For those of us who did not live through World War II, it's easy not to realize that there was considerable discussion in this country about the war, FDR's leadership, and many domestic labor issues. If nothing else seeing this cartoon might make some younger views scurry to the library to learn more about this time in American history.

A Political Cartoon, on the other hand, will just make them scurry away from the television sets. This long (almost 30 minutes) live-action/animated film is a drawn-out satire about a campaign manager engineering the election of a cartoon character to the White House. Written and directed by animation historian Joe Adamson, James Murrow, and Davis Stone, the crudely shot live-action footage isn't helped by some simplistic animation. The end scene, in which the political consultant turns to a puppet maker for his next candidate, underscores the message of the film with a heavy hand.

Ken Kimmelman's *Reaganocchio* is also fairly heavy-handed. Produced early in the Reagan presidency, the short uses Reagan sound bites to illustrate the gap between what Reagan was saying and what was actually happening.

Popeye for President is also included on this tape. The 1956 Famous Studio cartoon is a typical entry of the post-war *Popeye* shorts.

The tape also has several animated campaign commercials, new animation directed by Greg Ford, and a truly mind-boggling public service announcement from 1960 urging people to donate money to the party and candidate of their choice because "Your money is as important as your vote!"

Dinosaur Island
New Horizon Home Video

As long as *The Fantastic Four* gets a mention in *ANIMATO* [review follows] for its use of computer animation, I'd be remiss in not pointing out that low-budget old-fashioned stop-motion animation is alive and well in this direct-to-video release.

An affectionate send-up of those Fifties exploitation science-fiction films with guys getting marooned on lost islands inhabited by gorgeous cave women and extinct beasts, *Dinosaur Island* utilizes the dinosaur effects from *Carnosaur*, a man-in-a suit rig, a life-size prop dino and puppets. Unlike *Carnosaur*, though, there are several scenes with effective stop-motion work. The film has an effective cast including the lovely and talented Michelle Bauer.

Dinosaur Island is perhaps the best film either Fred Olen Ray and Jim Wynorski have made (the veteran filmmakers teamed up as co-producer and director on this production), and is an absolute perfect guilty pleasure for anyone who loves cheesy drive-in style movies and beautiful women.

The Fantastic Four

With its reliance on computer-animated special effects, *The Fantastic Four* deserves a mention here in *ANIMATO*. While *ANIMATO* does not encourage or condone video piracy, I have to admit that when a friend lent me a copy of the film, curiosity got the better of me.

This is the shelved Roger Corman co-production that supposedly will never receive any sort of official release as Steven Spielberg has bought the rights to the comic book characters for his own version. Along with *Carnosaur*, *The Fantastic Four* marked a new era with Corman producing more expensive films that would have limited theatrical releases and wide video releases.

Well, Corman and company are having the last laugh, as a bootleg tape of this film is readily available at comic book conventions. Fans will get to see the movie, although under less-than-ideal circumstances.

It's a shame, too, to see this film in the format of an umpteenth generation dub as it's perhaps the most successful production to date in translating Marvel Comic characters to the screen. Unlike the genuinely awful Captain America movie, this film actually stays largely faithful to the origin story of the FF, and attempts, within its limited budget, to bring the fantasy and science elements of the comic book to life.

The film sets up the origin of the FF and its chief nemesis, Dr. Doom. While there are very effective moments, including the friendship of Reed

Richards and Ben Grimm, and a touching earnestness with the tentative romance between Reed and Sue Storm, the film's story has just too many holes. The script relies too heavily on the assumed knowledge of the audience. For instance: how does Reed Richards finance his rocket experiments? How does Alicia Masters fall in love with Ben Grimm? How did the FF get back to the United States from Dr. Doom's castle? What country is Dr. Doom leading? When is this film set? Why don't their costumes tear up or catch on flame? These are questions that are never answered by the film

Also, the subplot involving the secondary villain, The Jeweler, is never really explained properly. Who is this guy? If he's so busy successfully robbing jewels, why does he live in squalor? The tone of the film reminds me somewhat of the *Superman* movies. At times, it's sincere, but also there are comic relief moments, which seem sort of out-of-place.

On the plus side, the film has a good look in costume, set, and make-up design, and has a very able cast. Ask any actor who's ever been in tights just how difficult it is to avoid looking ridiculous when bounding around a set being heroic. Fortunately, Alex Hyde-White as Reed Richards pulls it off well, as does the rest of the cast.

The special effects are . . . well . . . sort of cheap looking. The Thing suit is on the money, and the Invisible Girl gets invisible well enough, but Mr. Fantastic, well, there's a big problem. What was required was a complex morphing effect like *Terminator 2*. Unfortunately, the production had to use various prosthesis effects which look hokey, and a couple of instances of computer animation that look acceptable on this blurry dub. How they would have looked on the big screen is a guess.

The Human Torch's big moment when he flames on entirely and flies are handled completely with computer animation, which had a similar character design to that of *Lawnmower Man*. The effect just doesn't look real enough. The scenes in which Johnny flames on just his arm to shoot fireballs are much better.

I had the chance of talking with Alex Hyde-White at the Video Software Distributors Association show in July [1994], and he expressed regret that the film will not, in the immediate future, see release. He believed the production team had done the best job they could have with the budget they had, and that the film could have had a chance at some of the *Ace Ventura* money. In other words, that the target audience for the film (young teenagers, families), would have been the same. The film would have been undoubtedly rated PG-13.

For more on this film, log onto http://www.teako170.com/ffmovie. html.

Felix!
Black and white and color; 60 minutes; Milestone Film & Video #MILE022; $39.95
Presenting Felix the Cat, Volumes One and Two
Bosko Video; $29.95

Thanks to animation historian and animator John Canemaker, the reputation of Felix the Cat and his principal creator, Otto Messmer, had been academically established in a fine book and a series of articles. Now, however, thanks to Bosko Video and Milestone Video, animation fans will be able to see what only Canemaker and other animation historians with archival access have been raving about.

It's ironic that within a period of just a few months there has been greater fan access to the silent Felix the Cat shorts than in the last ten years. With the release of the recent Milestone Felix compilation and now the release of two volumes of Felix cartoons for Bosko Video (with several more volumes promised to follow), animation buffs will be able to evaluate the cartoons that have been described as the most popular of the silent era.

The new tape from Milestone boasts of five silent shorts, one early talkie, and some late-in-life footage of Messmer working on what we can assume is some sort of animation project. The print quality is quite good (with source material from the Cinematheque Quebecoise), and the musical score is adequate.

If pressed to admit, though, which collection I enjoyed more, I'd have to say the Bosko collection is superior to the Milestone tape. That is not to say the Milestone tape is not impressive. There are only two cartoons that are featured on both the Milestone and Bosko collections, so owning both is not a hardship.

The advantage the Bosko tape has is several-fold. The cartoons have been slightly window-boxed to preserve their original ratio, and the new score by organist Dave Wickersham is magnificent. His work on a vintage pipe organ lends an appreciated feeling of being back in the Twenties enjoying these shorts in a movie palace. The soundtrack was recorded in digital stereo for optimum effect. The quality of the prints ranges from good to excellent.

For me, though, the real plus is the presentation of the first Paramount Screen Magazine from 1919 that introduced Felix. While the Milestone tape also included this cartoon, Dave Butler of Bosko Video gives us the *entire* animation segment of the short subject, meaning we get several other cartoons as well, including an Earl Hurd *Bobby Bumps* cartoon. This is the kind of fascinating historical presentation that distinguishes the Bosko's (and other small companies') releases from the animation tapes produced by larger companies.

If your vision of Felix is the Joe Oriolo-produced shorts of the early Sixties, well, you're in for a bit of a shock. Don't expect to see Poindexter, the Professor or Rock Bottom on the Bosko tapes. And say goodbye to the Magic Bag.

This Felix is a city-wise alley cat whose adventures blend a feline characterization with the more surreal possibilities of the animated cartoon. Felix is independent. He doesn't have a re-occurring owner (not at least on these two tapes), but that doesn't mean he's against helping people out with their problems. In the best cartoon tradition, his tail is detachable, and can be used for a variety of purposes.

The conventional wisdom about Felix has been that he was the most popular cartoon star of the Twenties, the only one with a personality, and the funniest animated star. I don't ever try to argue with issues of popularity (for instance, I still don't understand what made Mickey Mouse so appealing), but I don't agree with the critical assessment that Felix was the only silent cartoon star with a personality or the best-defined personality. Nor can I say having viewed these three collections that the Felix shorts were the funniest.

The animation directed by Otto Messmer is smooth and accomplished.

If Pat Sullivan was Felix's biological father, then Messmer was the adoptive dad who actually raised him. The success of the Felix series can be directly attributed to Messmer's skills as an animator. Apparently, Messmer didn't care to use close-up shots very much, and didn't vary perspective often. Most of the action in his cartoons is seen in a medium or long shot.

Despite this moderately stodgy approach, many of the Felix shorts are enjoyable, and Felix does have a recognizable personality. Felix is a loner whose slumped head walk, whenever pondering a subject, became his trademark. His personality is an interesting contrast to the other widely popular cartoon character of the Twenties, Max Fleischer's Ko-Ko the Clown. Felix was the street-smart cat trying to survive, and Ko-Ko was the Peck's Bad Boy, an innocent who got into trouble with his boss, Max Fleischer, because of his own curiosity about the real world.

While not as technically inventive as the Ko-Ko shorts, the Felix cartoons are fun to watch, are sometimes quite funny, and are never as tedious as other silent cartoons, such as Paul Terry's *Farmer Alfalfa* series.

Under the heavy hand of Pat Sullivan, Felix did not make the transition to sound with much grace. A handful of crudely done sound shorts were produced in 1930, but they apparently made too little impact to counter the nation's fancy with Walt Disney's Mickey Mouse. A nicely produced series of color cartoons starring Felix from Van Beuren also failed to rekindle Felix mania. Felix remained a fixture in the nation's comic pages for years afterwards, though, and is back in comic books thanks to Joe Oriolo's son, Don.

I can only wish that Bosko does for Ko-Ko what the company has done for Felix. If you're a fan of silent animation, then do yourself a favor, and get these two tapes from Bosko. They're essential viewing.

FernGully 2: The Magical Rescue
20th Century-Fox Home Video

I've always thought that *FernGully* was an under-appreciated animated feature. With its vivid color design and ecological message, *FernGully* was certainly a different, and welcomed, direction in theatrical animation. Now comes *FernGully 2: The Magical Rescue*, and while this direct-to-video feature is not as successful as the first, children should find this sequel very entertaining.

FernGully 2 tells the story of the rain forest fairies rescuing a group of baby animals taken by a pair of poachers intent on selling them to overseas markets. Naturally, this means the fairies must come in contact with the human world which turns out to be just as dangerous as the mean-spirited hunters.

While the original film was aimed at both a youthful and adult audience, the sequel is definitely a movie for kids. The ecological themes are muted in this production and are replaced with a more standard animal-in-peril storyline. Of course to make this theme more frightening for children, the animals are *babies*, an obvious calculated move on the part of the filmmakers.

The filmmakers make a real mistake at the beginning of the movie. There is no real set-up for the story. The filmmakers assume their audience knows all about FernGully and the fairies and their fairies' role in maintaining the health of the rainforest. Once, however, the film gets rolling, it tells its story quite well.

Perhaps the most remarkable thing is that *FernGully 2* reportedly only had a budget of $3 million. It is a handsome-looking film with nice backgrounds and very respectable animation. Produced in San Francisco by Wild Brain, Inc., *FernGully 2* shows much feature potential for this studio that has made some great commercials.

Follow The Bouncing Ball Volume One; 82 minutes; Follow The Bouncing Ball Volume Two; 80 minutes; $29.95 each; Bosko Video

It's difficult to imagine that today's audiences would actually feel enough of a community spirit while in their nearest shopping mall multi-plex to join in with their neighbor in singing a song, but the new video releases from Dave Butler's Bosko Video takes you back to a time when people actually did just that.

Follow the Bouncing Ball Volumes One and Two re-introduces audiences to a long-running cartoon series produced by the Fleischer Studio. Although part of the old U.M. &M syndication package and once a programming staple of local television stations, the *Screen Song* cartoons haven't been released by Republic Home Video as the Betty Boop cartoons have. Butler sought out those *Screen Songs* that were in the public domain, and then found collectors who had prints. The results are two collections that will be of great interest to fans of the Fleischer Studio and classic 1930s animation. The print quality varies from fair to very good, and the video transfer is excellent with moderate window-boxing to insure a complete image.

The Fleischer Studio started the *Screen Songs* series in 1925. They were an out-growth of a common feature found in many movie houses at the time, a sing-along with glass slides with the lyrics of a popular song projected onto the screen. The theater's orchestra, organist or pianist would provide the music for the number.

The Fleischers hit upon a technique that would allow them to direct an audience to sing along . . . a bouncing ball that would establish the beat and tell people what words they should be singing. Rather than animate the ball, the Fleischers glued a ping-pong ball at the end of a dowel and painted the dowel black. The lyrics would be printed in white ink on black paper and mounted on a black circular drum. A cameraman would photograph one of the Fleischer staffers bouncing the ball over the printed lyrics and moving the drum to advance the next line.

There was plenty of animation in the silent *Screen Songs* (which were originally called *Ko-Ko Song Car-Tunes*), by the way, although the format of the cartoon allowed for greater repetition. Between the non-animated ball and the repeating scenes, these cartoons were less expensive to make than the studio's Ko-Ko shorts.

Despite their economy, the silent *Screen Songs* were a big hit with audiences and exhibitors. Their secret was featuring popular songs such as "By the Light of the Silvery Moon" and "Has Anyone Here Seen Kelly?" which people undoubtedly sung in their homes. It's easy to forget that having a musical instrument in a home, such as piano, was something far more common 60 years ago than today, and that playing and singing the popular songs of the day was as common as listening to one's CD player today.

The *Screen Songs* were the first cartoons that had sound-on-film synchronized soundtracks. Years before Disney's first experiment with sound, Max Fleischer collaborated with Dr. Lee DeForrest, the inventor of the vacuum tube and the developer of a sound process for motion pictures. Fleischer and DeForrest made several *Screen Songs* that were released with soundtrack for those theaters adventurous enough to be wired for DeForrest's system. Naturally, they were also released in silent versions.

While DeForrest proved himself to be ahead of his time, and was forced to discontinue his motion picture production, Fleischer's *Screen Songs* became a popular release from the studio that endured through 1937. The series underwent several changes in format as the two tapes attest.

Volume One presents 11 *Screen Songs* with the earliest, *Margie*, dating back to 1925, and presented with its DeForrest soundtrack. Shorter than the Ko-Kos, the silent *Screen Songs* were designed to highlight the song and little else. They not only featured the Bouncing Ball highlighting the lyrics, but also an animated segment with a cartoon character bouncing along the top the words. This segment was usually repeated twice, and oftentimes featured clever visual puns.

With the coming sound, the *Screen Songs* became little musicals with the song integrated into the action of an animated story. *In the Good Old Summertime* (1930), *In the Shade of the Old Apple Tree* (1930), *La Paloma* (1931), *In My Merry Oldsmobile* (1931) and *I Wonder Who's Kissing Her Now* (1932) all show this transitional stage. Like many early Fleischer talkies the studio's distinctive look hadn't quite yet gelled, although the pre-Production Code sensibilities certainly manifested themselves. *In the Shade of the Old Apple Tree* had the first and only breastfeeding gag I've seen in a cartoon, and a joke in which a character touches a woman's breast! *In My Merry Oldsmobile* (which was actually an advertising short commissioned by the Oldsmobile people), there's noticeable cleavage, peeping toms, and implied sexual assault.

For me, the height of the *Screen Song* came in its next incarnation. The Fleischer Studio took advantage of its ties to Paramount Pictures and its New York location, and featured notable radio, Broadway and recording stars in live-action performances in their *Screen Songs*. Any fan of the popular music of the 1930s would love these cartoons for their presentation of these vintage artists.

These later *Screen Songs* tried to tie in the song and the artists themselves into the animated framing story. Sometimes the tie-ins were logical and sometimes they were oblique to say the least, but that was part of the fun. *When It's Sleepy Time Down South* (1932) featured the Boswell Sisters, the act after which the better-known Andrews Sisters patterned themselves. *Ain't She Sweet* (1933) featured an absolutely hyper Lillian Roth. The prize on this tape, though, is *Dinah* (1933) performed by the Mills Brothers. The popular quartet performed not only the title song, but also the cartoon's entire musical track.

I have to admit I enjoyed *Volume One* much better than *Volume Two* because out of the eleven cartoons on the second tape four of them are without their song! Dave Butler said that one of the sources for his prints had edited the songs out because he was more interested in the animation than the music. This is regrettable, but until Republic Home Video puts out their own volume, this is the best representation of the *Screen Songs* available for fans.

This tape, though, really should be subtitled "The Best of Whiffle Piffle." Who or what was Whiffle Piffle? The character was developed as a supporting character in the Betty Boop series in the mid-Thirties, and can best be described as a case in which the parts are greater than the sum. A grotesque design, a wonderfully funny walk and a neat voice supplied by Jack Mercer were all part of Whiffle Piffle, but a personality wasn't part of the package. I do enjoy him, though, as a sort of guilty pleasure, and this tape has five Whiffle Piffle shorts.

Volume Two shows the last stage of the *Screen Song* in which there was far less of an effort to integrate the live-action performer into the story, and far less an attempt at a story. The *Screen Songs* began relying on a framework for spot gags. For instance, in this collection there are three shorts which feature take-offs on newsreels. The song is merely another feature on the cartoon screen. It's clear the series was running out of steam.

Among the highlights on *Volume Two* are *Reaching For the Moon* (1933), with the popular radio performer Arthur Tracy, and *This Little Piggy Went to Market* with another radio favorite, Singing Sam. And, of course, Whiffle Piffle.

General Chaos: Uncensored Animation
Manga Home Video
Now in theatrical release

Manga Home Entertainment's entry in the touring animation festival field is a very mixed bag. The good news is the outstanding material greatly outweighs the mediocre.

Any collection which features the hilarious Bill Plympton's *Sex and Violence* short, the mind-boggling *The Saint Inspector* by Mike Booth, the sick, sick, sick *Oh Julie*, and the very creepy *Donor Party* is well worth my time.

Unfortunately, there are some real dead spots in the collection. *Junky*, concerning a parrot with a cracker addiction, is quite tedious, as is *Body Directions*. Why do I have to sit through old material such as *Performance Art: Starring Chainsaw Bob* and *Mutilator*?

There are a couple of gag shorts that succeed; the funniest being *Beat the Meatles*. I loved the animation on *Killing Heinz*, but the punch line was a let down as was the case in *Looks Can Kill*.

The worst film was the inexplicable *The Hungry Hungry Nipples*. Oh, I guess these kids today get the "in" material that just goes over the head of the Animation Geezer, but after repeated viewings I still don't get it.

In any case, I look forward to the next edition of *General Chaos*.

Golden Boy 5
A.D.V. Films
30 minutes
Red blooded teenage boy fantasy sex
Subtitled

Here is indeed a very guilty pleasure for any man who has ever had fantasies about great looking women who wear skin-tight-leather outfits while cruising around the countryside on their souped-up motorcycles. Our hero Kintaro is a young man who bicycles around Japan, taking what jobs he can find while learning about life. While employed as part of the house staff at the estate of a wealthy family, he becomes hopelessly infatuated with the rich man's daughter. Little does he realize until he follows her to a secret garage that this prim and proper woman is actually the buxom raven-haired motorcycle rider with whom he had a chance encounter. It seems that Reiko has contempt for all men and is literally in love with her bike (proving it in front of our hero). She agrees, though, that she will sleep with Kintaro if he can beat her in a race: his bicycle against her motorcycle. Funny and sexy, this is one "adult" anime that didn't leave me wondering just what the hell it was all about. The race was particularly well animated.

History of Animation, 55 minutes
Willis O'Brien Primitives, 60 minutes
Attack of the Cohl Pumpkins, 60 minutes
Available from A-1 Video, P.O. Box 8808, Michigan City, IN, 46360
All are $15

A-1 Video is an independent video company, and its specialty is early silent cinema. The source material for the company's tape includes both 8mm and 16mm prints of public domain subjects. If you're interested in silent Laurel and Hardy, Mack Sennett, Hal Roach comedies or pre-World War I Griffith films, A-1 is one of the few companies which regularly present this kind of film. For the fantasy fan, A-1 also carries three collections of Georges Meliés films, and a volume of trick films from the Pathé Freres. Animation fans can witness the birth of the medium through three tapes, *History of Animation, Willis O'Brien Primitives,* and *Attack of the Cohl Pumpkins.* The first tape features some of the films by J. Stuart Blackton, including one of the first animated films, *Humorous Phases of Funny Faces.* After watching this tape, one realizes that so much of the techniques of animation were discovered very early in the development of motion pictures.

The *Willis O'Brien Primitives* is a collection of the animated shorts O'Brien did at the Edison Studio. Some stop-motion fans might be disappointed to learn that these films are fairly standard slapstick outings with most of the footage dedicated to animated cave people, instead of the dinosaurs! The animation is amazingly smooth in many sequences, though, and the model work, although certainly primitive, is ingenious. The tape ends with a very odd sound short which uses silent footage from *The Lost World.*

The early work of Emile Cohl, another animation pioneer, is featured on the third tape, although most of the tape is actually a collection of some of the very first motion pictures produced by the Lumiére Brothers before the turn of the century. Cohl worked both in stop motion and in cartoon techniques, and his films have a wit and style which is not expected at this early point in the medium's development. Be aware that on this tape, some of the Cohl films have their original French inter-titles.

Of course, the question on all of these tapes is the quality of the source material. I'm not the sort of person who enjoys squinting at a 16th-generation copy of something, but I certainly found the quality acceptable. One should keep in mind that many of these films were taken from their paper prints at the Library of Congress, or transferred from 16mm copies made from the original nitrate.

All in all, these three tapes represent a fascinating look at animation's beginnings.

The Incredible 1930s Van Beuren Cartoons Volume Four: The Rainbow Parades #1
70 minutes; color; $29.95; Bosko Video

The trials and tribulations of the Van Beuren Studios have been documented in past reviews, and this collection from Bosko Video features some cartoons that were included in the Kino On Video *Cartoons That Time Forgot* series. Again, the print quality varies from fair to good, while the video transfer is top notch. The image is window-boxed.

The cartoons of the Van Beuren Studios are an acquired taste. While their contemporaries at Disney, Fleischer, and Iwerks definitely had recognizable styles, the animators at Van Beuren never seemed to successfully find their niche. The nine cartoons on this tape are a decent sampling of the best of the Van Beuren output in its last years. Of the nine cartoons on this tape, there are four that are new to home video, and they are excellent examples of campy 1930s animation.

The *Rainbow Parade* series was the Van Beuren effort to compete with the Disney *Silly Symphonies*. Several of the productions on this tape are not in Technicolor, but rather in the red and blue process known as Cinecolor. These Cinecolor shorts are indeed rare, and, despite the limitations of that color process, the shorts are, for the most part, enjoyable.

A word to the wise, though, if you're diabetic, you might want to avoid a coma and fast-forward through the two Molly Moo Cow shorts. I didn't think anyone could make a more cloying cartoon than Disney until I saw these!

Joe's Apartment

Viacom, the media giant, which owns almost everything not included in the Time-Warner/Ted Turner merger, has decreed that its lucrative cable TV arms should produce theatrical motion pictures bearing the logos of Nickelodeon and MTV. On paper, the move seems to make sense; capitalize on the millions of moviegoers who also happen to watch both cable networks. After all, videos of MTV and Nick shows and spin-offs have done well enough and the Nick toy line is a success. Movies seem logical.

So this summer we've seen the first Nick movie, *Harriet the Spy*, which has done mediocre business. It undoubtedly will do great on home video where anything rated G is snapped up by anxious parents.

The MTV debut movie sunk like a stone at theaters, though. *Joe's Apartment* was based on clever short films featuring animated cockroaches seen on MTV, and to green light a feature-length film based on these gloried station i.d. bumpers was a gutsy one.

After all, if MTV had wanted to insure some great box-office, a 90-minute film of Jenny McCarthy playing beach volleyball or grocery shopping or doing her laundry, would probably have fit the bill.

I admire their decision because making an urban comic love story featuring talking cockroaches took true moxie. Making a film about Jenny McCarthy would have been the easy way, but it wouldn't have been the Cowboy Way!

Still, someone in the marketing department or research and development must have realized the awful truth. No matter how clever, witty or hip the finished film might be, it is still about . . . roaches. And not those roaches that people light up while watching MTV, either.

Hey, ants are hard-working; ladybugs have got families; crickets can be good luck; grasshoppers and katydids sing . . . cockroaches spread disease. People don't like cockroaches. They are not a cute kind of bug, and with the exception of Don Marquis' "Archy and Mehitabel" stories and poems, cockroaches have never been the objects of affection.

So, roll the dice and make a film about a farm boy from Iowa who moves to New York and who lucks onto an incredibly dirty, but rent-controlled, apartment only to find that his new best friends are the 20,000 singing, talking, dancing roaches in his place. The film's humor and funky charm will disarm the natural aversion to roaches and the fledging MTV will attract millions.

Well, not quite.

Joe's Apartment didn't deserve its fate. A well-made romantic comedy, it tries to translate the hip MTV atmosphere to a feature-length narrative. Rather than make a movie about music (probably a wise move considering how quickly musical tastes can change), the network made a feature which sums up its attitude.

Wise guy and film producer David Friedman once said that you sell the sizzle, not the steak. In this case, the MTV attitude is both the steak and the sizzle, and it works for *Joe's Apartment*.

Joe's Apartment serves up one disgusting vision of New York City that begins with a roaches' eye view of the city. As the singing roaches fly through the New York skyline, you can't miss the filmmaker's point . . . viewed from the right distance all of us resemble tiny scurrying insects. (Hmmm, I wonder if this is also a homage to *Mr. Bug Goes to Town?*)

Jerry O'Connell plays our hero with naive sincerity. He suffers through many hardships only to land an apartment in a doomed building. He doesn't mind the mess he's inherited and is a slob of the first water himself. When he unwittingly provides food for the roaches that expect instead to be killed, he's made thousands of friends without knowing it.

The film is very clever in setting up a roach society (they even have their own television show), and a roach philosophy (they don't understand the concept or need for privacy). They are loyal romantics who'd make excellent friends, except they are roaches!

The use of stop-motion animation, computer-generated animation, and real roaches (that's the point at which my wife decided she couldn't see the film) creates a seamless illusion that makes this must viewing for animation fans.

Put aside your petty prejudices and fears, and see *Joe's Apartment* when it makes its way to video.

Journey to the Beginning of Time
Goodtimes Home Video

This sell-through offering from Goodtimes Home Video (regrettably recorded in the LP speed) is the only easily accessible film for American audiences by the talented and prolific Czech animator and director Karel Zeman. Zeman, who will be the subject of a more in-depth article in an upcoming issue of *Animation Planet*, made a number of animated and live-action features from the mid-Fifties to the late Sixties. Although some of his films did see American theatrical release and some have been offered on home video, Zeman's work hasn't received the attention it so richly deserves.

Unlike other filmmakers who would use one form of animation for their production, Zeman combined a variety of animation techniques within a single film. Zeman combined cel animation with stop-motion model and paper cut-outs in order to get the effect he needed. His films, particularly his version of the Baron Munchausen legend and *The Mysterious World of Jules Verne,* are visually arresting.

Journey, however, is not pure Zeman. American producer William Cayton bought the rights to Zeman's 1954 film about a group of four boys who are literally rowing up a river through time and witnessing evolution. Cayton hired Fred Ladd to film a prologue that takes place in New York City, which has the four boys visiting the American Museum of Natural History and then hiring a rowboat in Central Park. Once they row into a mysterious cave, they begin to go back through time.

If the old *Boys' Life* Magazine had ever financed a movie, I imagine it would have looked a lot like this one. *Journey* is educational and imaginative, and it boasts the four most prepared, unflappable, dedicated young explorers ever to have been accidentally propelled back through time. No hysterics for these guys! For a rowing trip through Central Park, these kids come prepared with a complete camping rig. I'm not sure that was Zeman's original introduction, but the American version's set-up is unintentionally comical.

Once the viewer gets past the first act, Zeman's vision takes over. Zeman used stop-motion animation, plus ingenious hand puppets and cel animation to achieve his various prehistoric beasts. The final sequence of the film, at which the boys approach the literal creation of the world, seems to be tacked-on as its over-lapping colored light effects with a somber narration about God, doesn't match the style or tone of Zeman's footage.

The print used for the tape has some noticeable scratches, but is acceptable. Despite its adulterated form, *Journey* is a film that should interest any stop-motion fan.

The Library of Congress Video Collection
Volume Three: Origins of American Animation
ISBN 1-56098-479-1; 84 minutes

This collection of 21 complete films (and two fragments) is a serious examination of the beginnings of animation in this country. Beginning with J. Stuart Blackton's *The Enchanted Drawing* (1900) and ending with *Tony Sarg's Almanac: The First Circus* (1921), this collection affords the serious animation fan the opportunity of seeing some of the early productions one has read about for years.

Here are examples of Earl Hurd *Bobby Bumps* series, the Hearst/International Film Service adaptations of King Features comic strips, noted live-action director Gregory LaCava animation work, and stop-motion work by Willis O'Brien. There are completely obscure films such as Howard Moss' *Mary and Gretel*, which evidently was part of a stop-motion series from 1917. The tape comes with an informative booklet about the collection.

Those viewers who are expecting laughs will be sorely disappointed by this collection. The humor and animation in many of these films is indeed crude and predictable. If you watch this tape hoping to learn about how animation developed in this country, you will enjoy it.

I suppose my only real complaint is that some of the selections border on being animation esoterica, and I think the early work of people such as Paul Terry and Max Fleischer should have been included.

The print quality is uniformly good, and the transfer is excellent, although I would have preferred seeing the image window-boxed. This collection is a solid addition to any serious animation collection.

The Lost World
Animation Legend Winsor McCay
The Cameraman's Revenge
Milestone Video

I'm not sure what is worse for a film buff . . . reading glowing descriptions about films they can't see outside of an archive or paying for the right to develop eyestrain by attempting to watch scratchy, dupey prints or muddied video tapes. In animation, there have been certain titles that have been apparently doomed to these two situations. Long ago, I wanted to see bright, sharp prints of the Winsor McCay films, and I certainly wanted to see a complete version of Willis O'Brien's *The Lost World*.

Now, after plodding through innumerable bad tapes of these productions, we can see the definitive video editions. Milestone Film and Video has released not only *Animation Legend: Winsor McCay* and *The Lost World*, but also a collection of films by pioneer model animator Wladislaw Starewicz entitled *The Cameraman's Revenge and Other Fantastic Tales*. These tapes will be available beginning Dec. 1, 1993, and will retail for $39.95.

In an era of low-budget cartoon shock animation and high budget state-of-the-art computer-generated puppet animation, one might wonder if animation fans who are not already familiar with these works will give them a chance. After all, will an unsuspecting viewer be tempted to journey to *The Lost World*, when he or she has already been to *Jurassic Park*?

Technically, Willis O'Brien's 1925 adaptation of Arthur Conan Doyle's scientific romance is certainly primitive when compared with Spielberg's film. I'd hazard a guess, though, that without O'Brien's film, there wouldn't have been a *Jurassic Park*. What I like most about the film is its sense of wonder. In an era when species of animals were still being discovered and considerable parts of the world were still relatively unexplored, the magic of *The Lost World* is its "what if?" quality.

Thankfully, that attribute has not diminished with age, and still is very appealing to those of us who are armchair explorers. Long a subject for the public domain tape producers, *The Lost World* is presented here in its most complete version. Professor Challenger's beloved Brontosaurus never before looked this good on videotape.

Most existing versions of the film are based on the 16mm Kodascope prints abridged for the home market in the Thirties. The original film was quite a bit longer and contained information that fleshed out the characterizations and several plot points. Film historian Scott MacQueen was responsible for this tape, which originally saw release as a LumiVision Laserdisc. MacQueen used footage from a number of archives to construct the most complete and best possible pictorial quality restoration. The film is also carefully tinted as it would have been in its original release.

At the end of the film, MacQueen constructs the missing footage through stills and dialogue from the original inter-titles. Here, we see how the producers of the Kodascope print eliminated several key plot points, and shortened the expedition's journey through the Amazon rain forest to the Lost World.

The character of Professor Challenger was definitely altered by the shortened version. With the additional footage, Challenger just doesn't appear as a single-minded eccentric academic, but rather as a somewhat sinister figure. Film historians have long thought the Kodascope version lacked a dinosaur sequence. While I can't imagine why anyone would cut the very footage which makes the film so unique, nevertheless, MacQueen includes a description of the Brontosaurus poking his head through the window of a men's club, and disrupting a card game. How much of this scene was animated and how much involved the use of a full-scale Bronto head and neck model is not known. No stills apparently exist from the scene, although MacQueen did find a clipping from a magazine describing the scene with an illustration of stagehands holding a full-scale model.

Animation Legend: Winsor McCay (produced in association with Lumi-Vision McCay's collection) not only includes a wonderful print of *Gertie the Dinosaur*, but also the unfinished sequel is the only collection of McCay's films worth owning.

For the first time on video that I've ever seen, not only are McCay's complete films featured, but his uncompleted projects as well. Using both 16mm and 35mm sources, this collection shows just how tremendous an animator this legendary comic strip artist really was. It's been too easy for many animation fans to watch *Gertie the Dinosaur* and give McCay lip service as being a great animator. Now thanks to this collection, I think a lot of people will truly discover an animator whose contribution to the field is practically indescribable.

McCay never tried to maintain a production schedule such as his pioneering contemporary Emile Cohl. Animation was definitely a sideline for him. His lack of total commercial dedication to animation, though, didn't prevent him from setting high artistic standards for the industry, and establishing the idea that animation could be used for everything from serious subjects such as his *The Sinking of the Lusitania* to situation comedy (*The Flying House*).

The highpoints of this tape for me has to be the opportunity of seeing McCay's unfinished films, *Gertie on Tour, Flip's Circus,* and *The Centaurs.* The *Gertie* footage has the same charm as the original, while *The Centaurs* has a wistful sentimentality.

While the animation on *Flip's Circus* is fascinating, one can't help but wonder just where McCay was going with the narrative. McCay's weak points as an animator were his story sense and his timing. Too often, movements are repeated to the point of diminishing their effect. *Bug Vaudeville* and *The Flying House* are the worst examples of this problem.

For many animation fans the real discovery of these three tapes will be *The Cameraman's Revenge and Other Fantastic Tales.* Wladislaw Starewicz, who first began his animation work in his native Russia before the fall of the Czar, is a true animation pioneer who has been unfairly overlooked.

The first film on this tape, *The Cameraman's Revenge,* is a slightly sordid, but funny, tale of marital infidelity and revenge with animated insects. Starewicz used real insect bodies as his animation figures, and got some hideously life-like results.

Starewicz immigrated to France after the Russian revolution, and continued his filmmaking career there. Another silent offering on this tape is *The Song of the Nightingale,* a beautifully sentimental story of a little girl and a nightingale that masterfully mixes live action and animation. To top off the film, the entire short is hand tinted with a precision that is truly astonishing.

His best-known film, though, is *The Mascot,* a 20-minute short which rose to a certain prominence among modern audiences in the early Eighties when an excerpt of the short received repeated airplay over the cable *Night Flight* program and through exposure on various public domain videotapes.

This print of *The Mascot* is one of the best I've seen, and is complete. *The Mascot* tells a story of love and devotion. A poor Parisian doll maker struggles to make a living to support her daughter. While making a puppy doll, her tears fall into the stuffing, and the puppy comes to life. The daughter would like an orange, and the puppy decides to get her one.

His experiences make up the rest of the film, and while the first half is conventionally sentimental, the second is genuinely surreal. Many people may be familiar with the second half of the film as it is the part that has been excerpted under titles such as "The Devil's Party." With really no reason, our puppy hero finds himself at a party presided over by a doll in the shape of a devil. At the party, walking, talking vegetables, other dolls, and toys, try to pick each other up in a sequence with a strong sexual atmosphere. It's easy to think the filmmaker had two ideas that he wanted to combine.

The Mascot may be very odd, but it's visually fascinating and a film not easily forgotten. Beautifully transferred and accompanied with new effective musical scores, these three Milestone tapes are important additions to any serious animation library.

My Neighbor Totoro
Fox Video; #4276; 87 minutes

At long last, this Hayao Miyazaki production has come to the video market legally. One of several Japanese animated productions, which have been staples of the bootleggers' tables at conventions, *Totoro* is finally being seen in a gorgeous video presentation. The transfer preserves Miyazaki's photorealistic backgrounds and intricate colors.

For those animation fans that are used to anime, *Totoro* will be a bit of a shock. Just because it's Japanese, don't expect to see any outer space princesses, nudity or gore. Also, unlike anime, which is often very plot-heavy, *Totoro* is a movie that the viewer slowly, but surely gets inside a story that has genuine sentiment. This is not a movie with a plot that can be summed up in a few sentences, nor is it a manipulative tearjerker.

Totoro tell the story of a university professor who moves his two young daughters to a house in rural Japan. His wife is ill and staying in a hospital. While some of the children in the area say their house is haunted, the sisters see their new home as a place of magic; some real, like the soot spirits, and some imagined.

The magic intensifies when the youngest girl discovers the Totoros, mystical cat-like creatures who live in the woods near their home. Only children can see them (and only *some* children).

Now, if this was an American film, there would have to be a big conflict and resolution, and undoubtedly, the screenwriters would tie the Totoros into healing the sick mother. Well, thankfully, Miyazaki isn't interested in telling that kind of story. This film has a wonderful open-ended air about it, and it that makes you feel that you've heard one story from someone's childhood and you expect to hear another in the future.

The animation, though more limited in technique than current Disney theatrical animation, is still quite good, and is superior to most of the anime animation I've seen.

Record of Lodoss War
Tape 1; U.S. Manga Corps

This 1990 made-for-television anime production is a re-packaging of classic sword and sorcery elements; a group of unlikely heroes is headed off on a quest to fight the evil that threatens their home. We have Parn, who is determined to set right again his father's reputation as a knight; Deedlit, a female elf who is not only an experienced fighter, but is the love interest for Parn; Ghim, a battle-hardened dwarf; Etoh, a young priest who is in awe of Slayn, a more experienced magician; and finally the required voice of cynicism and all-around wise guy, Woodchuck, a thief Parn saves from prison.

What makes these tired old ingredients produce something fresh and involving is the engaging characterizations, the more-than-competent animation, and the sense the filmmakers truly wants to create an epic saga. There seems to be a respect for the material and for the audience, and even potentially clichéd situations are handled in a way that avoids the pitfalls of stereotypes. Even more refreshing is that most members of the family can watch *Record of Lodoss War*. There is a minimum of bloodshed and no sexually explicit material.

The dubbing is quite acceptable and three installments are presented in the 75-minute tape. There is also a short documentary on the making of the series.

ReiRei
Missionary of Love
A.D.V. Films
60 minutes
Sex, sex, and more sex; hypnotic goddess breasts
Dubbed

Oooooph! This is another one of those "erotic" anime productions in which the lead character is able to solve people's emotional problems through various sex acts. Kaguya is some sort of goddess of love who wants to heal the world through boffing. Aided by her troll manservant Pipi ("My lady! Don't leave without your Pipi!"), Kaguya drops her top, takes the afflicted person into some other dimensions, gets sweaty with them, and solves everyone's problems. Naturally, this all supposed to be erotic and funny.

Two episodes are on this tape. The first involves a girl who has a crush on her female doctor who in turn wants to end the relationship by killing her (funny stuff here!). The second has the goddess helping what appears to be a seventh grader get over his fear of women and get some sweet, sweet junior high loving.

Unremarkable crap.

Rock-A-Doodle
1992, HBO Home Video, $24.95

What the hell is this film about? Don Bluth's latest effort continues his artistic tradition of being an ex-Disney employee who apes much of the style of his former studio in his work. If nothing else this is Bluth's version of a *Silly Symphony*.

There's something of a plot about a bunch of barnyard animals (who all wear clothes) needing the services of their rooster to make the sun rise because if he doesn't make the sun rise the evil giant magical Duke of Owls (who hates the light) will eat everyone.

Got that?!

The rooster left the farm after being tricked into thinking the sun rose without his crow, and is now in The City starring at a nightclub as a singer known as "The King." A group of animals from the farm go to find him, and we discover this is all in a little boy's storybook. Only *his* family's farm is facing torrential rains, and the Duke *is* real, and turns the boy into a kitten with a blow of his magical breath, and he then joins in on the storybook quest.

Huh?!

Disney voice regular Phil Harris does the narration, which often seems like an attempt to tie this loose story all together, and Glen Campbell provides the voice of the Elvis-like rooster. The animation is fluid and colorful, and the characters are all those one-joke type frequently found in the worst Disney movies (i.e., there's a magpie who likes to eat, an intelligent mouse who wears glasses named Peepers, etc.). Naturally, they have some people with expressive voices (Eddie Deezen as the magpie, Sandy Duncan as the mouse, Charles Nelson Reilly as an inept killer owl) to help make up for the one-dimensional characterization.

Children, I've been told, like the film. Save the children!

Space Jam

You may not realize it, but *Space Jam* is a very important movie event. No, not because the Warner Brothers characters are finally making their first feature film appearance (I don't count those compilation films of the '70s), and not because Michael Jordan makes the leap from sports to acting.

No, *Space Jam* is an important film to the animation business because if it succeeds beyond the expectations of its producers, it will prove that companies other than Disney can make an animated blockbuster. Let's face it, most non-Disney animated films use their theatrical release as a marketing device to insure some sort of name recognition for the impending home video release.

Most G-rated animated features do quite well on video regardless of the film's box-office success or critical history. There is an insatiable hunger in this country for material considered "safe" by parents and the steady stream of harmless mediocre animated features have done well to fill this growing market.

The success of *Space Jam* in theaters is a real test. Not since *Bebe's Kids* (an uneven but admirable effort to do something different) has a non-Disney animated feature taken as many chances as *Space Jam*. The film isn't based on a fairy tale, a contemporary children's book, or a TV series. It's based on a sneaker commercial of all things. The live-action star is not an actor, but a sports hero. Its animated characters are all beloved and revered, but have not been the subjects of new animation for years. The film breaks out of the G ghetto and includes several slightly off-color jokes to earn a . . . shudder . . . PG rating.

Do the chances payoff? Well, yes and no. I was definitely entertained, something I couldn't say about *The Lion King* or *Hunchback of Notre Dame* or any Bluth feature I've seen in the past five years. I wanted more, though. The film opens with a long (and slow) sequence involving Michael Jordan and ends with a long Jordan sequence. Just what did I pay my money to see? Jordan or the Looney Tunes? Da Tunes!

The plot is – let's be charitable – convoluted. Aliens from another world who run an amusement park decide to kidnap all the Warner Brothers characters as their new attractions. The WB folks challenge the little space creatures to a basketball game to decide if they will go willingly to "Moron Mountain," but the aliens tip the scales in their favor by assuming the talents of five top NBA players. In order to even up the teams, the Looney Tunes grab superstar Michael Jordan.

Animation fans could spend the next ten years debating just why Warners wanted to make this story into a movie, however, from a marketing point of view, *Space Jam* has its strengths. The film makes no effort to compete with Disney in the fairy tale field. It wants to be different. It wants to appeal to adults and teens by presenting them the ever popular Michael Jordan in a way they've never before seen him. The film is designed to be as hip and contemporary as it can be and still capture the traditional family market.

My biggest complaint about *Space Jam* is that too much screen time is given to Michael Jordan. In their quest to grab new audiences, the producers wound up giving more screen time to Jordan than to the animated characters that have been beloved for the better part of 50 years. I wanted more time for the animation, because what I saw was quite good.

It was especially good considering the break-neck production schedule for this film. The end credits say it all; it seems that almost every animation outfit on the planet got an assignment from the *Space Jam* producers, and it shows every now and then on screen. Some of the characters do look slightly different from scene to scene.

Generally, though, the animation is slick. The voice work has been the subject of much debate from animation fans as whether or not the new group of voice actors will capture the sound and match the acting ability of the late Mel Blanc.

Generally, I believe they do, and I want to congratulate Billy West on how well he handled the high-pressure assignment of Bugs Bunny. I want to remind readers that West and all of the voice performers were performing to meet the criteria set by the film's director and producers. If a voice didn't sound exactly like Blanc, it's obvious the makers of the film wanted it to sound a different way, and rather than complain about an actor's performance, the criticism should be leveled at the decision boys.

It should also be noted that the voices that were traditionally played back at a higher speed (Porky is the big example) were in real time for this film. A special recognition should also go to June Foray, the original voice actress for Granny, who gets her first big screen credit for the role. June never received voice credit on the Warner shorts for her work as Granny, Witch Hazel or other characterizations, and it's long overdue.

Is the film funny? Yes, there are some great lines (several killer animation in-jokes which kid Disney and the Warner Brothers licensing juggernaut) and sight gags, but the animation doesn't get really cooking until the second half of the basketball game sequence. That's a problem for me. The film takes a lot of time establishing who is Michael Jordan (undoubtedly in part to prepare foreign audiences who are unfamiliar with the basketball player) and not enough time setting up the Looney Tunes.

We never really learn just how or why they exist, unlike the more carefully constructed *Who Framed Roger Rabbit.*

Generally, they are used as supporting players for Jordan rather than individual characters. Bugs and Daffy get to shine, but that's about it. Clearly, the goal of the filmmakers was to put nearly every character who-ever appeared in a Warners cartoon on the screen, which gives it a nice nostalgic feel. Some of these characters get to do a little business (Sniffle's scene is pretty funny, for instance), but they don't get to do enough!

Perhaps if *Space Jam* does well enough, the Powers That Be at Warners will have the courage to make another animated feature without having the crutch of basing it on a shoe ad and without putting a non actor as the film's star. Let's hope so.

The Tune - 1992 (1993 video release)
Triboro Entertainment Group; 80 minutes

Writing something less than a greatly enthusiastic review of Bill Plympton's *The Tune* is practically an act of heresy for an animation fan such as myself. Plympton is one the few independent animators who has risen from the animation festival ranks to establish a name for himself outside of anima-tion circles. His work on MTV and various television ad campaigns has given him the financial resources to tackle producing a feature-length ani-mated musical.

The good news is that Plympton has remained very true to his unique technique. While his use of colored pencils is somewhat more polished here than on some of his shorts, it still has that distinctive rough and im-mediate style. His trademark transformations and cheerful sadism is also present in *The Tune.*

The problem is Plympton's transition in going from short gag-oriented cartoons to a feature with a plot and sympathetic characterizations. *The Tune* is the story of songwriter named Del who is searching for a song. By taking the wrong exit off of a highway cloverleaf he winds up in the town of Flooby Nooby where bursting into spontaneous compositions is com-monplace. This cheerfully surreal aspect of the film is wonderful. Gener-ally, the songs are clever, and Plympton's animation is a delight.

Where the film has difficulties is several scenes in which the tone changes. Del and his girlfriend may be breaking up because of his inability to write. Del reveals he really didn't love her, but was using her to get to her boss, the owner of a music-publishing house. This somber plotline seems truly out of place. It's very difficult to blend a melodramatic plot with surreal slapstick, and I don't think Plympton pulls it off.

Despite my reservations, though, *The Tune* is an example of totally original filmmaking, as opposed to Disney clone features (such as the sugary Hanna-Barbera's *Once Upon a Forest* and Filmation's *Snow White* rip-off *Happily Ever After*), and is well worth your time. As an added bonus, a making-of short follows the feature.

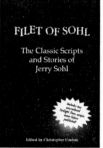

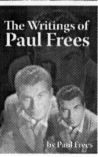

Printed in the United States
200210BV00003B/1-9/A